Felicia Skene of Oxford; a memoir by E.C. Rickards. With numerous portraits and other illustrations

Edith C Rickards

Observations

- Catholic influences in childhood and education
- Travel - lived in France as a young child
    - lived in Greece for 6-7 years from age of 14
    (Brother later a travel writer) (see below)
        - Is 'Hidden Depths' a travel story?

- Sexuality? Pg 36

- Travel Writing 'Wayfaring Sketches among the Greeks and Turks' - travel writing among foreigners like 'Hidden Depths'
    - foreigness of lower classes.

- Felicia longs for a role in life (Pg 81) cf Ernestine in 'Hidden Depths'

FELICIA SKENE OF OXFORD

FIRST EDITION, . *February* 1902
Reprinted, ... *April* 1902

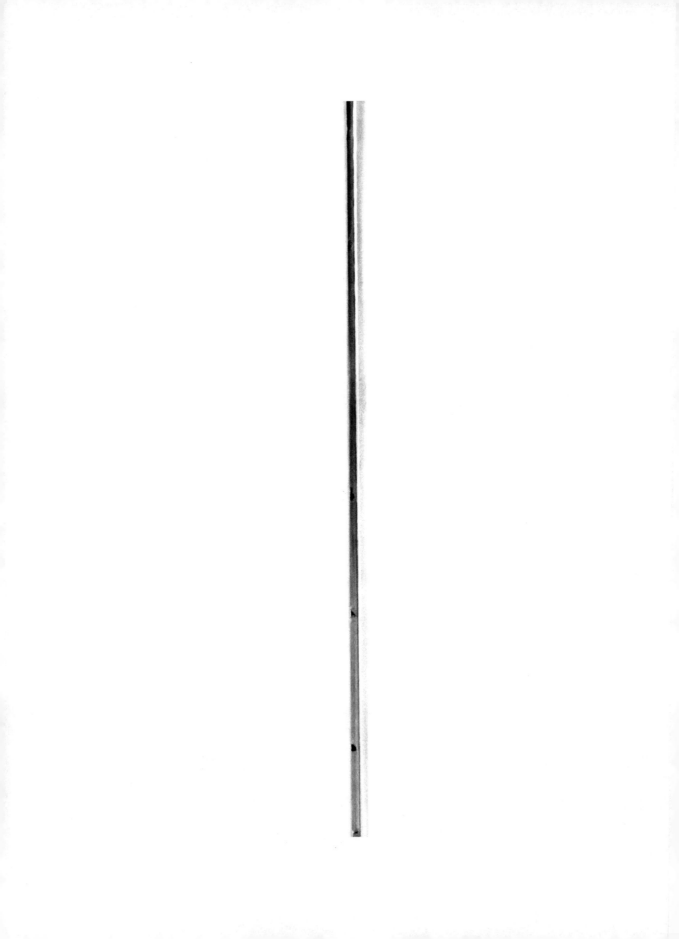

Geo. Romney, Pinxit.

Betty, Lady Forbes.

FELICIA SKENE
OF OXFORD
A MEMOIR

By E. C. RICKARDS

WITH NUMEROUS PORTRAITS AND OTHER ILLUSTRATIONS

LONDON
JOHN MURRAY, ALBEMARLE STREET
1902

DEDICATED TO

Z. T.

TO WHOM I OWE THE PRIVILEGE OF RECORDING THE LIFE

OF ONE DEAR TO HER BY TIES OF KINDRED

AND TO BOTH OF US BY FRIENDSHIP

AND REVERENCE FOR THE

BEAUTY OF HER

CHARACTER

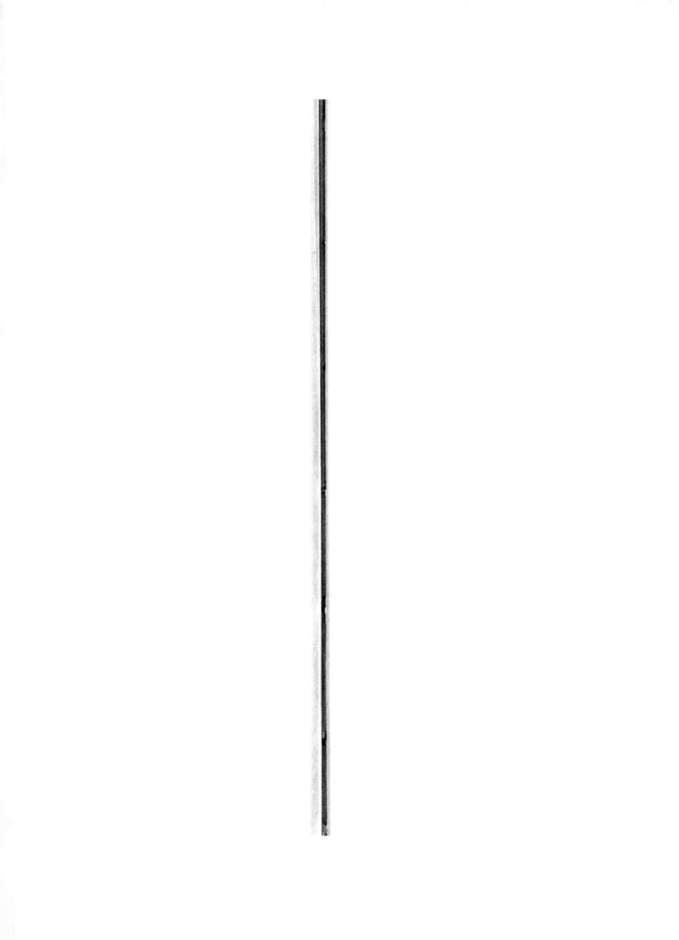

INTRODUCTION

IN carrying out the delightful task of giving some account of the life depicted in this volume, I feel how much I am indebted to the many kind friends and acquaintances who have helped me to accomplish it. I have to thank Miss Frances Power Cobbe, Mrs Humphry Ward, Miss Wordsworth, Sister Harriet of St Thomas-the-Martyr, Oxford, Lady Rose Weigall, Lady Sophia Palmer, Mr Charles Wood, Editor of the *Argosy*, the Rev. R. L. Phelps, Major Griffiths, and Dr Doyne, for the interesting reminiscences of Miss Skene, which they have contributed to this volume.

To others I owe sincere thanks for giving me information, or allowing me to make use of letters. Among these are the Hon. Mrs William Lyttelton, Mrs Max Müller, Mrs Miller of Shotover, the Mothers Superior of the Sisterhood at St Thomas-the-Martyr, and of the Convent, Oxford; Sister Louisa and Miss Mabel Wilson, Mrs Edmund Simeon, Mrs Irving Davies, Mrs Wilson, daughter of the late Dr Norman Macleod, Mrs Leslie, Miss J. and Miss C. Cooke, Dr George MacDonald, the Rev. H. Bevan, the Rev. Rosslyn Bruce, and Mr Harvey Bruce, the Rev. F. Newton, formerly Chaplain at Oxford Gaol, Sir David Hunter Blair, the Rev. Father Parkinson, Colonel Isaacson, former Governor of Oxford Gaol, and Mr Pullan, the present Governor; Mr Tallack of the Howard Association, Mr W. Shepherd Allen, Mrs Jordan, Miss Webbe, Mrs Young, and Mrs Whitaker.

I wish also to thank the Publishers and Editors of Magazines, who have given me permission to quote passages from various writings of Miss Skene's. I have to thank those who have kindly allowed pictures in their possession to be copied for this book. To Miss Venables I am indebted for the photographs taken with the camera lent by Miss Acland, of Frewen Hall,[1] of Miss Skene's house in St Michael's Street, and her grave in St Thomas' churchyard.

[1] By kind permission of Dr Shadwell.

Above all, my warmest thanks are due to Mrs Thomson, niece of Miss Skene, and the Rev. Algernon Barrington Simeon and Mrs Simeon. Without their constant and ever-ready help, I could not have attempted my task.

In estimates formed of the character and opinions of the same person by different friends, it is inevitable that the views taken by various writers should in some respects be divergent. In regard to the Impressions appended to this volume, it must be clearly understood that each contributor is solely and entirely responsible for his or her own statements.

I feel deeply the difficulty of giving any adequate picture of the life which was a blessing to all who came in contact with it. Only a glimpse of all Felicia Skene was, and of all she did, can be shown here; the rest is known to God alone. It is a privilege to have enjoyed her friendship while she was with us. It is a happiness to have been once more brought, as it were, into her presence, by the study of her noble life.

E. C. RICKARDS.

Christmas, 1901.

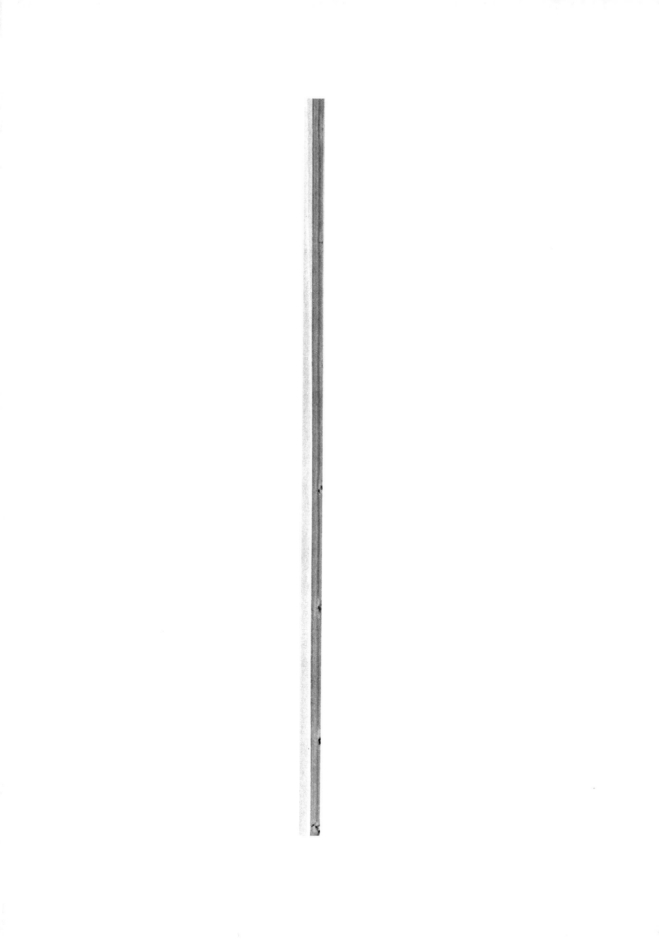

CONTENTS

PART I

PREPARATION FOR WORK

PART II

WORKING DAYS

CONTENTS

LIST OF ILLUSTRATIONS

xiii

PART I

PREPARATION FOR WORK

"Take Joy home,
And make a place in thy great heart for her
And give her time to grow and cherish her!
Then will she come and often sing to thee,
When thou are working with the furrows, aye,
Or weeding in the sacred hour of dawn.
It is a comely fashion to be glad—
Joy is the grace we say to God."

—JEAN INGELOW.

ERRATA

Page 100, *line* 1. *For* "Le Divine Maître," *read* "Le Divin Maitre."

Page 358, *line* 10. *For* "in which she was delighted," *read* "in which she delighted."

Pages 316, 345. *For* "Lady Jane Antrim," *read* "Jane, Countess of Antrim," *and in Index.*

Page 110, *line* 17. *After* "bold enterprise," *add* "are somewhat changed."

Page 146, *line* 2. *For* "Tatters," *read* "Toby."

FELICIA SKENE OF OXFORD

—·····┼·····—

CHAPTER I

FAMILY HISTORY

ON the 23rd of May 1821, a little girl was
born at Aix in Provence, to whom the
Christian names of Felicia Mary Frances were
given. The first of these, which she owed to her
godmother, a certain Comtesse Felicité, could
not have been better bestowed, for she was
blessed with those elements of character which
make for happiness both for self and for others.
She was happy also in the surroundings
in which she found herself on her entry into
the world, for, if we may be allowed a favourite
modern expression, she " had chosen her parents
well."

The name of her father, Mr James Skene of
Rubislaw, is not likely to be forgotten as long
as the poems of Sir Walter Scott are read ; for
the warm friendship between the two men is

A

touchingly described in the Introduction to the fourth canto of "Marmion." Their summer walks, their talks, whose topics ranged "from grave to gay," their sports pursued in "social silence," the one intent on his sketching, the other on the study of antique legends; their "blithesome nights,"

> "When fires were bright and lamps beamed gay,"

all deepened a friendship in which

> "Through many a varied scene,
> Unkindness never came between,"

and were among Scott's happiest memories.

But stronger even than friendship was another link between the two men, connected with a passion that coloured the whole of Sir Walter's life. James Skene's wife was sister to Sir William Forbes, who married the beautiful Williamina Stuart, to whom Scott had been deeply attached in his early youth. It was this Sir William Forbes who, upon the visit of George IV. to Scotland, made this spirited reply to the king's offer to restore, by a new creation, the title of Pitsligo, forfeited by his Jacobite uncle at the attainder of 1745: "I have done nothing to deserve a new peerage, but I have a right to my old one." The king demurred on the ground that if he restored a title in one case, he must do it in all, and the matter dropped.

In a paper in the *Century Magazine*, written

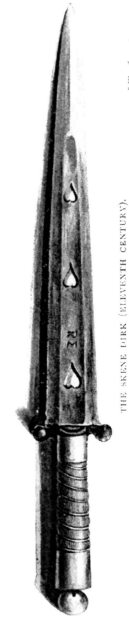

THE SKENE DIRK (ELEVENTH CENTURY).

[*To face p. 2.*

by Felicia in 1899, called " Sir Walter Scott's First Love," she touchingly relates the story of the poet's love, what it had been, and what it ever was to him as long as life lasted.   Scott's death, thirty years before that of James Skene, was one of the deepest griefs that Felicia's father had to bear.   It was a strong proof of the profound impression made on him by that friendship, that shortly before his death, in his ninetieth year, he was convinced that the poet came to see him, and sat with him a long time talking over the old happy days together.

If hereditary influences count for much, Felicia had all the advantages which descent from the high-minded and cultivated families of both parents could bring her.

The history of the Skene family goes back to an early period, as far as the eleventh century. The old legend, on the authority of one of its members, Alexander Skene, who in 1678 devoted himself to the study of the pedigree, was that a son of the founder of the family, the Laird of Struans, had his first donation from the king for killing "ane devouring wolfe in the forest of Aberdeen."   The legend is preserved in an old MS.

"King Malcolm Kenmore being 'fiercely purshewed by a devouring woulfe,' . . . a second son of Donald of the Isles perceiving the fierceness of the woulfe with his open mouth coming upon the king, wrapt his plaid about his left arme, and thrust in his mouth, and interposed himself to the furie of the wyld beast, rather than have his prince in hazard; and then with his right hand, drew his Skene, and under his arme that was in the mouth of the woulfe, struck in his Skeine at his head, and cut off his head and delivered it to King Malcombe, for the quhilk Malcome gave him the lands of Skene, and caused him to be called Skene of that ilk, as lykways the great Laik or Loch of Skene, being sax miles of circuit, well plenished with fresh water fishes, Elk Bulls and croched Cows on the sides thereof, who have but on ear or lug, and gives exceeding mutch milk, and are never seen to Bule, but its vulgarly reported that these Elfe Bules come out in the night season, and return with a great Bulying in the Watter."

There is a picture of the old skean or dirk in the family chest of charters, and it is believed that from the time that the lands were erected into a barony, in 1317, the dirk was used as a symbol of investiture.

The Skenes soon developed into a large clan. Some dozen branches are described in Mr William Forbes Skene's history of the family. Our concern is only with the Skenes of Rubislaw, the first of whom was George, the son of David of the Mylne of Potterton. He attained to the dignity of Provost of Aberdeen in 1676, and was afterward knighted as Sir George Skene of Fintray.

ARMS OF SIR GEORGE SKENE.
FROM A STONE FORMERLY IN THE HOUSE OF RUBISLAW.

[*To face p.* 4.

His elder brother sent him to Poland when he was quite a boy, and there he became first apprentice and afterwards merchant of Dantzick. On his return to Scotland he spent part of the fortune he had made, in acquiring the estate of Rubislaw. There is a charming picture in Mr William Skene's "Memorials of the Family" of the old-fashioned country-house, homely and substantial, with its long staircase up to the front door, over which hangs the coat of arms. Here George took up his abode when he was not in his town-house in Aberdeen.

He seems to have been a deeply religious man, judging from papers in the Rubislaw chest in which are found copies of two prayers he wrote. One is entitled, "Ane holy Divorce and Solemn Renunciation of all and every sin, and of my sins in a special manner, from this day henceforth and for ever"; the other, "A Solemn Vow and Covenant Betwixt the Almighty Lord God of Hosts and George Skene, from this day from henceforth and for ever." Both prayers breathe a deeply and sincerely religious spirit, assuring the Almighty of his "fixt resolution," more particularly "to guard against any idol sin, never to give it a kyndly look any more," . . . "solemnly joyning himself in a marriage covenant to be Christ's for ever, and taking Him as his alone Lord and Saviour, and his head and husband for ever."

One of his successors was of a very different character.   George Skene, the father of James and grandfather of Felicia, succeeded to Rubislaw in 1757, and the following quaint description is given of his disposition:—

"Being of too lively a cast for so plodding a profession (as the law) . . . he yielded to the conviviality of his disposition, giving up his time to gaiety and amusement, and soon became the delight of the society he frequented in Aberdeen. He sang well, played on various instruments, composed humorous songs, caricatures and lampoons, constantly inventing some amusing frolic of which his uncle, Portlethen, a pompous, portly man, and his cousin, Miss Finnie, a starched antiquated virgin, were frequent subjects.   Indeed he not unfrequently subjected the whole inhabitants of the town to his frolics, by various successful and amusing hoaxes, which to this day continue to afford merriment in the narration."

In vain was he prevailed upon to go to Edinburgh to study law; for having little "taste for that dry pursuit . . . he returned to pass the remainder of his life at Rubislaw, in the fulness of convivial indulgence, which soon ushered in its train that surly monitor the gout," of which he died, in 1776, at the age of forty.

If the jovial George Skene had no specially fine qualities to transmit to his descendants, at least he did his best for posterity by marrying into the staunch old stock of the Moirs, whose loyalty to the Stuart family has been related by Dr John Brown in his essay called "A Jacobite Family," in "Horæ Subsecivæ." The adventures of Moir of Stoneywood and his servant John Gunn are worthy to have formed the plot of one of the Waverley Novels. It was through the Moirs that the Bible which Charles I. put into the hands of Bishop Juxon on the scaffold, with the word "Remember," came into the possession of Miss Skene of Rubislaw. On its light blue velvet cover, adorned with gold and silver lace, are the crown and the Prince of Wales' feathers—the latter showing that it had once belonged to the Prince. The alteration of the initials on the cover can be plainly seen; for "C. P." has been obviously changed into "C. R." by the addition of a little tail to the second letter. But, alas! the title-page containing the royal autograph has been torn out. How that came to pass—through the dishonesty of a servant, assisted by her lover, a blacksmith, and the subsequent rascality of a bookseller—is related by Dr John Brown. One Margaret Grant, a maid in the service of Miss Moir of Stoneywood, conceived the wicked thought of stealing and selling the precious Bible. Her lover, who was a blacksmith, having opened the family charter chest in which the book was kept, the woman then offered it for sale in Aberdeen. Taking fright afterwards lest the theft should be discovered

and proved against her, since it was well known
in the neighbourhood that the Bible was an heir-
loom in the Moir family, she took the book by
night to Stoneywood, and placed it at the foot of
a large chestnut tree near the house, where it
was discovered next morning.   But alas! the
blank leaf on which was inscribed the autograph
of King Charles had been torn out by a bookseller to whom the Bible had been offered, and
ingeniously inserted into another, which he sold
for a large sum to the Earl of Fife, in whose
library it figured as the genuine book.   The
King's own Bible descended, minus the royal
signature, to Miss Skene of Rubislaw, together
with the life-size portraits of Prince Charlie, the
Duke of York and his parents, presented by the
Prince to Moir of Stoneywood.

Mr George Skene's son, Felicia's uncle, was
a great improvement on his parent.   He died
at the early age of twenty-one, a martyr to
his self-denying and chivalrous devotion to
two noble ladies, the Duchesses of Gordon and
Bedford.   Travelling on horse-back to visit the
Highlands, "he stopped at Nairn on a very
stormy night of rain, when a family with ladies
arrived late, whom, as the house was full, it was
impossible to accommodate; and they being
averse to proceed further during bad weather,
unfortunately applied to Mr Skene to give up
his room.   With this request he generously

THE PRAYER BOOK OF CHARLES I.

[*To face p.* 8.

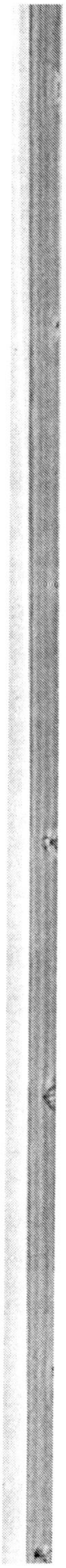

complied, though unwell at the time, and set
off to ride to Inverness in a cold and stormy
night.   An access of fever was the natural
consequence, which he incautiously disregarded,
and proceeded next day to visit Beauly." Two
days afterwards he expired at Ettles Inn, in the
presence of the landlord.

To him succeeded James Skene, the able, the
cultivated and the excellent father of the subject
of this Memoir. He was born in 1775, and his
mother became a widow the following year.
She then went to live in Edinburgh for the
education of the children, and James was placed
at the High School, there making acquaintance
with many boys who became distinguished in
after life.   He became the owner of Rubislaw at
sixteen; but before settling down in his own
country he went to Germany to study languages.
On returning to Edinburgh he joined the
Scottish Bar, and then began his friendship
with Walter Scott, and his association with him
in the organisation of the Edinburgh Regiment
of Light Horse Volunteers.

In 1802 he went abroad again for several years,
during which he travelled over the greater part
of Europe. The mental activity and breadth of
mind which afterwards distinguished his daughter
Felicia, were probably derived from him; for
no subject seemed to come amiss to him—
geology, antiquities, literature, art, science,

history, all attracted his interest, and won a
welcome for him into many learned Societies.
But he was not merely a learned man; he was
what is better and rarer, a wise one, full of
practical ability, which stood him in good stead
during the many years when he was Secretary
to the Board of Trustees and Manufacturers in
Edinburgh, and also in his philanthropic work in
Oxford years afterwards. The great attraction
of his character, however, lay in his gentle
manner, his love of all that was beautiful in art
and nature, his enjoyment of manly exercise, and,
above all, in his loyal and affectionate nature.
In 1806 he married Jane, daughter of Sir
William Forbes, nephew and heir of the famous
Jacobite, Lord Pitsligo and Monymusk, whose
romantic character and hairbreadth escapes in
the rising of 1745 were related by Felicia in an
article in *Temple Bar*, in September 1894.

He had taken part in the first attempt to
recover the throne for the Stuarts in 1715, and
now, when he was approaching his seventieth
year, he joined the army of the young Pretender.
Just before he started he went to take leave
of an old friend; and as he prepared to mount
his horse to ride away, one of the children
of the house brought him a stool to assist him.

"My little fellow," said Lord Pitsligo, "this is
the severest reproof I have met with for pre-
suming to go on such an expedition."

But the old war-horse was not to be kept from the battle. Through the long winter months he was with the Prince's army, and when that was broken up, Lord Pitsligo found himself in the position of a fugitive with a price set on his head. From place to place he wandered, sometimes in the disguise of a beggar, at another of a cobbler. Now we find him taking refuge in a cave, then in the granary of a farmhouse, or behind a wainscot. On one occasion, when the dragoons came to search the house where he lay concealed, he owed his escape to the unexpectedly shrewd reply of an idiot to the searching questions of the soldiers. Lord Pitsligo had in former days shown great kindness to the poor fellow, who, on hearing the arrival of the soldiers sent to look for his lord, broke out into such piteous lamentations as at once to arouse their suspicion. "Who is that beggar?" they asked, pointing to the disguised Jacobite.

It was a moment of terrible suspense, relieved by the delightful surprise of hearing the idiot reply that the man was once a prosperous farmer, but had been ruined by the loss of all his stock.

On another occasion he was saved by the presence of mind shown by a lady, in the house where he was taking refuge. The bed in which she slept was placed in front of a wainscot, behind which was a recess where Lord Pitsligo lay concealed. The bad air of his narrow hiding-place brought on an attack of asthma, and after the soldiers had searched every nook and corner of the room, as they believed, the lady was terrified to hear the sounds of loud asthmatic breathing, which she thought would certainly betray him. She prudently indulged in so loud a fit of coughing as to drown the old gentleman's gasps, and the search was happily abandoned. It was characteristic of him that as soon as he could leave his black hole, he begged that a hot breakfast might be provided for the soldiers as it was a bitter cold morning.

The Jacobite leanings of ancestors, on the side of both parents, were inherited by one member at any rate of Mr James Skene's family—his eldest son George, a handsome and clever young man, who had a distinguished career as Professor of Universal Law in the University of Edinburgh, and afterwards as Professor of Law at Glasgow. Perhaps his strong taste for family history increased his sympathy for hereditary rights; and certainly his ancestral relations, the Moirs and the Pitsligos, would have hailed their Jacobite descendant as worthy of his race.

Mrs James Skene was a woman of a good deal of charm of mind and character and easy, agreeable manners. Raeburn's portrait of her shows that she had an attractive, intelligent countenance, though she did not inherit the

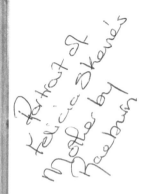

Jacobite leanings

Portrait of Felicia Skene's Mother by Raeburn

From the Picture by   Sir Henry Raeburn, R.A.
SIR WILLIAM FORBES OF PITSLIGO AND MONYMUSK, SIXTH BARONET.

[To face p. 12.

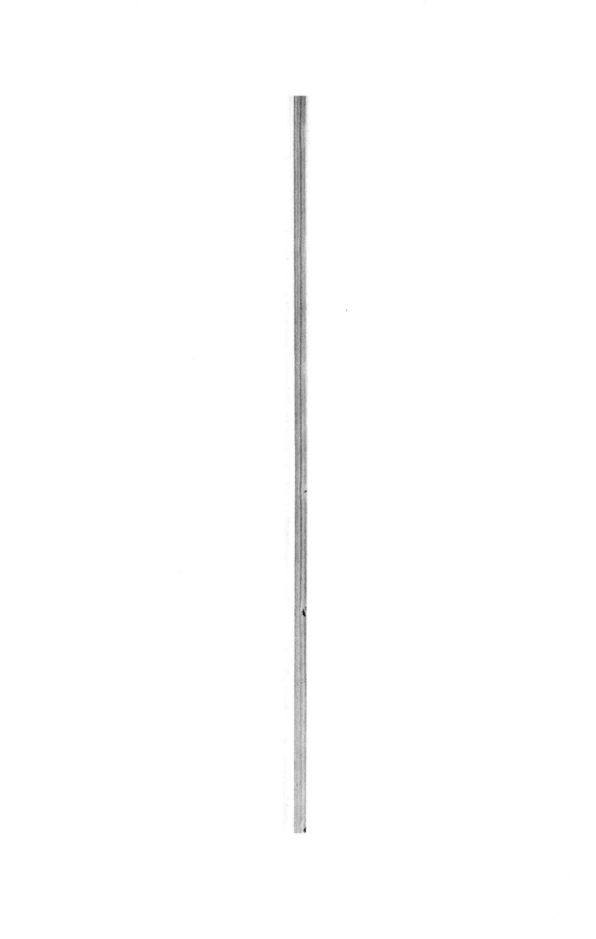

rare beauty of her mother, the daughter of Sir James Hay, and wife of Sir William Forbes, sixth Baronet. Romney's famous picture of this lovely woman (which forms the frontispiece to this book), in a large shady hat, has been lately exhibited in the "Gallery of Fair Women," at the Grafton. Judging by Raeburn's picture of her husband, which we give here, they must have been as striking-looking a couple as could well be met. Her brother, Sir John Hay (whose portrait is also given), had much of the charm of his sister, and is described as having been one of the most delightful of country gentlemen.

Mrs Skene fully shared in Sir Walter Scott's friendship for her husband, and received from the great Unknown the honour of being the only woman to whom the secret of the authorship of the Waverley Novels was confided.

But the proof of his trust in her which must have touched her still more deeply was that bestowed upon her only a few years before his death. After all intercourse between Sir Walter and the family of his first love, the beautiful Williamina Forbes, had long ceased, the poet received from her mother, Lady Louisa Stuart, a letter begging him in affectionate terms to come and visit her.

Even after that long spell of years Sir Walter was so shaken by the request that he felt he could not face the interview alone, and wrote to Mrs Skene, the sister of his first love's husband, begging her to accompany him ; and she was present at the interview, which she describes as having been extremely affecting.

Of all the pathetic passages in Lockhart's "Life of Scott," there are none more touching than the reference to that visit in the poet's diary, ending with the words, " The dead will feel no pain."

CHAPTER II

CHILDHOOD

THE home-party which encircled Felicia in childhood was a large and lively one. The different ages of the family of three boys and four girls ranged over a period of fourteen years, giving all the variety of a drawing-room, a school-room and a nursery party. The youngest of a family has, generally speaking, every chance of receiving a double portion of notice, and little Felicia possessed, in addition to the advantage of that position, just the qualities that would make her the pet and darling of them all. Full of life and spirit, active in mind and body, merry and affectionate, she was the life of the house wherever she was.

Sir John Gray.

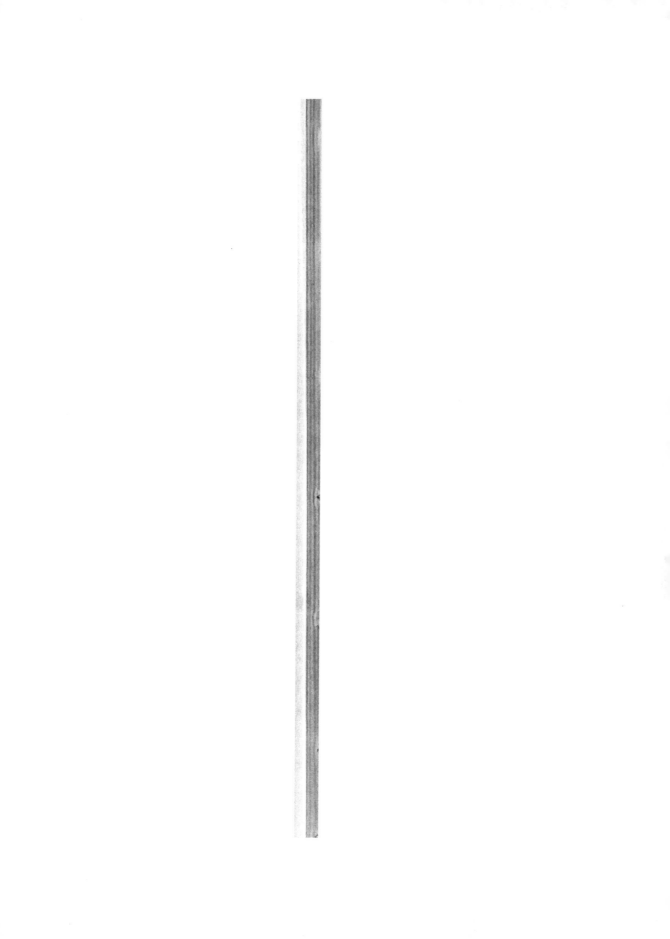

To her mother she was enthusiastically devoted, imploring her to live to be eighty, and having to content herself with Mrs Skene's promise, " I will not die if I can help it." Her strong imagination—one great source of her power over others in after life—was not likely to be lacking then, and it is the quality that gives its greatest charm to childhood.

There are some children who seem to be born grown-up, precocious little men and women of the world, who move about in an existence new to them without wonder or curiosity. Mighty dull and prosy do they grow up.

There are others to whom everything in life is strange and interesting, something to exercise their imaginations upon. The world to them is full of strange beings, whether biped or quadruped—a stage for exciting adventures and marvellous possibilities. They have no conventional ideas or time-worn prejudices, and look at everything from their own personal point of view; and you can never tell beforehand how anything will strike their minds and lead to the unexpected remark which is the delight and amusement of the elders. To the latter class of original investigators of Wonderland did Felicia belong.

It must have been a happy remembrance to her in later life, that this gift of imagination cheered for a short time one of the darkest

moments in the experience of her father's
greatest friend. Towards the close of her life
Felicia related the story in a paper in
Blackwood's Magazine, called "Glimpses of
Some Vanished Celebrities," which came out in
July 1895. From this, through the kindness of
Mr Blackwood, we are permitted to quote :—

On hearing of the total wreck of his fortunes,
"Scott," she writes, "had come for quiet and
refuge from visitors to my father's house, where
he was as free as in his own ; but he said frankly,
he felt unequal to any society but that of his
friend's youngest child, who would amuse him
with her merry *bavardage.* So I was left alone
with him that afternoon, and the scene is present
with me as if it were yesterday. Sir Walter,
addressing me with the gentle 'dearie' he was
wont to apply to little children, told me that
he did not wish to speak himself at all, but he
would be glad to listen to some fairy stories
if I had any to tell him. Nothing was easier
to me, as fairies and hobgoblins were the
constant companions of my thoughts at that
period of my existence. I plunged at once
into a wild invention of what I imagined to
be the manners and customs of such frolicsome
beings, to all of which he listened patiently for
a long time, and often laughed out heartily in
spite of his overhanging gloom. I was very sorry
when a grave person in authority came to take me
back to my school-room, and leave the greatest
of all story-tellers to forget the child's fantastic
romance in his own dark thoughts."

Felicia & Waverley novels of Scott

She relates in the same article another story with regard to him that redounds less to her credit—a saucy little trick to discover how authors would look and behave on finding some one engaged in reading their books—"What could be their feelings? Would they be dreadfully ashamed, or perhaps very proud; or would they snatch the book away, and pretend they had nothing to do with it?"

An opportunity of answering these questions occurred. Sir Walter was spending the evening at her father's, and just before dinner was over, Felicia repaired to the drawing-room and perched herself on a little stool by the fire, with one of the Waverleys open on her lap:—

"I waited till the heavy, halting step of the great author sounded on the stair, and he came into the room, leaning as usual on the strong stick which his lameness made necessary. He came towards me at once, with his accustomed cordial kindness to children, and seeing me apparently engaged in reading, he said with a smile, 'Well, my little lady, what have you got there? I suppose it is the "Arabian Nights."' I raised my head very solemnly and fixed my eyes with scrutinizing gaze on his kind face as I said slowly, 'No, it is a book called "The Abbot."' For a moment he looked much astonished at the audacity of this mite of a child, for whom, in any case, his novels could not at that time be considered suitable

B

reading, as being far beyond her comprehension; then his expression changed to one of decided displeasure, and he half turned to my father, who had not noticed me; but remembering apparently that he might draw down vials of wrath on my head if he made known my impertinence, he gave me a look which showed me that I was at once to close the book and put it away; and then he left me and engaged my father in conversation, so that my small escapade should not be known, which it never was till I now reveal it some sixty years later."

Felicia's favourite playmate and specially dear sister, both in childhood and throughout her life, was the next one in age to her, Caroline, whose curly pate suggested to Sir Walter the nickname of "Curlinda." The two little girls seemed to have had an equal part in Scott's devotion—an honour shared with his wonderful little friend, Pet Marjorie. But with most people Curlinda's portion was that of the lion; for Felicia says that when her sister was present, no one could notice *her*. Caroline's beauty and her lovable character attracted all, young and old, while a certain pride and independence of nature gave piquancy to intercourse with her. This is amusingly shown in one of Felicia's early recollections. Like many lively-minded children, Curlinda took it into her head to write her own Memoir, which opened in the following manner :—

" When people write their lives they generally

begin by saying that they were born of respectable parents.   Now I beg to say that my parents are a great deal more than respectable."

And then to prove her own words she makes an excursion into the family pedigree.

Very different lots awaited the two sisters in after life, but through all changes and separations their mutual devotion remained the same.   Great trials were to come to each, the one in married, the other in single life, and the title which Felicia chose in after years for a short memoir which she wrote of Caroline, " A Noble Life," [1] would be equally applicable to her own.

When Felicia was six years old her parents went to live in Paris for the sake of their children's education.   Two reminiscences of that visit stood out clearly in her memory afterwards —a sight of the great lumbering coach-and-six, accompanied by mounted soldiers, rolling slowly along, conveying the melancholy-looking monarch, Charles X., who was soon afterwards to leave his country and take refuge at Holyrood: the other, a drawing-room scene at the pianoforte, at which a music-lesson was being given; the frightened pupil, one of Felicia's sisters; the teacher—a wild-looking, long-haired, excited man, whose patience was not proof against the girl's blunders—the great musician, Liszt.

The next move was to Versailles, where Felicia

[1] *The Argosy*, January 1898.

attained to the dignity of going to a day-school, escorted occasionally in state by the old Scottish butler. It was supposed to be the highest class of school to be found. If so, what the lowest could be it would be difficult to imagine; for she describes the arrangements as being worse than would be found in any parish school now-a-days. Boys and girls sat together, placed alternately on wooden benches without any back.

" I believe," she writes, " I was the only representative of Great Britain, the other pupils being chiefly French, with just a sprinkling of Italians and Spaniards. I sat in the front row, as one of the youngest; and facing us was a raised daïs, on which, in a magisterial-looking chair, sat our sole instructress, Mademoiselle Henriette. A very vivacious elderly French lady she was, coming down sharply upon us for any breach of politeness or good manners; but I am unable to recall any one item of even the most rudimentary learning which I acquired at her hands. I could already read and write; but the varied list of attainments supposed to be taught in the school, geography, arithmetic, etc., seems never to have come my way at all." [1]

Of this she gives evidence from the fact that on her return home in the evening her governess would offer a prize of a bon-bon for any piece of knowledge acquired at school; and not one did

[1] "Some Episodes in a Long Life."—*Blackwood's Magazine*, June 1896.

she ever win. The only advantage she thought she acquired was a fluency in chattering French, and this was gained by talking to the other pupils, not from her teacher, Mademoiselle Henriette.

When the Skenes returned to Edinburgh the girls' education was carried on by a governess, Miss Palmer, whose surname the children took the liberty of turning into " Pompey." She was a shy and rather prim lady, and these characteristics were soon taken advantage of by her mischievous little pupil Felicia ; for in their daily walks they would often pass some of the officers commanding the soldiers quartered in the city, and it was the child's delight to slip her arm through her governess's in order to give a sly pull to the long veil which modestly covered that lady's face, so as to force her to make an involuntary bow to any officer they might chance to meet. Poor Pompey's blushes and discomfiture were keenly relished by Felicia. Her power of enjoyment and sense of humour were gifts that were to stand her in good stead throughout her life. If she had not been able to appreciate the humorous side in the strange characters and tragic scenes with which she was hereafter to be brought into close contact, her sensitive mind could scarcely have borne the painful revelation of the sins and sufferings of human nature.

Two friendships stood out most clearly in her remembrances of childhood in Edinburgh. One

was with the Lockhart family, with whom the
Skenes often stayed ; the other with the little
French Princes and Princesses in the Palace of
Holyrood.

The three Lockhart children had been Felicia's
playmates from her nursery days—the clever
Littlejohn, the darling of his father and grandfather, whose early death was keenly felt by his
girl-friend ; the handsome, merry Walter, soon to
be called away like his brother, and Charlotte,
Felicia's particular friend, of whose sweet nature
and beautiful voice she was warm in admiration.

As the two girls grew older, the enjoyment
which each felt in the literary and artistic society
which met at their parents' houses, was doubled by
being shared.   Their red-letter days were those
on which they were allowed the dear delight of
taking part in a " grown-up " dinner, before they
had formally come out.   Felicia's memories of
her friend's father are kindly and tender.   Though
reserved and stern in manner to the outside
world, " the devoted care and affection he
lavished on his delicate boy, Johnnie, who was
never out of his arms when he had a moment to
spare for him," made a deep impression upon
her, and she describes the household as having
been one of singular brightness and charm.
With Mrs Lockhart's sister, Anne, the intimacy
lasted for many years, and was kept up by the
long visits she paid to the Skenes,

The other friendship with the children of the murdered Duc de Berri — Henri, Duc de Bordeaux, afterwards Comte de Chambord, and his sister, Louise, the future Duchess of Parma, sprang out of an acquaintance between the Duchesse de Gontaut, who had charge of the royal children, and Mr and Mrs Skene. Many were the meetings that took place between the young people, for Mademoiselle often spent the day at Felicia's home, though the Duke was guarded more carefully and only allowed to go there occasionally.   The Skene children would, however, have plenty of opportunities of seeing him when they spent the day at the Palace.

"A more delightful companion than Mademoiselle," writes Felicia, "could not have been granted to us.   She was a bright, vivacious child, full of intelligence and feeling; and although merry enough when engaged in play with us, she was yet perfectly conscious of her own position and the reverses of her family, and often speculated in the quaintest manner as to what her own fate was likely to be—whether she was to find herself on some European throne or in neglected obscurity, perhaps in a prison. Sometimes, in accordance with these previsions, we would vary our amusements from hide-and-seek and other games to the arrangement of a mimic Court, in which Mademoiselle was perched on a throne formed of cushions piled upon the table, while we acted as ladies-in-waiting and went through all the ceremonies of presentations and solemn petitions humbly laid at her Majesty's feet. On these occasions the little Princess conducted herself with the most perfect dignity, and showed the keenest recollections of all the etiquette of her royal home in the beloved Paris she was to see no more. Mademoiselle's visits to our house came to an abrupt and painful end, by the dastardly action of a French revolutionary who waylaid her as she was alighting from her carriage at our door, and heaped curses on all who bore the name of Bourbon, with the fiercest invectives. Her governess, with the help of our butler, succeeded in hurrying the terrified child into the house and closing the door on the miscreant, who would have followed, but poor Mademoiselle came flying into the drawing-room, sobbing out her indignation and terror.

"'*Il a dit des injures de mon cher grand-père,*' she repeated over and over again as we tried to pacify her, and it was some time before she recovered her composure."[1]

It was well that the Princess could not have her curiosity about her future lot satisfied, for a dark tragedy awaited her in the assassination of the Italian duke whom she was to marry.

On one of the evenings spent at Holyrood with the Prince and Princess, an amusing little incident occurred. The children were playing at a charade game, in which the syllables of the word given had to be illustrated by drawing

[1] "Glimpses of Some Vanished Celebrities." — *Blackwood's Magazine.*

instead of acting.   A certain M. d'Hardevillier, one of the gentlemen in attendance, who was a good artist, was to give his sketch of the subject to the child whose drawing he considered the best.   The word was " Courtship."

" The scene," she writes, " is before me now. The Duc de Bordeaux, a quiet, fair-haired boy, laboriously setting to work in perfect silence; Mademoiselle, full of animation and excitement, talking rapidly in French and expressing her hopes of winning the coveted prize.   I was the youngest child in the room, and my attempts must have been of the crudest description. What I made of the Court scene I do not remember, but when it came to the ship I portrayed, I added a flag to it which was about twice the size of the vessel itself.   Then it occurred to me that my conspicuous banner would be the better of some ornamentation, so I drew some flowers upon it, entirely the offspring of my own fancy.   When the finished drawings were collected for judgment, my flowery flag instantly attracted the attention of the loyal French exiles, and a universal cry arose: ' *Les fleurs de lis! les fleurs de lis!* the dear sympathetic child has drawn the *fleurs de lis* in honour of France!! *Ô la chère petite! la charmante enfant!* to her must the prize be awarded without doubt.'

" I was much too shy and shamefaced to make any avowal of the fact that I knew nothing whatever about the *fleurs de lis*, and that no sentiment towards France had inspired me in executing the meaningless hieroglyphics on my flag. So M. d'Hardevillier's beautiful drawing was presented to me, most unworthy of it, and it is in my possession to this day, a graceful representation of the different meanings of the charade."

For about two years of their girlhood, in the transition period of the 'teens, Caroline and Felicia were sent to a school at Leamington, highly thought of, and kept by two charming French ladies. Though they were Roman Catholics themselves, they were careful never to interfere with the religious opinions of their pupils. The school was a small one, consisting of six or eight pupils, so that plenty of attention could be given to each.

Felicia was at that time going through the shy, silent, awkward stage that often comes upon girls at that period of their existence, and was daunted by her conviction that she was extremely plain.

Like most people she set the highest value on the quality that she thought she lacked, and which she admired so much in her sister Caroline, who could always shine, both in appearance and conversation, in the parties given at the school. The shyness was but a passing phase, soon to vanish in the novel surroundings in which she was to find herself.

Among the many distinguished friends of Mr James Skene, few could have been more valued

dev. of Felicia's
Christian Faith

than Dean Ramsay, the witty and the saintly.
If, as Felicia tells us, his character had a powerful influence on all who knew him, he had the best
opportunity of leaving his mark on her, for he it
was who, when the time came, prepared her for
Confirmation. She was one of those persons who
are sometimes described as having a natural
genius for religion. It was a necessity of her
nature, and she could say with M. Coppée, " J'ai
toujours eu le besoin de Dieu." With her
capacity for devotion and self-sacrifice, her
longing after goodness, and conviction of the
existence of an unseen world, all of which grew
stronger with her strength, she would have been
restless and miserable without that satisfaction of
her deepest needs which Christianity offered her.
But there was no forcing of the spiritual life
within. It grew up naturally under the good
training received and the bright examples around
her. What different changes and developments
it assumed in after years we shall see later on.
Stagnant and unaltered it could not remain,
in one whose mind was open, as hers was, to the
different sides which truth presents. But in the
great essentials of devotion to her Saviour, and
in loving service to man, it was ever the same.

CHAPTER III

LIFE IN GREECE

IN 1838 a great change took place in Felicia's life, just when she was at the impressionable age of seventeen, on the threshold of woman-hood, when the power of enjoyment is fresh and keen, the mind active, and enthusiasm and imagination at their warmest and liveliest :— Mr and Mrs James Skene and their family left Scotland and went to live in Greece.

The great move came about in the following way :—the second son, James Skene, who had been in the 73rd Regiment, had been quartered in Malta. Being fond of sport, he had, when a chance offered, crossed over to Greece for shooting, made friends among the Greeks, and met at a party a beautiful Greek girl, Rhalou, daughter of Jakovaki de Rangabé, the head of an old and influential Phanariot family. He fell in love with her on the spot, and succeeded in winning her hand. Selling his commission, he settled down in Greece, being at the time of his marriage twenty-one years of age, while his bride was sixteen.

He was eventually to enter the diplomatic

service, and to occupy his leisure in literature, for he became the author of several books of travels—"The Frontier Lands of the Christian and the Turk"; "Anadol, the Last House of the Faithful"; "Rambles in the Syrian Deserts," and "With Lord Stratford in the Crimean War."

In one of his visits to his family in Edinburgh, he found the subject of a move to a warmer climate, on account of his mother's delicate health, under discussion. He soon persuaded his parents to give up the idea of the Riviera, and take a more unaccustomed flight to Greece.

When they all set out on their journey they probably little guessed how long they would stay there, for it was to be their home for between six and seven years.

If the anxiety of convoying a family so far afield was no light one, the beauty of the journey must have been a great compensation. They drove at their convenience in their own carriage, taking plenty of time to enjoy all the interesting places they passed by the way. Their route took them by the Rhine and Tyrol to Trieste, where they stayed some time before embarking for Greece. There were delightful expeditions to be made in the neighbourhood of the Adriatic port — the romantic castle of Lueg, frowning down from the heights of a precipitous rock; the grotto of Adelsberg in Styria, with its underground

lake and long meandering caves and passages
—all these must be visited.   Here it was that
the adventurous Caroline gave her family what
could hardly be called a pleasing excitement.
In her eagerness to enjoy all she could of the
romantic spot, she boldly set off alone to explore
the long, branching subterranean caves and
corridors, and was drawn on by the beauty of the
stalactites which hung from the roofs and sides
of the rock further and further into the depths
of the cave.

Soon the cry was raised, " Where is Caroline ?"
and her father, filled with alarm, which was
certainly justified by the fact that the guides
were unable to direct him, started off in search
of her.

Perhaps she remembered the story of Blondel
and Richard Cœur de Lion, only in her case it
was the sought and not the seeker who called
music to her aid ; for she began singing at
the top of her clear voice an old ballad, which
directed her father to the right spot.

Caroline was the heroine too of a more
romantic story in the course of their travels ; for
before they crossed the Alps she made an
amusing conquest.   The Skene family fell in
with a splendid Hungarian gentleman, travelling
in all the pomp and glory of a fine carriage
and horses and a large escort of servants.   On an
acquaintance being struck up, he at once lost

his heart to the charming girl. What though he was obliged to own that, *pour son malheur*, he was already provided with a wife at home; that was but a trifling impediment, to be brushed aside with the greatest ease; for he had only to go to Vienna, where a divorce could be obtained as readily as he could purchase a new hat. That he took the polite refusal he received in good part was proved by a present he afterwards sent the family, of many bottles of a valuable Tokay wine.

As we shall see later, Caroline was to meet her future husband before the journey ended, but we will reserve her love story for the present.

It did not take long for the Skenes to settle down happily at Athens, and to feel quite at home in that beautiful city. Mr Skene, finding that the life there suited them all so well, decided on building a villa just outside Athens. It was to be large enough to take in his own family and that of his son, and there, after the Greek custom, they would live together in patriarchal fashion. His daughter-in-law's nursery was full of merry little folk, one of whom, the elder little girl Zoe—who had inherited her mother's beauty, and was some day to be the wife of a future Archbishop of York—was to prove one of the greatest blessings of Felicia's life. What the tender friendship between aunt and niece became to both we shall see later. In those early days Felicia was teacher, playfellow, elder sister and aunt in one.

As the children grew bigger and needed more room on the one hand, the home party diminished on the other; for in the second year after the arrival in Greece, Mr Skene's eldest daughter married the Baron Charles de Heidenstam, Swedish Minister in Athens; another of Felicia's sisters became in the following year the wife of Mr Foster Grierson, Queen's Printer for Ireland, who carried off his handsome bride to his home in that country, while Caroline at the same period was to set up a home of her own.

So, ere long, Felicia found herself the only home-daughter, and a devoted one she was, the pride of her father's heart, sharing his intellectual interests and enjoying the company of his many distinguished friends, who found the villa near Athens a delightful house of call. She was the companion of his long adventurous rides into the wild mountainous regions, in whose lonely recesses brigands were not merely romantic pictures of the imagination but dangerous realities. Felicia tells us in her " Wayfaring Sketches," that she was fortunate in never seeing a brigand *entire* while they lived in Greece.

" I once saw," she writes, " the head of one which a peasant was exultingly carrying past the windows on his way to claim his reward from Government; he told us that he had found the poor robber, wounded severely by a *gend'arme*, lying in a wood, and that he had kindly *cured* him."

But happily it was not ghastly but beautiful sights that were wont to greet her eyes; and to go about with such a cultivated man as her father, visiting the classical and historical remains in Athens and the surrounding country, was a more stimulating mode of education than any systematic course of lessons, lectures or classes could be.

How thoroughly she had entered into the spirit of the poetic and artistic associations of Greece was shown in a paper she wrote years afterwards in a little local magazine at Oxford, after the performance of the *Agamemnon* in Balliol Hall. The article is called "Agamemnon in Mycenæ—Athens—Oxford," and she writes as one admitted into the secret of the tragic beauty of the Greek poet.

But if she imbibed, for the most part without direct instruction, the teaching of her surroundings, the regular methods were not discarded; and in one branch of education especially, she went through a severe training. She was gifted with a rich and powerful contralto voice, the tones of which lent a charm even to her ordinary speech, and always formed one of her great

C

attractions. Her mother, determined that her singing should have every chance of rising above the performance of the ordinary amateur, sent for the *maestro* of the Opera, who, after hearing her, remarked that he had never taught a lady before, and that if Miss Skene became his pupil he should insist on giving her the same training as a *prima donna*. His proposal was accepted; and those who in after years heard her rendering of some of Handel's solos had cause to rejoice that the *maestro* had his way. He deeply deplored that, with so fine a voice, it was impossible that she should become a public singer. It was of unusual compass, and was of the kind that has sufficient *body* in it to last almost to old age; and when she was between sixty and seventy, and was staying at Bishopthorpe, Mrs Thomson relates that one day when she took her aunt and other friends to see the Festival Concert Room at York, Felicia was persuaded to sing some Italian songs; and that her voice came ringing down the great room in a way that astonished her audience. Music became an absorbing delight to her at Athens, where at one time she used to go three times a week to a box which her father took at the Opera.

Any talent she possessed for drawing was likely to meet with every help and encouragement from her father, with whom sketching had always been a favourite pursuit, from the time when a glance at his illustrated diary supplied Sir Walter Scott with ideas and suggestions for the Waverley Novels.

" The last news which I hear from Edinburgh," writes Sir Walter in the Dedicatory Epistle of " Ivanhoe," " is that the gentleman who fills the situation of Secretary to the Antiquaries of Scotland is the best amateur draughtsman in that kingdom." And he explains in a note—" Mr Skene of Rubislaw is here intimated, to whose taste and skill the author is indebted for a series of etchings exhibiting the various localities alluded to in these novels."

The Skenes had the *entrée* to the best society that Athens afforded, and Felicia was much at Court, where she learnt to know and admire Queen Amélie, about whose beauty and grace she writes warmly.

One proceeding of Her Majesty, however, as regarded herself, she was scarcely likely to appreciate. Felicia was a daring rider. If her horse was so spirited and mischievous as to give a spice of danger to her rides, so much the bettter for her ! On one occasion she was riding with a favourite maid-of-honour of Queen Amélie, when her horse took to kicking out violently against that of her companion. This was not to be borne, and Felicia retired to the shelter of a stone quarry to have it out with him. The Queen passing by and hearing what had occurred took alarm for the safety of her court lady, and forbade any more rides with so dangerous a companion.

It is difficult to say whether Felicia found the winter with its social gaieties, or summer with its long out-door rides and expeditions, in beautiful scenery, and with exciting adventures, the more enjoyable. Always there were the interests of art and antiquity to attract her, the beautiful ruins, the statues, the ancient sepulchres. That she was worthy of the sight of these treasures is proved by the descriptions she gives of them in her book about Greece, written evidently *con amore*. It is enough to quote one passage, in which she describes a statue in words which show how fully she entered into the meaning of the artist who carved it :—

"There is one statue—lost in the remotest island of the Cyclades, which, if once seen, for ever after haunts the memory like a ghost; it is the size of life, and has evidently been intended as the portrait of a young female; every fold of the flowing, graceful drapery, every vein on the small white feet, has been exquisitely given; but the face, the divine face, that for countless ages has worn that beseeching look of gentlest, most mournful entreaty, how marvellously lovely it is! We know not what is the timid petition that seems just passing from her parted lips, but so perfectly has the expression been conveyed in every line of those delicate features, that we could almost imagine the living form had grown to marble in the breathless suspense which followed her unanswered prayer." [1]

The peasants too in their picturesque costumes were a pleasure to her artistic eye, especially the young girls, whom she declared to be as beautiful in early youth as they became ugly in middle age. One of the little maidens, a silk-winder, she describes as being more like the most exquisite statue than a mortal being.

But her interest went beyond their outward appearance. She soon learnt to talk modern Greek—an accomplishment which she put to good use on occasion, years afterwards at Oxford. The work, the pleasures, the superstitions, the quarrels, the love-affairs of the peasants, were all interesting to her, through her gifts of imagination and sympathy. The stories she tells of life in Greece are as vivid as any she ever wrote. Some of them are of the experiences of the friends and acquaintances she made among rich and poor; others are of her own, for she found herself frequently taking part in exciting incidents. Indeed there seemed to be a natural affinity between Felicia and adventure. Miss Austen tells us in the opening chapter of "Northanger Abbey," that if a young lady is born to be a heroine, the perseverance of forty surrounding families

[1] "Wayfaring Sketches."

cannot prevent her. Felicia, being just of the character and in the position that would attract adventures, drew them like a magnet; starting with a natural advantage over Catherine Morland, who, Miss Austen remarks, had nothing in her nature and circumstances to assist her.

As to romantic tales, they gravitated towards her as inevitably as Sir Isaac Newton's historic apple towards the earth; and all her acquaintances, high and low, poured their love-stories into her ear, and even went so far as to open their cupboard doors and allow her a glance at their family skeletons. And she certainly did not spoil her stories in the telling; for the actors in them live and move before our eyes. Had her lot been cast in the most prosaic suburb of London, the tragedies and comedies of life would still have been revealed to her quick insight. In romantic Greece they lay open before her eyes. The story of the headsman of Egina, which she relates in the introduction to her " Wayfaring Sketches," is as thrilling as it is dramatically related.

As specimens of the kind of adventures she and her father met with in their long rides into the wilds of the country, the following may be mentioned :—

They had set off in search of various interesting classical remains, and their first night was passed on the Plain of Marathon, where her sense of the ludicrous was much tickled by a Prussian gentleman, one of the party, who, being afraid of the heat by day, went out to inspect the battlefield in the darkest hour of a moonless night, with his servant carrying a candle before him.

The next day was spent in wandering among the mountains, seeking for the remains of a temple of Nemesis, of which they at last discovered a few broken columns of pure white marble, though the presence of a huge, angry snake—which evidently entered into the spirit of the locality—acting sentry at the ruin, prevented them from approaching close to it.

The site of the tomb of Iphigenia, priestess of Diana, was their next object; having attained which, they set off in search of a certain village, where they hoped to find shelter for their second night.

But it seemed likely to remain a hope, for cold and darkness soon set in; the horses were tired out and there was no path, and having realised that they had lost their bearings, they left the choice of the way to their horses. But they proved to be equally at fault. Stumbling and weary they plodded on under a sky heavy with clouds, and no prospect of a shelter, the howling of hungry jackals in the distance falling on their ears. But presently one of the servants gave a cry of joy as he pointed

to a twinkling light a long way off. They urged
their horses to a fresh effort, and soon found
themselves in a wild Albanian hamlet, inhabited
by shepherds and their families. The best of the
huts was at once placed at their service and
gratefully accepted. The weary travellers took
their places on the sheep-skins spread out on the
floor round a blazing fire, with their host and
his wife, their married daughter of fourteen and
her husband of twenty. The one room of which
the hut consisted was also shared by the riding-
horses of the new-comers, and the ass, the pig,
and the innumerable cocks and hens belonging
to the Albanian shepherd. At the door stood a
group of the villagers, anxious to make the most
of a rare chance of seeing and speaking to strangers.

The forks and spoons produced from the
saddlebags, and the air-cushions, which they
seemed to think were bewitched, gave their hosts
as much pleasure as new toys to children, and
very funny were some of the questions asked.
Why, for instance, should their guests comb
their hair, when no doubt that function had
been performed on Easter day?

The crowd were at last dismissed with an
invitation from the shepherd to return and see
the rest of the exhibition next morning. After
the family had said their evening prayers before
a sacred print lighted up by a small lamp, they
wrapped themselves up in their sheep-skins and

were soon asleep. If it had not been for the
restlessness of the pig, and for a serenade performed by the braying ass, the travellers might
have done the same. But they got what rest
and sleep they could before their early start at
three o'clock next morning.

Another riding adventure led to hospitality
being shown under more comfortable circumstances, though preceded by equal fatigue,
similar loss of the mountain road, and anxiety
about finding a shelter.

By permission of Mr Blackwood we quote the
story in Felicia's own words.

The hospitality in this case was offered by the
venerable *Egoumenos* (Abbot) of a monastery
hidden away among the hills that look on
Marathon !

" I had come to the quaint old building where
he dwelt with his monks, very late one evening,
after having been fourteen hours on horseback.
My father and I, with my Greek brother-
in-law, had been travelling in the interior
of the country, and we had lost our way, and
only succeeded in arriving, long after sunset, at
the isolated monastery—our sole hope of shelter
for the night. The door was opened wide, and
the *Egoumenos* came out to greet us, followed
by several of his monks. Such a gentle, amiable-
looking old man he was, with the clear-cut
features of his race, and the dignified dress believed by members of the Greek Church to be

the same as that worn by the apostles, and never, certainly, having been altered within any period known to history, the same simple black robe with its wide sleeves, and the high cap of the same hue resting on his flowing white hair." To their request for hospitality, "the kind old man said he would be delighted to receive M. de Rangabé, whose name he knew well, and my father and our servants (all Greeks) and our horses—but the lady—alas! no, that was impossible: she belonged to the dangerous class which was never allowed to pass the threshold of the monastery."

In this apparent *impasse*, Felicia was equal to the occasion. "I drew my horse close to the old man, and addressed him with all the reverential Greek titles due to his ecclesiastical rank. I told him I was so tired that if he did not allow me a shelter I should drop to the ground and be found there dead in the morning. I said I would sleep in any outside shed if he liked, only in the name of charity he must not send me from his door. He looked quite tenderly at me while he mused for a few minutes. Then he said he had thought of an expedient. His own sleeping-room was situated quite apart from the dormitories of the monks, and he would give it up to me. My father and brother should occupy two of their cells in the body of the house, and none of them would even see me or know that I was there." Thither Felicia was conducted, and left alone for the night's rest. "There was nothing in the room but a sacred icon on the wall, a small table under the window (on which stood a classical-shaped vase filled with cold water) and the bed. It consisted of a long wooden board, on which

was laid a piece of carpet; another slip of the
same was to be used as a counterpane, and there
was a stiff, narrow pillow at the head. Without
doubt it was the hardest bed I ever lay on in my
life—but I was at the age when slumber comes
easily, and I only woke when I saw through the
barred window the glowing Greek sunrise light-
ing up the lovely hills around. I had been up
and dressed some time when there was a little
knock at the door, and there was the *Egoumenos*
smiling upon me with the sweet expression
which was his special characteristic. He spoke
some gentle words of blessing and then said:
'Forgive me, my child, for disturbing you; but
there is a little matter here which I require.' He
went towards the bed, and lifting the pillow, he
took from under it a leathern bag, from which
there came the sound of coins shaken together as
he held it **up** before me. 'There,' he said, 'in
this little sack is all the money the monastery
possesses—not a drachma have we anywhere else!'
'So, you let your whole fortune lie under my
head all night!' I exclaimed; 'were you not afraid
I might steal it and ride away with it?'—'Ah
no,' he answered with his gentle smile, 'you are
Inglesa, and the travellers from that country do
not steal or cheat. They are good Christians.'
I said I was glad he thought so well of my com-
patriots, and then I thanked him very warmly
for his kindness in giving up his room to me.
He brought me some black coffee, without sugar
or milk, and some brown bread for my breakfast,
and then we remounted and rode away." [1]

[1] "Some Episodes in a Long Life."—*Blackwood's Magazine*, June 1896.

A tragic interest is connected with this adventure, for the good old man was afterwards captured by brigands, and before he could be rescued or ransomed, was shot by the villains, who tied his dead body to the back of the mule he had ridden. The faithful animal carried it back to the monastery, where it was mournfully received by the monks.

An amusing adventure, which she dwells on with delight, was one which took place at the reputed tomb of Agamemnon, where they met with two young Englishmen of the common tourist order, who seemed to regard the classic spot as a "jolly old place," wondering why "that fellow Agamemnon" had needed so much room for his remains. The sudden apparition of a lady in white at the doorway, so startled and terrified them that, declaring it was nothing earthly, they fled in haste, assured no doubt that they had encountered the ghost of the hero's avenging widow.

Felicia's rides were made the more enjoyable by the companionship of her father's friends, who would often join him and his daughter, and who, when he was unable to go, would be her escort instead. For a whole year, when Mr Skene was prevented from taking his usual exercise, Lord Lyons, the English ambassador, arranged that she should ride with him in the evening whenever he had time to go ; and Sir Richard Church,

who was then living in Athens after fulfilling his
task of suppressing brigandage in Italy, often
joined them. That Lord Lyons had not forgotten those pleasant rides, Felicia tells us that
she had proof long years afterwards, when he
came to Oxford to receive his "D.C.L." "Shall
we take a ride to Kephissa?" he asked her, as
they met after leaving the Sheldonian.

The visits to Athens of English friends were a
great refreshment to the Skene family. Dean
Stanley, whose historic enthusiasm in the Greek
capital may be imagined, was one of the welcome
travellers, and preached to the small congregation
at the English chapel. Felicia gratefully notes
that he let them off for once the almost invari-
able topic chosen by other holiday parsons of
Paul preaching at Athens.

Captain Basil Hall, whose painful mental
disease was then beginning, and the widow of
Sir Humphry Davy, who amused Felicia by the
innocent flirtation she set up with Mr Skene,
whom she evidently admired greatly, were among
other distinguished guests.

They had, of course, frequent opportunities of
making acquaintance with interesting foreigners.
One of these, whom Felicia met at a Court ball,
was no less a personage than King Otho's brother
Maximilian, at that time Crown Prince of
Bavaria. His opening remark to her, after she
was presented to him, was somewhat over-

whelming. "I hear you have been a great poet from your earliest childhood," he remarked. She was prompt to disclaim the compliment. But the topic was a fortunate one, for it launched them into an interesting talk about several English poets whose works the Prince knew well.

But the foreign acquaintance on which she dwells with perhaps greater pleasure was one made on board the steamer which conveyed her and her family to Venice. They were leaving Greece for a few months to be spent in Italy, when they found themselves in the company of Count Gonfalonieri, the friend and fellow-prisoner of Silvio Pellico. Fresh from the reading of the fascinating book which describes their captivity, Felicia felt deep interest in seeing and conversing with the venerable-looking man of striking appearance, with his white hair, dark, flashing eyes, and melancholy expression. Just before they parted at Venice he came up to her with an earnest request. Would she, he whispered, take charge of and convey to shore in her luggage some political documents he had with him, which might, if discovered, risk both his liberty and his life? Her boxes would not be likely to arouse suspicion, and she could afterwards safely restore the papers to him at the hotel.

She performed the commission duly, rather to

the consternation of her father afterwards, when she told him the part she had been playing in a political scheme.

It is a curious thing that she undertook a rather similar commission for a Frenchman devoted to the interests of the Orleans family. He asked her to post letters for him, from time to time, to the exiled Louis Philippe at Claremont, which she did till the ex-monarch's death.

The expeditions made by Felicia and her family by sea were as enjoyable as those made on land, and they took place under the most agreeable conditions. For the king often lent Mr Skene the royal yacht, in which the lovely coasts and islands of Greece were visited and explored.

When the great heats of the Greek summer are over, the families who have fled to the cooler regions of the country, return to the capital, and social gatherings begin.

Besides enjoying the Court society, Felicia and her sisters went to many parties among the *Corps Diplomatique*, with whom the marriages that had taken place in the family especially threw them. The society was lively and varied, from the number of nationalities that met at Athens, among whom French was generally spoken as the common language. A ball at the Palace was a scene never to be forgotten. The king and queen were the best of hosts, managing to blend harmoniously the different elements of which their parties were composed. There would be met the *capitani*, or native chiefs, in Greek costume, whose wives, in bejewelled dresses and red caps with tassels made of strings of pearls, vied with the ladies of other European countries, arrayed in brilliant dresses of a different fashion.

Few amongst the company could have been more popular than Felicia, with her tall aristocratic figure, animated expression and lively talk, and it was only to be expected that, like her sisters, she should have many lovers. Her natural gift of sympathy and essential good breeding set her at ease in any company, so that all her life she found no difficulty in drawing any one out, and could adapt herself with equal readiness to a duke or a costermonger, while the fun and mischief with which she was bubbling over, and her ready wit, drew friends and admirers round her wherever she went.

" Sure, and I'm not following you, me lady, for your money, but for your ilegant conversation," remarked an old beggar-woman, a few years after, when Felicia was staying with a friend in Ireland. And her " ilegant conversation," drew other followers than Irish beggars.

Though not regularly handsome, she had quite sufficient good looks to win admiration. The point in her personal appearance which was an affliction to her was her hair. In the

Red hair

matter of its abundance she had no cause to complain, for even after middle-life had passed, it remained as long and as thick as in her early days; but she thought nature had been unkind to her as to its colour, and highly disapproved of its dark red hue. "Every one thought my red hair ugly in my youth," she writes to her niece in one of her later letters. "I was much depressed and snubbed in consequence; and now it is admired."

The sister whose companionship was most missed by Felicia on her marriage was her beloved Caroline; but as to retaining the pretty, lively girl—*l'ange aux yeux bleus*, as one of her lovers called her—the family must soon have realized that there was little chance of that.

At the first moment of their landing at the Piræus, Caroline met her fate—and a fortunate one it proved in the end, though the course of true love was to run very roughly for some time. Alexander Rizo de Rangabé, brother of Mrs James Henry Skene — who met the travellers on their arrival and escorted them to Athens—succumbed at once to Caroline's charms, and he was a lover to be proud of. He belonged to one of the most ancient families in Greece. The "Livre d'Or"—which in that country answers to the "Almanach de Gotha"—traces the lineage as far back as the beginning

D

of the eighth century to Patrice Rangabé,
founder of the family. He was the grandfather
of the Byzantine Emperor Michel de Rangabé,
who married one of the daughters of Charle-
magne. That certainly takes us far enough
back. But to come down to modern times,
Caroline had every reason in the present to
feel proud of her lover's family; for her
future father in-law, Prince Rizo de Rangabé,
held the high position of Minister of Foreign
Affairs in Wallachia, and was distinguished as
an author and poet.

His son inherited his poetic tastes, and Felicia
declares that it was Caroline's pretty remark
addressed to the young man in French, as he
did not understand English, when first she
caught sight of the Acropolis with the new
town lying at its base: "La ville moderne
s'agenouille devant l'Acropole," which sealed her
conquest over Alexander de Rangabé's poetical
mind. After the Greek War of Independence,
titles were abolished in that country, and the
de Rangabés were no longer addressed by their
hereditary title of prince.

The gifts and talents which won fame to
Caroline's admirer in his after career, as
poet, statesman, and archæologist, made his
company and conversation delightful from the
first. When to these attractions were added a
noble, upright character and a devotion to herself,

the force of which was only increased by the opposition of circumstances, no wonder Caroline soon completely lost her heart. Felicia's sympathies were at once drawn out by the troubles of the lovers.

According to the tenets of the Greek Church a double marriage between members of two families ought not to be allowed, and her brother had anticipated her by marrying a de Rangabé. When therefore the young man and maiden were told that they must renounce all hope of a union, and that they were not even to be allowed to meet, the only comfort they had in their misery was in exchanging promises to remain faithful to one another for ever. When they were nearly reduced to despair, a ray of light came to cheer them. The ecclesiastical authorities yielded so far as to say that if the bride would become a member of the Greek Church, the impediment to marriage might be removed. A careless or shallow girl would have consented at once, but, like the present Czarina of Russia, Caroline would not yield until she had conscientiously studied the points at issue, and could honestly say that there was nothing in the Greek creed in any essential point which seemed to her to contradict the religious system in which she had been brought up.

And the marriage took place.

Alexander de Rangabé, who was Professor of Archæology in the University of Athens, took his bride to live with his parents, where they remained until he gave up his post to become Minister of Foreign Affairs at Athens. He afterwards entered the Diplomatic Service, and became Minister at Washington, Paris, Constantinople and Berlin. He had many distinguished friends, beginning with the great Emperor William of Germany, who had a high regard for him, and bestowed on him the Order of the Red Eagle. Mr Gladstone was always eager to see him when he visited England, and sent urgent messages to him in his absence, through his niece Mrs Thomson, on political matters. "Mind you tell your uncle," he would say to her, "to be sure to unite Greek interests with the Slavs." In literary matters there would be a strong bond of interest between them, both being enthusiastic about Greek history, poetry and archæology, on which they employed their busy pens.

Caroline's home and children henceforth became a new happiness for Felicia. Little Cleon, the eldest of her six de Rangabé nephews, some day to follow in his father's footsteps, and to be Greek Ambassador at Berlin; his younger brothers, and three handsome sisters, the future Princess Bibica Rosetti, Madame de Pétroff, and the Princess Chariclea Lobanow, were always a pride

and delight to Felicia's heart. What a good
angel she proved to the de Rangabés in the
heavy sorrows that befell them in after years we
shall see later. Every large family should be
possessed of one single sister at least, who may
act the *deus ex máchina* to the married members,
as successfully as the rich bachelor uncle in
Australia who comes to the rescue in play or
novel. Felicia was ready to play the part
in her family throughout her life, and, in most
exceptional circumstances, for the benefit of her
sister Caroline and her children. Those days of
need, however, were far ahead, and in her girlhood
in Greece, life was at its most brilliant for her,
and in strongest contrast with the scenes of sin
and sorrow which she was voluntarily to enter
that she might bring light to those who were in
gloom. Yet the bright, gay time was all to be of
use in the work of her life. She laid up then a
fund of mirth and good spirits, as the sunshine of
summer is said to be stored up in our systems
against the winter cold, to be drawn upon as a
reserve force in many a painful scene. And the
variety of nationalities, classes and characters
with which she came in contact in Athens
widened her mind, enlarged her sympathies, and
prevented the narrowness of view and confinement of thought in one groove, which is so
often the bane of good women.

CHAPTER IV

FIRST LITERARY EFFORTS

IT was while she lived in Greece that Felicia made her first literary effort, and, as is generally the case, the launch was made in poetry. Romantic subjects lay ready to hand, and ballads and narrative poems, which seem to have borrowed form and inspiration from Scott and Byron, were the result. Among the old MS. books in her possession was one she must always have regarded with peculiar tenderness as a memento of her father's affectionate pride in her. It is a copy in his delicate hand-writing, paper and ink both discoloured with age, of her first poetical effusions, illustrated by his own sketches.

The book begins with a poem called *Ianthe*, followed by *Greek Fanaticism*—a narrative poem relating an event which had recently taken place in a peasant family. It was written about a year after the move to Athens. Then follow a few more—*The Deformed, Evening, Night* and *Madness;* and the volume ends with a poem in French, in which language she was almost as much at home as in English.

It must be confessed that the sketches, some

of which are really exquisite in delicacy of outline and colour, and which would have delighted the soul of Mr Ruskin, are of far more value than the verse they illustrate. The views of Athens from the Piræus road, of the Temple of Jupiter, and the Plain of Marathon, would be hard to beat.

The poems, though they show signs of the vigour of imagination and wealth of language of Felicia's later writings, do not rise in merit above those of most young maidens who are blessed with a vein of poetry in their composition, and are moved to give early expression to it. She herself wrote of them in later life as "simply worthless and defying all rules of versification." But the time and thought given to them were not thrown away, if it is true that the composition of verse is the best training that can be given for the writing of good prose, since it teaches dexterity in the handling of words, and trains the ear in rhythmic balance of phrase and harmony of language. She would not have attained to such good prose afterwards if she had not tried her 'prentice hand on poetry.

A later volume of her poems, called "The Isles of Greece," was probably an improvement on those in MS., as it was deemed worthy of the dignity of print.

But her first literary success was the book before referred to, called. " Wayfaring Sketches

among the Greeks and Turks." The introductory chapter gives a short account of the
life and surroundings at Athens. The rest of
the book describes the long journey she and
her family made on their way back to England.

It was anything but a direct one, for they
diverged eastward before going west. Till they
arrived at Linz, beyond Vienna, they went
by water, either river or sea. The beautiful
isles of the Archipelago and the coast of Asia
Minor were the first objects of interest. Then,
passing through the Straits of the Dardanelles,
they entered the little Sea of Marmora, and
halted for a few days at Constantinople. From
thence they had to endure a horrid tossing
in a severe storm on the Black Sea; and she
gives an amusing account of the "confused
din consisting of lamentations in Turkish,
anathemas in Greek, angry mutterings of misery
in French, abrupt and comprehensive groans
in German," and "the mingled invocations to
St Nicholas and the Prophet," arising from the
polyglot crew below deck. When the dreary
night of the storm was over, she alone had
strength to crawl round to the different berths
and offer what assistance she could, "receiving
no other answer than an entreaty that I would
put a speedy termination to their existence."

When they reached the mouths of the
Danube, their long river-voyage began, by

Bulgaria, Roumania, Servia, and Hungary. Halts of a few days were made at Pesth and at Vienna; and when they arrived at the pretty little town of Linz, they parted company with the river, and Felicia's account of their travels comes to an end.

When we consider the variety of scenes and places, of nationalities and characters, that this list of names implies, we can imagine how stimulating the journey must have been to a mind like hers, ready to be interested in everything and everybody.

It may be said of many folk—

"Far ha'e they travelled, and muckle ha'e they seen"—

and yet they return home as dull as when they started.

That was not her case. Her travels enlarged her sympathies with foreigners of all kinds. A brown, a yellow, or a black skin, was no bar to intercourse with her; and she relates how a poor slave, in response to the look of interest with which she regarded him, "suddenly came forward, and timidly, almost fearfully, ventured to offer me one of his flowers. It was quite touching to see how his dusky face beamed with delighted surprise and joy when I took it and thanked him warmly. How rare to this poor slave must have been the look of kindness for which he could be so grateful!

I really think the face of a negro, when it is intelligent, is more expressive than that of a white man can ever be; strange as it seems to say so, the brightest smiles I have ever seen have been upon *black* lips."[1]

The only exception to her general fellow-feeling was with regard to the Turks as a nation, which arose from her warm sympathies with the recent struggles of Greece to free itself from the yoke of Turkey, and her joy at the success of the War of Independence. These feelings had been enlisted even before their arrival at Athens, by meeting on board ship Prince Mavrocordato, the Greek patriot, who had played a heroic part in the conflict; and seven years' residence in Greece had naturally deepened them. Yet she found it impossible to restrain her usual friendly spirit with regard to individuals among the Turks. One of them she persuaded to teach her to sing the call to prayers of the Muezzins. With another, a gentleman of great *hauteur* and solemnity, she had a game of chess. He loftily brushed aside the young Frenchman who was to have been her opponent, and took his place opposite to her. The game was something of an "awful joy." Neither understood the language of the other; but she soon learnt to her cost what *chok pasha!* meant, and after a

[1] "Wayfaring Sketches."

few such challenges to her king she found herself beaten in ten moves.

The two events at Constantinople which made the deepest impression on her mind were of a very different kind—the one delightful, the other painful.

The first was the intercourse they had with her father's old friend Sir Stratford Canning, afterwards Lord Stratford de Redcliffe, known to the natives as "the Great Elchi." He had visited Mr and Mrs Skene at Athens, and now returned their hospitality. If his high position and somewhat haughty manner alarmed Felicia a little at first, his real kindness soon allayed her fears.

"I went," she writes, "one day to dine with my father at the Embassy. It happened that there was no other lady-guest at the party, excepting the members of his own family, so he took me down to the dining-room, and placed me next to himself at table; there, to my surprise, I found the habitually reserved, silent man transformed into the most kind and genial host imaginable, doing his best to entertain his insignificant guest with the utmost cordiality, and such he continued to be during all the occasions when we met him afterwards during our stay in Constantinople."[1]

That she made a favourable impression on her host was shown a few years later. When the Crimean War broke out, and the need arose for

[1] "Some Episodes in a Long Life."—*Blackwood's Magazine*, June 1896

nurses to be sent out for the wounded soldiers, he wrote to her, begging her to do all she could to help Miss Nightingale and Lady Canning to select suitable women.

The painful reminiscence was the sight of the slave market, which she describes with disgust :—

"It was a long, low building, forming a square of a considerable size. On a large platform, divided into pens shut in by railings, were confined the black slaves, while through the open doors leading into the house itself could be seen the veiled forms of the white women grouped behind a wooden screen. On benches so placed as to command a view of both were the buyers— coarse-looking Turks—whose calm, searching gaze seemed to take in every detail. The merchant conducting the sale stood before them, talking and gesticulating with great vehemence. He turned to one of the pens which was filled with young Circassian women, most of whom were very handsome. They were seated close together on the ground in an attitude of listless despondency, their white garments flowing round them, and as they gazed up at me with their sad, dark eyes, I felt painfully how they must envy the free and happy stranger. . . . The slave-trader came forward, followed by a phlegmatic-looking Turk, and seizing one of the women by the arm, forced her to stand up before this man who, it appeared, wished to buy her, and inspected her very much in the same manner as he might have examined a horse or a dog, and his decision was unfavourable. He turned away with a contemptuous movement of the head, and the slave-merchant in a rage thrust back the unfortunate girl, who sank down trembling among her companions in captivity. This scene was as much as we could stand, and we left the place hurriedly at once. It is well indeed that such sights can be witnessed no more, at least in Europe." [1]

Felicia was, as we have said, one of those people who have a talent for picking up wonderful stories, either because they were confided to her, or because her quick observation revealed to her the incidents passing around, which others overlooked. And what she saw and vividly realised remained in her memory, to be reproduced at will, and, rare case where the imagination is lively, reproduced accurately. She did not even need to write down any statistics of numbers, size, etc., for these dry details printed themselves on her memory as deeply as the more lively and amusing features of a scene. She once astonished a friend by repeating a long passage, word for word, from a letter read over once years before. It was a proof of the vigour of her mental grasp. She gripped the facts and held them fast. Being a born narrator, she tells in her " Wayfaring Sketches " tale after tale, with a natural ease and skill that carry the reader along and make him feel he cannot stop, but must positively know what happened next. The

[1] "Some Episodes in a Long Life."—*Blackwood's Magazine,* June 1896.

history of Carripèze, the French headsman,
shows considerable dramatic power, and makes
one understand the request she received in later
years from a literary American gentleman that
he might adapt one of her stories as a play.

If "Wayfaring Sketches" had been purely
narrative, we might say there was not a dull page
in it.   Unfortunately there are too many moral
reflections, and when she indulges in them, she
abandons her brisk, lively style and becomes
quite Johnsonian in her grandiloquence.   The
book was originally written in French for the
benefit of her brothers, and she was persuaded to
translate and publish it.   If the reflections were
conscientiously read and digested by the young
men, they must have been very unlike those of
the present day.   We can scarcely forbear a
smile at the lofty language and rolling sentences
in which she utters her sentiments.   The style
has gone completely out of fashion.   But perhaps,
after all, there is as much to be said for it as for
the smartness that is now in vogue; and it is
free from certain other modern failings, for it is
never ungrammatical or slipshod.   Each sentence
is rightly organized in all its parts.   You are
sure when you begin it that you will arrive,
without halt or hitch, safely at the end.

The   whole   book   glows   with   imagination
enough to supply a society of authors, while
her metaphors and images are often striking;

moral reflections

'Wayfaring Sketches' originally written in French

and when we add that she lays a good sub-
stratum of solid facts in describing the various
institutions, educational, political and religious,
which she visited in the different countries she
passed through, and that the book is full of
the humour which delighted in the comic side of
the adventures described, we cannot wonder that
" Wayfaring Sketches " soon reached a second
edition.

The family party had been pleasantly enlarged
by the addition of the younger Mr James Skene's
two little girls, Zoe and Janie, whose father and
mother had consented to their accompanying their
grandparents to England for education.   They
were enlivening elements in the party until they
reached Antwerp, when poor little Zoe seemed
to realize for the first time that she had left her
home and country, and wept during the whole
passage till they reached the English coast.   But
the new home was to be a very happy one for the
children, and Felicia was to prove an ideal aunt.

Among fellow-travellers on board their
different steamers, they met with various
agreeable or entertaining people, whom they
selected as their special companions.   The most
distinguished was M. de Saulcy, a great traveller,
linguist, archæologist and writer.   If he did not
actually become a declared suitor of Felicia, his
admiration for her was evident, and the friendship
then begun was life-long.

A certain M. de B. and his nephew Ernest—
typical Frenchmen in their passion for Paris, its
gaieties and luxuries—added greatly to the mirth
of the party, especially when the young man, on
the strength of a prize gained at College for
German, vainly tried to make himself understood
in that language.   Every failure was accentuated
by the disappointed exclamation of his uncle:
"Et pourtant, Ernest, vous avez gagné le prix
pour l'allemand à l'Université."   What could
the unsuccessful competitors have been like?
Their amusement reached its height when the
following scene took place :—

They were going over a palace at Offen near
Pesth under the guidance of a remarkably stupid
Swiss, "whose attempts to comprehend the
questions with which the young Frenchman
assailed him with the greatest volubility and in his
own peculiar German, were most amusing.
Sometimes he put on an expression of the most
hopeless despondency, and turned to me as though
he thought I should have been able to understand him, saying piteously, 'What does the
little gentleman want?'   At last, when he
seemed about to usher us out without our having
seen the famous crown, Monsieur Ernest became
highly excited, and his impatience rendering him
still more incoherent, the poor man grew quite
bewildered, and not having the smallest idea of
what he was asking for, the conversation between
them was most ludicrous.   'Sie haben ein
Kron?' (' you have got a crown?') said M. Ernest

to him very decidedly. 'Ich? Armer Mensch!
Ich habe kein Kron.' ('I? a poor man! I have
got no crown'). 'Yes, you have; you have got a
crown, a sceptre.' 'Holy Saint Nicholas! I have
neither crown nor sceptre! I am a poor man
with a large family.' 'A king's crown!' shouted
Monsieur Ernest, 'and a sceptre and a mantle.'
'I am no king,' he answered doggedly, 'and I
have not got a sceptre; I keep the keys.' At
last, catching at a word, he made out his meaning, and told us the crown was at Vienna; when
Monsieur de B. wound up the whole by remarking, 'Et pourtant, Ernest, vous avez gagné le
prix,'[1] etc. But the joke of the party was a
certain American, whom, from his frequent
references to his native city, they nicknamed
'Kentucky.' He was a sort of *enfant terrible*,
who said and did the most extraordinary things.
His American mind seemed quite unable to
grasp the ideas and prejudices of the old world,
and his cool off-hand proceedings often set his
fellow-travellers on tenterhooks."

On one occasion at Widdein in Bulgaria,
Felicia with one or two companions had been
invited to visit the palace of a certain pasha.
With her usual *savoir-faire*, she went through
all the proper ceremonies of bowing and placing
her hand on heart, head and forehead in respect-
ful salutation of the pasha, whenever coffee or
sweetmeats were handed to her. She also took
the jewelled pipe offered her, as if she had

[1] "Wayfaring Sketches."

E

been accustomed to one all her life. In the
midst of this solemn function Kentucky suddenly
appeared at the door, hat on head and cane in
hand, having made his way through the guards.
Having taken a good stare at His Highness, he
remarked to Felicia, "I calculate he never saw
an American afore." If a look could have
withered him, the indignant gaze of the pasha
would have done so. We are not told whether
he was turned out of the room by force, but as
he had the grace to show signs of uneasiness, let
us hope he turned and fled.

Felicia's visit to her host's harem, and her
admiration of the beautiful Georgian and
Circassian slave-girls who attended on the
magnificent sultana, are prettily described. As
if to the manner born, she again went through
the correct compliments and salutations as she
accepted the seat offered her on the divan by the
great lady, and puffed away valiantly at a long
pipe, one end of which was held up by a kneeling slave. She admired her hostess's dress with
all the eloquence at her command; she answered
the extraordinary questions put to her; she made
friends with the four children, for whom, in order
to allay all anxieties on the mother's part lest her
visitor should have an evil eye, she at once
expressed the wish that they might live for ever,
and acceded to the proposal that she and the
sultana should henceforth be sisters. Before she

Felicia's visit to a harem

left, the interpreter was told to inform her that her highness had once before seen a Christian, who was not at all like her. This Felicia could well believe.

The proposed sisterhood was sealed by the present from the great lady of a diamond ring, so handsome that the guest hesitated to accept it, and thereby found she was giving great offence. " Oh! if the lady wished for something better," remarked the sultana with a frown, " a more valuable present should be found."

So, with polite explanations and many expressions of gratitude, Felicia put the ring on her finger.

Their adventures were not always so agreeable. In one Bulgarian town where they landed to take a stroll, the Mahommedan inhabitants scowled at them with threatening looks, soon followed by cries of, " Giaours, dogs of Christians "—which Felicia had sufficient knowledge of the language to understand—hurled against themselves and their ancestors for many generations. Worst of all, volleys of stones followed, and they had to take to their heels and run for their lives.

It was like a nightmare, for poor Monsieur de B. could not make much way. " Courrez, mon oncle," shouted Monsieur Ernest; but the efforts to obey only landed the poor man panting and puffing against a tree, after which he fell and rolled down a grassy bank. "Nous faisons toujours du chemin," cried the nephew encouragingly, as he picked the elder gentleman up and set him on his feet again, making Felicia laugh, even in that moment of terror, to see the energy with which they continued their flight. The goal was reached safely at last, and the travellers took refuge in a little boat sent for their rescue by the captain, though not before Felicia had been hit on the shoulder by a stone.

But the enjoyments of their travels far outweighed any risks or inconveniences that they had gone through, and left a store of happy memories on which to draw for the rest of their lives.

Felicia ends her account of their long journey with the visit they paid to the pretty little town of Linz, where they said a reluctant good-bye to the river. Before they reached it, they had already parted with some of their companions. Monsieur de B. and his nephew were wild to return to their beloved Paris, and had set forth thither.

Kentucky was last seen by Felicia on the staircase of the hotel at Vienna, wondering whether "as he had come all the way up the Danube, it would not be very good fun to go down again."

CHAPTER V

VISITS—LEAMINGTON

FOR the first two years after the return of the wanderers from Greece Mr Skene and his family settled once more in Scotland as their head-quarters, spending their winters in Edinburgh and their summers in a house in the country. After Felicia's long absence from her native land, it was natural that her friends and relations should be clamouring for her company, and that she should pay a series of visits among them to their mutual pleasure.

With her usual luck she generally met some interesting personage, either on her journeys or her visits. At one time it was Sir Edwin Landseer, and while travelling together by coach they soon got upon a subject particularly congenial to both, she not having an idea at the time who he was. He puzzled her by informing her that stags were animals that he found particularly useful, though he neither shot them nor had any special partiality for venison. From stags they got upon the subject of dogs, and Felicia, being a born dog-lover, listened with delight to the stories he related of his canine pets.

Not till they parted did he tell her that he was the well-known artist.

Mr Robert Chambers was another interesting fellow-traveller; and as they spent hours together on the Caledonian Canal, they had time enough to enjoy a long talk on a variety of topics, from his family concerns and his delight in his numerous daughters, to the mighty subject of the origin and vicissitudes of this earthly planet. When he expatiated on geology as they passed through beautiful scenery, she amused him by protesting against devoting their attention to the poor, naked bones of earth, instead of enjoying the lovely forms and colours of the landscape. It was a pity that they never had the opportunity of meeting again, though the friendship begun did not die out, but was kept up by the many pleasant letters that passed between them.

William Aytoun was another celebrity whom she was fortunate enough to sit next to, at a dinner-party, and whom she often met with afterwards. And he was not the only poet she had the happiness to talk to, for on another occasion she found herself staying in the same house with Walter Savage Landor. She thought him pleasant and courteous, but he did not attract her in the same way as did Long-fellow, with whom she made acquaintance on one of his visits to England, and whose personality deeply impressed her. And both then

and throughout her life she was one who would
always make the most of such opportunities.
Celebrities were not mere lions to be stared at.
Her quick sympathy with the ideals of great
men drew them towards her, and expanded and
enriched her own mind.

Felicia's first visit seems to have been to the
home in Ireland of her sister Mrs Grierson,
where the happy chance came to her of forming
a friendship, which lasted to the end of her days,
with one whose name is well known in literature.
How it began shall be told in that lady's own
words :—

RECOLLECTIONS OF FELICIA SKENE

BY FRANCES POWER COBBE

My first acquaintance with Felicia Skene was,
I think, in 1846, or possibly a year sooner.
She had recently returned with all her family
from Greece, where they had remained for many
years, and she came to Ireland to pay a visit
to one of her sisters who had married an Irish-
man, Mr John Grierson, one of the firm of the
Queen's Printers.   Mr Grierson, his brother, and
three quaint old sisters, all lived at the time in
a lovely shooting lodge belonging to my father,
in Glenasmoil—a valley in the Dublin mountains,
on the borders of Wicklow.   We saw the
Grierson family frequently, particularly Mrs
John Grierson, *née* Skene, who was a charming
and beautiful woman whom I greatly admired,

and when Miss Skene arrived I was early introduced to her.   She attracted me exceedingly as a
very powerful personality; strong and earnest in
no ordinary degree, and very different from the
young women of such society as existed then
in Ireland.   Moreover, her long residence in
Greece and familiarity with its glorious ruins
(of which I had made such study as was possible
for me from books and engravings) and her vivid
descriptions of such scenes as the Plain of
Marathon and the " marbled steep " of Sunium,
excited my youthful interest to the greatest
degree.   She had also recently published a
little book of poems, *The Isles of Greece*,
and was the first living author I had ever met;
and though the poems, alas! were distinctly
juvenile, and she soon regretted the too hasty
publication, there was a *verve* and lilt in them
which delighted my young ears.   Long years
afterwards I repeated—on the scene they describe
—these lines :

> " But who is he that hath made his rest
>   Where mortal shall never tread,
>   And chosen the blue sea's glorious breast
>   To pillow his weary head ?

> " Let Greece respond with the pride of yore,
>   ' All hallowed be those blue seas,
>   For every wave ere it reach the shore
>   Sighs o'er Themistocles ! ' "

I soon induced Miss Skene to come and pay
me a visit at my father's house (Newbridge,
Co. Dublin—not to be confounded with Newbridge, where the barracks are, Co. Kildare); and
my mother's fine social instincts immediately

discovered the high value of my new friend's character, and welcomed her with her own sweet cordiality.   She repeated these visits, sometimes alone, sometimes with her father and mother, or sister, many times in the remaining years of my mother's life, and was constantly more loved and esteemed by us all.

Felicia Skene must have been about twenty-four or twenty-five years old at this time. She was not at all handsome, but had then and always great distinction.   Nobody could mistake the fact that she was a well-born woman, and her simple, unaffected, but naturally dignified behaviour charmed every one.   She was rather tall and largely made, with hair of the colour which in those days was condemned as "red"; and at a more artistic period much admired.   She was always pale, and had rather large features, and grey eyes full of softness and intelligence. Her voice was a great charm.   It was a delightfully rich and full one in conversation, and, in singing, a superb contralto.   She sang a great deal in those days, specially religious music of the hymn sort, and I can well recall the magnificence of her rendering of one favourite canticle, of which the first part began with the words, *Quando corpus morietur.*   This was in tones of sepulchral depths and solemnity, while the second, describing the soul ascending to "paradise and glory," was a veritable song of Heaven.

Mr James Skene, Laird of Rubislaw, her father, to whom she was much attached, was, when I knew him, a grey-haired old gentleman of very gentle and reposeful manners.   I was too young to profit by all I might have learnt from him, both about Greece, with which he was probably better acquainted than any man of that generation (except Mr George Finlay, my friend in later years); and also about his own great friend, Walter Scott. The reader will remember that Scott dedicated Canto IV of *Marmion* to Mr Skene, and that, speaking of their excursions together among the hills, when Mr Skene sketched and Scott read old ballads to him, he describes their two dogs, with their genuine canine jealousies:

> " At either's feet a trusty squire,
>   Pandour and Camp with eyes of fire,
>   Jealous each other's motions viewed,
>   And scarce repressed the ancient feud."

Portraits of both Pandour and Camp, Miss Skene told me a few years ago, were still in the possession of her brother, Mr Skene. Mrs Skene, Felicia Skene's mother, daughter of Sir William Forbes of Pitsligo, was, like herself, a tall, dignified Scotchwoman, with frank and pleasant manners.

Felicia Skene and I soon formed a friendship so sound that it subsisted unbroken (even through the considerable strain of her refusal to form nearer ties with my family), for something like fifty-five years. We were, I suppose, not very like the majority of young women, for our interminable conversations nearly all turned on theology and on the hopes of a future life, which she maintained and preached with passionate persistency. She was then and always quite orthodox in her views, with the slight tinge of Ritualism just beginning to show itself at

Oxford, while I was already a heretic of the deepest dye, so that we had abundant fields for our discussions. Nothing could exceed her sweetness and amiability to me in all our arguments. She was also full of humour and very quick-witted. Some of her stories of her experiences in Greece were extremely funny, but my recollections of them, alas! have considerably faded.

I remember her telling me as a joke against herself, how, when a new English Church was to be opened in Athens, the chaplain and other clergymen of the place were eagerly arranging for her to lead the singing on the grand occasion, and in rehearsing the music to them, she had involuntarily sung out, in her great, deep voice, this extraordinary sentence:

"Whoever will be saved—without doubt he shall perish everlastingly!"

They naturally exclaimed, "What an awful doctrine, Miss Skene!"

M. de Saulcy, the distinguished French scholar, was a devoted friend of hers, and I could readily suppose (though on such topics we never talked), that he had desired to be something nearer. One day he brought her a copy of verses which he had just written, and began to read out the first lines. They opened with the somewhat ambiguous compliment to her large grey eyes:

"Vous avez des yeux singuliers, et qui me touchent——"

He had no time to reach the second line, for Felicia shut him up by exclaiming, "Est ce que

vous allez dire que je louche ? " Her self-control
and calmness under all circumstances formed
features of her character of which many instances may be recalled. I remember her telling
me, *à propos* of poisonous snakes, that she had
got up one morning at sunrise, from their yacht
(or camp), under Sunium, and had been sitting
long alone among the beautiful columns, when,
happening to look down, she saw a large snake
actually lying across her foot, motionless. It
was of a deadly sort, and had she followed her
natural impulse to start up, the reptile would in
all probability have bitten her. She had, however, the extreme courage to remain perfectly
still, till the snake, but half awakened in the
early morning, slowly, very slowly, drew itself
across the foot, and passed on its way, leaving
her unharmed.

From that distant epoch, some fifty-five years
ago, we met very rarely, when I happened to
go to Oxford. She was never able to accept
my urgent invitations to the home I shared with
my friend Miss Lloyd, for twenty years, in
South Kensington, nor to come to us in Wales,
where we spent our summers. But our correspondence never wholly dropped, and was always,
I think I may say on both sides, full of affectionate interest in one another.

She was always infinitely kind to various
nieces and nephews and cousins of mine, who
from time to time went to Oxford.

Her books and articles, it is needless to say,
interested me deeply, and I often longed to have
real talks with her, as in our far-off youth. She
warmly sympathised in my efforts to put a stop

to scientific cruelty to animals, and was at all times ready to give her name and assistance to our Anti-vivisection work in Oxford.

I had had no reason to feel any alarm about her health when I had the pang to read in the *Times* that she was dead. A life of sincerest devotion to God, and of self-sacrifice for her fellow-men ended (as she would have wished) very suddenly; but none who knew her goodness will ever cease to cherish tenderly her noble memory.

As Scotland proved too cold for Mrs Skene, who was then in delicate health, a new home had to be decided upon. The place chosen was Leamington, where the invalid could be under the care of the famous Dr Jephson, and here the next three years of Felicia's life were passed. It was not a town which suited her tastes, for both place and society seemed to her tame and uninteresting after the delights of Athens and Edinburgh.

Still, as usual, she found opportunities for real friendship. The closest of her intimacies at that time was with Miss Isabel Percy of Guy's Cliffe, daughter of Lord Charles Percy, who became a friend for life, to be welcomed in after years when she came to stay with Felicia Skene in the little house in New Inn Hall Street, Oxford.

Miss Percy's uncle, the late Duke of Northumberland, quite considered himself included in the

friendship, and many years after, not very long
before his death, he pleased her by sending her
his photograph as a token of his old regard.

Felicia Skene and Miss Percy were alike in
their intellectual tastes, and one great bond of
union between them was the joint composition
of a story they embarked in, describing the life
and adventures of one Mr Smith. Though his
name might not sound promising, they were as
determined as Mrs Walford in *her* story of a
hero of the same name, that he should prove
interesting to all who might make his acquaintance. They wrote alternate chapters, and many
were the meetings for discussion of the plot and
characters. One incident of the story gave Felicia
a chance, too tempting to resist, of playing a trick
on a friend, Lady Somerville. "Just read this,"
she said to her visitor, as she handed her a sheet
of note-paper. It was part of a letter to the
heroine of the tale, containing an offer of
marriage, to be inserted into the story. Felicia's
hopes that the lady would think it one just
received by herself were entirely fulfilled.

Lady Somerville fell into the trap at once.

"May I congratulate you?" she enquired in
solemn tones as she handed back the letter.

That Felicia had abundant opportunities for
studying the various ways in which proposals
may be made ought certainly to have proved of
use to her in the many novels she wrote; for in

the course of a long life she might have married
over and over again. One devoted lover is
reported to have proposed to her annually for
eighteen years, appealing to her pity at last, on
the ground that he was growing blind and
needed her care.

On one of the occasions on which he besought
her to accept him an amusing little incident
occurred. It was an idiosyncracy in the Forbes
family that they should be seized with sudden,
unaccountable volleys of sneezing. On the rejected lover returning to the drawing-room after
an interview with Felicia, he found Mrs Skene
sitting with her face buried in her pocket-
handkerchief while recovering from one of these
attacks. With an outburst of gratitude for what
he thought was the expression of her tearful
sympathy, he exclaimed, " *O Madame, que vous
êtes émue !* "

It was not likely that one who had once tasted
the sweets of literary success should not indulge
in further efforts, especially when there was an
abundant power of invention and fluency of expression ; and one of her early friends at Leamington records her impression that Felicia was
always writing. Her next book, written at
that place, and published the year she left it,
in 1849, by Messrs. Rivington, is a religious
novel, of a fervid, not to say perfervid, character,
called " Use and Abuse." The scene begins and

ends in the Arabian Desert, and carries us in the interval to Constantinople, Greece, Switzerland, and England.

Though it gives evidence of a good deal of mental power, there are too many purple patches in it. In those early days she had not shaken herself free of a superabundance of language—perhaps she never did entirely — so that the reader sometimes feels as if he were being drenched under Niagara. But there are few writers who would wish to be judged by their earliest writings.

The admiration she received at Leamington brought her more invitations than she cared for. If there were any agreeable gentleman-guest staying at a friend's house, Felicia must come and entertain him and ensure a successful evening. Young, middle-aged, old, whichever he might be, he would be sure to come under the influence of her spell.

And was she not a traveller and an authoress, at a time when travelling and authorship were less common than they are now, especially among ladies? Her niece, Mrs Thomson, remembers that as she and her aunt walked through the streets of Leamington, people would sometimes leave their shopping and run to the doors to look at her as she passed, and point her out as a lion, a character which she always had a horror of assuming.

But the gay life at Leamington did not suit her. "It is very bad for me being made so much of," she would say to her niece.

And in her secret soul she longed for some congenial sphere of real work into which she might throw herself. There were powers of heart and mind which found little scope at a gay health resort, and which made her feel restless and unsatisfied. But the time of waiting and longing was not to be for long, and "the stone that was fit for the wall, was not left in the way."

It was while she was at Leamington that she came under a very strong religious influence, which moulded her life and opinions for a long period.

One of the most earnest-minded of the clergy there, the Rev. J. Lincoln Galton, a member of the extreme High Church party then struggling into prominence, impressed her deeply by his devoted life and teaching. With youthful enthusiasm she adopted his views, accepting him unreservedly as her spiritual guide. In after years she regretted having surrendered too much of her religious liberty and independence. But if she erred, it was the mistake of a noble nature, eager for self-sacrifice.

A still stronger and more lasting influence was exercised over her by another clergyman, the Rev. Thomas Chamberlain of St Thomas-the-

Martyr, Oxford, with whom she first made acquaintance when he was staying with his relations at Leamington. Her interest in all that she learnt about his work was increased by a friendship she formed with his cousin, Miss Hughes, who was at the head of a Sisterhood he had established in his parish. With her Felicia stayed at the school for young ladies, which was under the care of the Sisters.

The more she saw of Oxford the more did she feel the attractions of the place, and long to persuade her parents to make their home in it. Every side of it appealed to her: the social, the intellectual, the religious—each offered her all that she most desired. Leamington seemed to her uninteresting and unsatisfying by comparison. Each visit she paid to the University town, whether it took her into a centre of work or play, increased the attraction. The dons found her an agreeable addition to every social gathering; and breakfast and other parties were got up that the guests might be introduced to the traveller and writer.

" I shall have to have all my dresses reversed, the front where the back should be, for my head is completely turned," she laughingly remarked to her family on returning home after a particularly delightful visit to her cousins, Lord and Lady Forbes, who were then living at Oxford, where she had made acquaintance with

From a Photo by   CLAUDET.

ZOË SKENE (MRS THOMSON).

[*To face p.* 82.

Mr Charles Marriott, Dean Burgon, and many other interesting men.

The love of Oxford then begun was to increase with her years, so that it was a real wrench to her in after life to tear herself away from it : and it was only her still stronger family affections, or the call of duty that could induce her ever to leave it.

Great was her satisfaction when her parents made a sort of trial trip to this city of delight, and showed every sign of appreciation of it.

The next stage was the taking of a house temporarily, that they might see how it suited them and the two young grand-daughters, Miss Zoë and Miss Janie Skene. Before long they had come to see Oxford through the eyes of the daughter to whom they were devoted, and they determined to take a house in the newly-built Beaumont Street, the then Belgravia of the town.

Thus began for Felicia the long spell of nearly fifty years of Oxford life, which was to bring so many blessings both to it and to herself.

PART II

WORKING DAYS

"To relieve the indigent; to single out the unhappy, from whom can be expected no returns either of present entertainment or future service, for the objects of our favours; to esteem a man's being friendless as a recommendation; dejection and incapacity of struggling through the world, as a motive for assisting him; in a word, to consider these circumstances of disadvantage, which are usually thought a sufficient reason for neglect and overlooking a person, as a motive for helping them forward; this is the course of benevolence which compassion marks out and directs us to; this is that humanity, which is so peculiarly becoming our nature and circumstances in this world."

—BISHOP BUTLER.

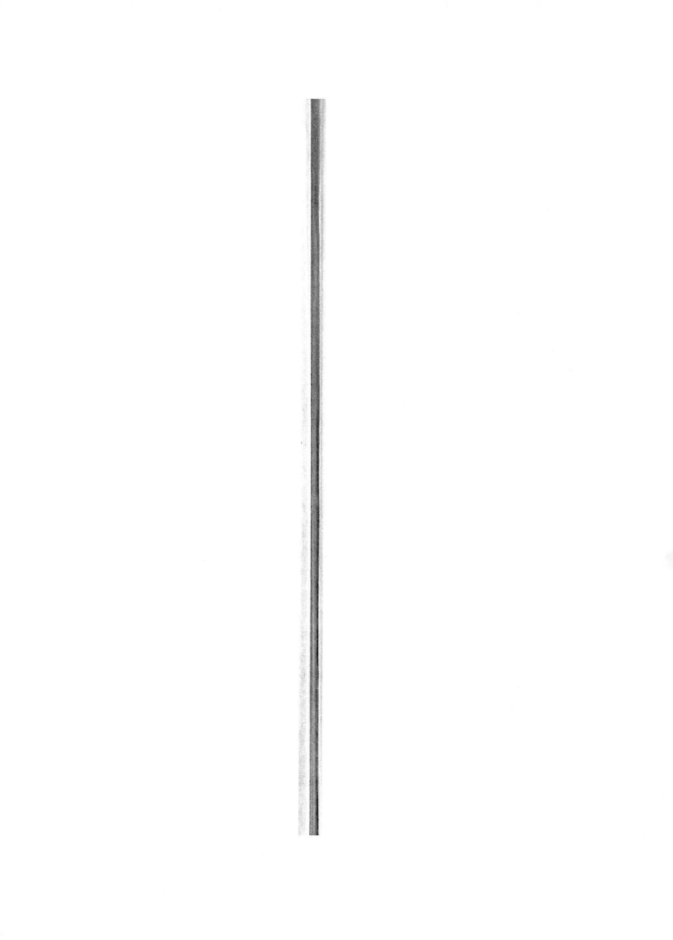

Work at St. Thomas-the-Martyr

CHAPTER VI

WORK AT ST THOMAS-THE-MARTYR

FELICIA'S life at Oxford was a remarkably full one. She was young and strong, and there were so many calls of duty and pleasure upon her, that the difficulty was how to crowd in what with most people would have been the occupations of two days, into one. Family duties to parents and nieces, friendship, society, literary work, and parish, were all pulling her in different directions. The last-mentioned became so predominant in her life at this time that we must give it our first consideration. The parish of St Thomas-the-Martyr being the central field of her operations, her labours in it could not be appreciated without some account of the history and character of the place, and of the remarkable man under whom she worked.

No one who visited to-day the rustic-looking church and pretty churchyard, with the vicarage, the sisterhood, the school, and some of the quiet-looking streets of small houses close by, would guess what a battlefield that oasis between the railway-station and the noisy thoroughfares close by had once been. There are plenty of less attractive-looking streets within the boundaries of the parish, but the immediate surroundings of the church look like a quiet haven.

Poor St Thomas's had been a sort of blacksheep among the parishes of Oxford. Every kind of evil had flourished in that unlucky spot, which has been described in a short Memoir of the Rev. Thomas Chamberlain, by the Rev. A. Barrington-Simeon, as a sort of Lazarus, full of sores, lying at the very gates of wealthy Christ Church, " neglected, poor, forsaken, the haunt of thieves and harlots," abounding in houses of ill-fame and in every kind of wickedness.

Since the Reformation it had had no resident clergyman, and the church was nearly empty.

The history of the church was an interesting one. It had been founded in 1141 by the Canons of Osney Abbey, and dedicated to St Nicholas of Myra. It seemed as if there were to be a contest between two saints for its name; for, after the murder of Thomas-a-Becket, St Nicholas had to give way to that prelate, whose name it received and retained until Henry VIII. re-dedicated it to St Nicholas.

Thomas-a-Becket was conqueror in the end, and it was a particular satisfaction to Mr Chamberlain to stamp the church books with a representation of the archbishop, with whose high views of ecclesiastical authority he was in full sympathy. Had he lived himself in the reign of Henry II., and occupied the throne at Canterbury, there would, we feel sure, have been no alteration in the history and the tragic termination of the struggle between king and prelate.

Mr Chamberlain was a man of striking appearance, strong personality, and decided uncompromising views. Of the Tractarian party a more vigorous representative could scarcely have been found. He certainly justified in his own person the title of Church Militant, for there was war to the knife between him and the terrible evils with which his parish was rife. The strong arm of the law was evoked to suppress the houses of evil repute. He drew forth from his ecclesiastical armoury every weapon provided by the Catholic revival in the Church of England. Convinced that for the ignorant, teaching through the eye is the most effective, he adopted all the ritualistic practices which he considered that certain rubrics would allow. Daily services, choral Celebrations, the establishment of a sisterhood, incessant parochial visiting, the starting of a musical society for the practice of Gregorian music, the founding of the " Englishman's Library "—in which tales of such distinctively High Church teaching as those by Paget, and Gresley's " Siege of Lichfield," were published—

the editing for more than twenty years of a periodical called *The Ecclesiastic*, all testified to his zeal in the line of attack he had laid down.

Like all hard-working vicars, he soon attracted a band of curates as eager as himself to carry on the battle. Felicia's cousin, Mr Alexander Forbes, afterwards Bishop of Brechin, had worked under him before Mr and Mrs Skene went to live in Oxford, and had been an indefatigable fellow-labourer, as Felicia testified in a short Memoir which she wrote of him in 1875. The Rev. H. F. Jones, Prebendary Miller, and, at a later period, the Rev. Algernon Simeon, were other zealous fellow-workers.

If Mr Chamberlain was stern in his requirements of others, he was equally rigid with himself. He was prepared to lead a forlorn hope against the evils he attacked, at any hour of the day or night, regardless of abuse and of the actual personal danger which he sometimes encountered.

The fact that the reforms he attempted, and the theological principles which he put in practice, might excite an angry mob to attack him, affected his determination no whit. The immediate cause of one of these riots was his refusal to allow the body of a notorious and unrepentant evil-liver to be carried into the church before burial. He marched boldly on, regardless of the abuse and the missiles hurled at him, and would not have hesitated to walk up to the stake if required.

It was long before any way could be made in such an apparently unequal struggle. It was not until a visitation of cholera and smallpox ravaged the parish, giving the clergy the opportunity of showing their unselfish devotion in their ministrations among the sufferers, that the fierce opposition began to die away. The hottest of the fight was over when Felicia began her activities in the parish.

Mr Chamberlain's influence soon grew strong upon her. The fact that he was fighting on the side of the minority would at once appeal to her generous nature. Whether she fully sympathised in all his measures and theological tenets or not, she was loyal in carrying out his orders and responding to all his demands. If his nature was less wide and sympathetic than her own, the force of his character and convictions would fully make amends; for strength has a fascination for women, especially those of warm feelings and emotional temperament. We can trace his influence in every page of a story she published not long after her new home was established in Oxford, and see in Mr Chesterfield of St Albans, Mr Chamberlain of St Thomas-the-Martyr. Yet we need hardly say that while working under the guidance of her vicar, it was the Divine Master, the Centre of her religious

life, the Object of her passionate devotion, for
Whom she loved to labour with all the powers
of her heart and mind.   For Him she was ready
to draw upon every talent and accomplishment
she possessed, whether of the lighter and more
secular kind, her singing, her agreeable conversation, her ready wit and humour, her personal
charm; or of a more solid and serious nature.
Teaching, nursing, temperance and rescue-work,
all needed her help, and whether the work went
against the grain or not, mattered not to her.

She tells us in one of her articles that she had
no faculty whatsoever for teaching, and where
that is the case it must always be more or less a
drudgery.   Yet every day would she appear at
the Rewley School for young ladies, managed by
the Sisters, to teach music, French, or drawing.
That school was a hobby of the vicar's, on which
he set special store; and a lady who was a good
linguist, first-rate singer, and something of an
artist, was too great a treasure not to be
utilized.

One of her pupils, now Sister Harriet of St
Thomas's, relates her reminiscences of Felicia's
daily visits.

" When first I saw Miss Skene, I was at school
at Rewley, in July 1857.   She used to come every
Sunday evening and sing to us in the school-room.
'Too late, too late,' was one of her songs.   She
had a beautiful contralto voice.   On Saturday

afternoons she used to come to take our marks.
There was one called 'Inattention,' which a
smile in church would incur. Woe be to any
one who gave it in! Not that Miss Skene ever
scolded, but her grave, grieved manner was quite
enough. She taught us French too, which she
pronounced with a lovely liquid accent, pure and
yet not affected. Her voice was particularly
musical. She used to get so tired that sometimes in the middle of a French *dictée* she would
fall asleep between the sentences and wake with,
'I beg your pardon, I had gone to sleep.' Only
for a moment though. She used always to come
to St Thomas's 9 A.M. Service, and the older girls
at Rewley used to think it a great privilege to
walk to church with her. She had to pass our
school (then in Worcester Street) on her way from
Beaumont Street. She was very lame at that
time and was glad of a prop. She would talk
kindly to us, but not lecture us on the way.
We took it in turns to walk with her, and used
to watch in a queer little sitting-room—where
also the marking was done—till she came along
with her dog Urisk. He was shut into the old
Vicarage during the hours of service. Miss
Skene used to come down in Holy Week, and
at the 8 o'clock Celebration used to sing and
play a beautiful Introit. 'Is it nothing to you?'
etc. I can hear her voice still. It gave one
one's first idea of the blessed solemnity of Holy
Week. Her father and mother used to come to
St Thomas's 11 o'clock Service. A fine, tall
couple they were. Miss Skene was always
gracious in her manner, queenly in her courtesy,
and always having time to give, or making it.

We were always sympathised with and encouraged by her."

It is satisfactory in every way to know that submissive as Felicia was to her vicar's wishes, there was one point, at any rate, in which she maintained her independence.

When his cousin, Miss Hughes, left St Thomas's and became head of another Sisterhood in Oxford, where she has been for years the honoured Mother Superior, Mr Chamberlain thought no one would take her place better than Felicia Skene, and earnestly desired her to become a Sister, with a view to her subsequently assuming the headship. It was a true instinct that led her firmly to refuse. If there are many who are exactly fitted for such a life, Felicia was certainly not one. She was a worker to whom a free hand must be given, to do justice to her powers, which could never have had full scope in community life for the variety of results they accomplished. It was not that she would not have forced herself to obey rules. Her extreme conscientiousness in keeping to all the regulations laid down, when she became a visitor at the prison, is proof enough of this.

But nature had marked her out as a free lance. She must be allowed to choose her own time and methods, often most unconventional, but generally the right ones in her hands. She might make blunders from time to time, but she must fight her own way to success. She must be free too to write her ideas, not only on philanthropic and social questions, but on any others about which she longed to express herself, in fiction, history, biography, essay, whatever the vehicle might be. She must be at full liberty to exercise her genius for friendship, one of her most marked characteristics to the end of her days. Young and old, rich and poor, men and women, unknown or famous, old friends or new, were the constant interest and refreshment of her life. And hers was a mind that had not only great enjoyment, but a real need, of masculine as well as feminine society, which she could not have had if she had yielded to Mr Chamberlain's persuasions.

Perhaps he secretly indulged a hope of ultimate success in his aim from observing the long, severe-looking black dress, made with big, loose sleeves, unlike that of other ladies, which she adopted at one time, and regarded it as a step to donning the official one of a regular Sister. But this dress did not give general satisfaction. Her family longed to see her in brighter colours, and her cousin, Bishop Forbes, remarked, as he gazed at her costume: "I like whole sisters; I don't like half ones."

After a time the dress was discarded for an ordinary one, and she took special pleasure in wearing a little bit of bright colour in every bonnet as a flag of independence.

Her energies were constantly employed in getting workers for the parish. To this end she wrote a little book called, " A Cry from the Foot of the Cross." The need of money which always comes to daunt the efforts of the philanthropist prompted her to give her industrious pen ample employment at all spare moments. Often would she sit up till the small hours of the morning, intent on her tales and novels, or on papers for Mr Chamberlain's Magazine.

It was her rule throughout her long life never to spend on herself what she gained from her writings, partly from her natural love of giving, partly from an old-fashioned idea that it was an undignified thing for a lady to earn money for her own personal advantage.

The only exception to this rule was in connection with her editorship of the *Churchman's Companion*, begun a few years later, and carried on by her for nearly twenty years. For this she received a salary, which she felt free to use as she chose for herself or for others.

Felicia's interest in the parish of St Thomas-the-Martyr lasted, through all changes and chances, to the end of her life. She never ceased to attend the services, or to help the clergy who succeeded Mr Chamberlain in the vicarage. One of them wrote to her near the close of her life saying how strongly he realized that the church and parish "mean perhaps more to her than they mean to any one else, and that the remembrance of her in her hidden corner in the early morning would always be a help and an encouragement to him."

Her grave, with its recumbent marble cross, is in that part of the churchyard which lies close to the window put up to the memory of her eldest brother.

Near that window she was wont to kneel. On the opposite side of the church are those in memory of her parents. The uncommon subjects of the pictures they contain, were chosen by herself from the book of Revelation.

Church and churchyard seem still under the spell of her loving presence.

CHAPTER VII

CHOLERA OUTBREAK AT OXFORD
THE CRIMEAN WAR

As was not unnatural, Felicia became more and more absorbed with her work of various kinds in St Thomas's parish, which she found it difficult to combine with home and social duties. In after years she reproached herself bitterly with not

G

having devoted herself sufficiently to her parents, and as we wish to give a faithful picture of her, it may be right to say that there was perhaps a time when she fell into the snare that often besets enthusiastic workers among the poor—of not giving due attention to home claims. But in reading her expressions of self-reproach, we must take into account the tenderness of an always exacting conscience, remembering at the same time the deep love and devotion she ever felt for her father and mother, which shine out constantly in her letters.

For herself it might have been better if she had at that time gone more into society, for, with her nature and the mentally exhausting work she undertook, a change of intellectual atmosphere would have been as wholesome as a blast of fresh air or a draught of spring water. Fortunately there were always plenty of callers, some of whom she could not avoid seeing, who brought a change of thought. Mr Skene's house was bound to be the resort of agreeable people, of old friends visiting Oxford, of dons and under-graduates; and his two grand-daughters, who were growing up into lively and charming girls, would make it the more attractive.

Of Felicia's inner spiritual life, during those early years at Oxford, the best reflection is given in her little book, "The Divine Master," published anonymously. It attained perhaps

Felicia's book (The Divine Master published anonymously

11 editions of "The Divine Master"

greater celebrity than any book she wrote. In 1852 it reached a second edition, and one after another was called for, until it attained to its eleventh in 1885.

The plan on which it is written is that of a dialogue, in which the Divine Teacher explains to His pupil the "Way of the Cross," in Repentance, Humility, the Sacraments, Obedience, Perseverance, Holy Zeal, Temptations, Suffering and Death. A chapter is devoted to each subject. While the Master instructs and explains, the pupil pours out his difficulties, fears and trials. The little book is written in the spirit of Thomas-à-Kempis; there are passages of great beauty, and not a page that does not breathe a spirit of lofty devotion. If it contains counsels of perfection to which the many may feel they cannot attain, the popularity of the little volume shows nevertheless that there were plenty to whom it did appeal. Some will think the language overstrained; and if it had been written at a later period of her life, there would probably have been more restraint. The passionate love to her Saviour that filled Felicia's heart never changed, but the expression of it might have been different.

It was a cause of annoyance to her that a charge was made against the author of publishing as original the translation of a French

book called, " Le Divine Maître "; and she was
careful to declare in a preface to the second
edition that she had never seen that book or
any translation from it.

In 1854 a fresh claim came upon her energies.
Oxford was once more attacked by cholera
and smallpox.   It was the worst visitation of
cholera there had been, numbering more victims
than either of the two previous ones.

Already, in 1849, Felicia had given her services
to the sufferers, so that she had had some experience of the terrible disease.   In St Thomas's
parish it was at its worst.   In one of the maps
in Sir Henry Acland's able " Memoir of the
Cholera at Oxford," the black spots, showing the
streets invaded by it, are more conspicuous in that
district than in any part of the city except the
County Gaol, where the mortality was highest.

A noble corps of workers among the doctors,
the   clergy,   and   others   banded   themselves
together   to   cope   with   the   scourge.   Terrible
disclosures   were   made   of   the   state   of   things
in   the   miserable   rooms   of   the   sufferers.   " It
was   not,"   Sir   Henry   Acland   tells   us,   " that
the   houses,   as   houses   are   counted   bad,   were
specially bad."   Often the worst sufferings arose
from mental and moral causes.   The kinds of
cases   with   which   Felicia   and   her   fellow-
labourers   had   to   deal   are   painful   even   to
read   about.   We   need   only   quote   one   that

Sir Henry mentions, to show the scenes in which she did not shrink from taking her part :—

" Soon after five one morning a woman awoke in the agony of cramps, with intense and sudden collapse. She was seen at six. There was in her room no article of furniture but one broken chair, no bed of any kind, no fire, no food; she lay on the bare boards; a bundle of old sacking served for a pillow; she had no blanket or any covering but the ragged cotton clothes she had on. She rolled screaming. One woman, scarcely sober, sat by; she sat with a pipe in her mouth, looking on. To treat her in this state was hopeless. She was to be removed. There was a press of work at the hospital and a delay. When the carriers came, her saturated-garments were stripped off, and in the finer linen and in the blankets of a wealthier woman she was borne away, and in the hospital she died.

Her room was cleaned out; the woman that cleaned it had next night the cholera. She and her husband were drunk in bed. The agony sobered her, but her husband went reeling about the room; in a room below were smokers and drinkers. Then a woman of the streets in her gaudiness came to see her. They would not hear reason, but drank more spirits. The victim of the disease cried out to the end that her soul was everlastingly lost; and she died." [1]

Memoir of the Cholera at Oxford," by Sir Henry Acland.

The plan of campaign adopted was a double one. Nursing must be carried on in some building in an airy spot apart from the town, for the reception of those patients who could be removed to it; and those who could not must be nursed in their own houses.

For the first, a field was found on which three old cattle-sheds were adapted for the use of patients, one for smallpox, two for cholera. Sleeping shelters were provided for members of the families of the sufferers; tents were erected for meals and for the reception of children coming from infected houses. There they could be carefully watched to see if symptoms of disease appeared, and removed to the temporary hospital if necessary. Every department on that "Field of Observation," as it was called, was admirably organised under Sir Henry Acland's orders, and he was assisted in his medical duties by Mr H. P. Mallam, Mr Thomson and others; Professor Rolleston also took a leading part. The clergy rose nobly to the occasion. Mr Charles Marriott was indefatigable in his labours amongst old and young, going from the bedside of some poor man or woman, whose miseries were increased by the memory of a life spent in evil practices, to the tent of the children, to play with them or sing hymns to them. Mr Venables (afterwards Bishop) was another of the clergy who

might be sent for at any time to minister to
the sick and dying.

The nursing itself was carried on under the
direction of Felicia's friend, Miss Hughes (Sister
Marion), of whose noble efforts for the comfort
and relief of her patients, whether in body, mind
or spirit, Sir Henry speaks with enthusiasm.
It was the human love shown by her and others
that sometimes helped the sufferers to realise what
the Divine might be, and enabled them to rise from
the despair into which their bad lives had plunged
them, to feelings of humble trust.   The other department of the nursing, that in which Felicia took
the leading part, had to be carried on in the homes
of the sick, and was probably the harder and more
trying of the two, from the dreadful condition
of some of the tenements in yards and alleys
where the sufferers lived.   Here were found the
worst cases of the disease, the patients being too
ill to be removed to the Field of Observation.

At first Felicia tried to carry on her labours
among them single-handed, but it soon became
necessary to enlist other helpers.   Mr Cart-
wright, Deputy Chairman of the Board of
Guardians, was made responsible for engaging
and dismissing a band of respectable women as
nurses, and Felicia was to superintend and
instruct them in their duties.

She had undertaken no light task, for if on
the whole they did their work satisfactorily,

many were ignorant and needed training. How she acquitted herself Sir Henry Acland shall testify :—

"Lastly," he writes, "because the most important, a lady (who desires her name to be withheld) visited daily every house within a certain area, to instruct the nurses, to comfort the sick, to cheer the disconsolate, and, where need was, herself to supply a sudden emergency, or to relieve a wearied attendant. By day and by night she plied this task; and when she rested, or where—as long at least as she knew of a house where disease had entered—is known to herself alone."[1]

At all hours Felicia might have been seen going about the lowest streets, carrying hot-water bottles or other comforts for the sufferers. If she were not sitting up at night with one of them, she was willing to be sent for at any moment. The front door of her house was kept on the latch, with a policeman walking up and down to guard it, to make her summons easy. The cholera cases were often awfully rapid. The patient would be suddenly seized with violent pains, and in a couple of hours all would be over.

The cases of natural smallpox she found even more painful and distressing. Those who were stricken down with it were often so changed as

[1] Acland's "Memoir of the Cholera at Oxford."

to look scarcely human, more like logs of wood, she said, than anything else. She would sometimes find the sick or dying left entirely alone in the house, and on her would fall the burden and responsibility of tending them through the hours of night. She would often have to lay out the dead; and if there were no friends or relations to attend the funeral, she would follow them to the grave herself.

Her fearlessness struck all with whom she worked, rendering her, fortunately, less liable to catch the disease herself. Like Isaac Walton's falcon, "her mettle made her careless of danger," though she took all reasonable precautions against infection for herself and others.

Her self-forgetfulness was the more remarkable, because she had an unusually keen sense of smell. In one room, she described the atmosphere as being enough to knock you down, and she thought as she entered, "if ever there is danger of infection, it is certainly here."

Neither had she that special taste and talent for nursing that makes it, quite apart from duty, a real pleasure to many women; though she had the moral qualities required, which have led to the saying, that it takes a good woman to be a good nurse. In that, as in so many branches of work, love helps to find out the way. Her quick sympathy gave her insight into the patients' needs. Her tenderness invited confidence, so that they could pour out the anxieties which weighed on their minds and retarded their recovery. Her courage and cheerfulness braced them to make an effort to get well. Her strong will ensured obedience to her orders. Her very presence with its vigorous vitality seemed to inspire them with hope and strength.

The love and gratitude she won were deep and lasting, though sometimes the expression given to them was not what she would have chosen.

After the outbreak had subsided, she was walking along a mean street with a friend one day, when a man reeled up to her and put his arm round her waist. Shrinking back in alarm, she begged her companion to call a policeman to free her from her tipsy admirer. His protection, however, was not required, for the man withdrew his arm, explaining that he only wished to show his gratitude to her for nursing his wife through the cholera and saving her life.

Another proof of appreciation of her nursing labours was less trying yet hardly welcome. There had been another outbreak of smallpox in Oxford, and as she was walking home in the dark one evening from the wooden shanty put up by the Local Board where the cases were received, an elderly farmer came up to her and begged to be allowed a few words with her.

He was simple and homely in appearance, and spoke with a broad provincial accent. On receiving permission to speak, he told her that he had been watching her for some time, as he passed every day to and fro in his gig, and that he had made up his mind to marry her. He could give an excellent account of his worldly affairs, was in a position to offer her an extremely comfortable home at his farm, and, in fact, he intended to make her his wife.

Felicia's sense of humour was so tickled by the astonishment she felt at receiving such an unexpected offer that she hardly knew how to restrain her laughter. Putting a strong force on herself to reply with becoming seriousness, she managed to express her gratitude for the honour he had done her, and her regret that she was unable to accede to his wishes.

A happier and more lasting result of the devotion she showed to the sick and dying was the friendship begun during the visitation of cholera with Sir Henry Acland. It was to be one of the happinesses of her life. They were near neighbours, and the intercourse between the two houses became close and constant.

As time went on he looked more and more to her for help and advice. She assisted him in his literary work, looking through and correcting his MSS.; she answered his letters for him when he was away from home. Above

all, when the infirmities of age had depressed
his spirit, he turned to her to strengthen his
faith and rekindle his hope. She would come
in at any time, sometimes twice in the day, to
answer some doubt, to read to him or write
for him. And the many notes that flitted from
Broad Street to her little house in St Michael
Street overflow with expressions of gratitude for
all her kindness.

Every sort of trouble appealed to her, so that
friends and acquaintances felt her to be a sure
resort, as a true daughter of consolation.

Among the letters she received at this time
are two touching ones from a clergyman on
whom one of the heaviest sorrows of life had
fallen. He had a request to make of her, which
he described as a very solemn one. His poor
wife was mentally afflicted and under restraint.
If he should be taken from this world before
his children were old enough to ascertain that
every possible comfort and alleviation were given
her, would she look in on her from time to time?
The knowledge that she would do so would be
an inexpressible comfort to him. The letter was
sent on Christmas Day, and on New Year's Day
he writes his warm thanks to his "dear kind
friend" for her compliance with his request.

A few years after he turned to her again
for sympathy; his poor son, always good and
kind to him, who had been recently married,

had taken his own life in a sudden attack of insanity.

And then, after another interval, there follows one more letter, recording the death of his daughter—his comfort and support for twenty years. Her mind, too, had been affected for a time, but she had recovered from her malady to be once more his constant companion, and now an attack of fever had robbed him of her after a few weeks' illness.

It was impossible for a person of Felicia's nature not to feel the strain which the constant giving out of sympathy entails. An old friend of hers remarked that one of her strongest characteristics was an unusual capacity for suffering. Happily, as is often the case, it was balanced by an equal capacity for enjoyment. A queer incident, a droll saying, an amusing specimen of eccentricity among the strange characters with whom she came into contact, would give her real enjoyment and make her laugh till the tears ran down her cheeks.

Felicia's work at the time of the cholera was to lead to fresh enterprise on her part, when in the following year the Crimean War began.

Her younger niece, Miss Janie Skene, then a girl of fifteen, was staying with her parents in Constantinople, and had gone with her mother to visit the wounded soldiers at Scutari. So shocked was she at the sight of the sufferings of the poor men, and the utter inadequacy of the means taken to relieve them, through the lack of good nurses and of hospital appliances and comforts of every kind, that she wrote a long letter to her grandfather, Mr Skene, on the subject. Struck by her forcible remarks, he immediately sent it to the *Times*, where it was inserted, and did much to stir up the feelings of the public and to lead to measures being taken to introduce a better state of things at Scutari.

It struck Felicia that having with great pains trained her corps of nurses for the cholera, they might now be utilized at Scutari, her great desire being to go out herself at the head of them. Had these events occurred at the present day, when ideas of what ladies, still young, may and may not do in the way of bold enterprise, perhaps she might have obtained her parents' permission to go. As it was, the notion was too new and startling to be taken into consideration; and she had to content herself with doing all she could at home to send out others.

Her zeal was quickened by a letter she received from Lord Stratford de Redcliffe, who had been much struck by her energy and ability, urging her to do all she could in England to send to the rescue.

At once she set to work as a pioneer in the undertaking, delighted to encourage her nurses to take their part in the patriotic task.

Florence Nightingale

Meantime Miss Nightingale was hard at work enlisting recruits, thankful to secure Felicia's services as agent in Oxford. She sent her friends Mr and Mrs Bracebridge down there, that they might inspect the volunteers and select the women they thought would be suitable.

The interviews took place in Mr Skene's dining-room, along the walls of which the candidates were ranged.

Kind-hearted as Mrs Bracebridge was, her proceedings were somewhat in the "Off with their heads!" style of the famous duchess in "Alice in Wonderland!" If the sudden questions fired at each in succession were not answered in a way she thought quite satisfactory,—"She won't do; send her out," was the decided command.

And Felicia had to administer balm to the wounded feelings of the rejected.

When the corps was complete, Felicia was requested to escort the party to London, to the house of Lady Canning, where they were to be provided with their outfit, and despatched without delay to the seat of war. Needless to say, Felicia was charmed with her beautiful hostess, "whose manners and speech were engaging and graceful to the utmost degree. She was so perfectly frank and sympathetic that we seemed to become friends immediately. She was enthusiastic in the cause of our soldiers, and eagerly desirous that everything should be done for their comfort. She left me in the drawing-room, while she went down to interview the nurses and send them off to the lodgings where they were to pass the night. Then she came back and entered clearly and carefully into the manner in which the home concerns of the nurses were to be left in my hands." [1]

When Felicia returned to Oxford, a close correspondence was begun between her and Miss Nightingale, who had many orders to give her about the investment of part of the nurses' salaries in the savings-bank. These were to pass through Felicia's hands. Like every one else, she was struck with Miss Nightingale's ability for business, every detail being as carefully arranged as if it were the sole one under her consideration.

CHAPTER VIII

PERSONAL TRAITS AND HABITS

In trying to present Felicia to the reader so that he may realise in some measure her strong individuality, we feel, as one of her friends said, " She was so utterly unlike any one else."

[1] " Some Episodes in a Long Life."—*Blackwood's Magazine.*

And we are struck at once by the fact that she differed in quantity, if we may use the expression, as well as quality, from ordinary people,—there was so much of her—she was cast in such a large mould.

"She nothing common did, or mean"

in any respect.

There was a streak of nobility even in her faults, which were for the most part virtues in excess. She could do nothing by halves. Whatever the matter might be, she threw her whole soul into it. This was notably the case in her friendships. When living in a house of her own, after her parents' death, she was free to open her hospitable doors in the evening to any undergraduate who liked to come in for a chat. It was not surprising that each one should feel himself the object of peculiar interest, for so he was—his own peculiar interest.

Her talent for friendship was one of her most marked characteristics, and one she exercised to the last year of her life. A new friendship was a fresh and delightful discovery. She never gave up the old ones, but she realized keenly the delight that comes with the first revelation of mutual attraction, when a spark of light and heat is, as it were, struck off in the contact.

Foreign visitors to Oxford felt lucky if they

H

got an introduction to her, for they were sure of a welcome.   She never felt any difficulty with regard to the Jewish precept, " Love ye, therefore, the stranger," partly from her natural disposition, partly from having been much thrown with men and women of different nationalities in her early days.   One of her foreign acquaintances, a learned Dutchman, Dr Müller, writes of her in a letter from Utrecht with great appreciation, " as a most lively person, lovely and lively."   He made acquaintance with her in a visit he paid to Oxford, their conversation being carried on in Greek. He pronounces Miss Skene and Lady Victoria Welby the two most interesting English ladies he ever met in his life.

Men and women were equally susceptible to her charm, and young people felt it as strongly in her old age as in her youth.   She did not seem ancient to them.   " She is as young as any of us," they would say.   And they generally found it easy to comply with her request that they would call her by her Christian name, or rather by its diminutive of " Fifie," by which she was always known.   She could not bear to be " Miss Skene" to any one she really cared for.   She always had her little court of young ladies-in-waiting, taking the greatest interest in all their affairs, especially their love-affairs, in which she was their trusted confidante.   She frankly owned herself a great matchmaker, and in an innocent and lady-like way she was; longing that others should enjoy the happiness she had often refused for herself. There were plenty of people to be thankful that she had declined to be appropriated by any one person, as it left her at greater liberty not only to devote herself to her own family, but to become a Mother in Israel, taking under her protecting wing all who came to her for shelter. In her later years she would make merry over her single-blessedness. "Only think what a bore it would be, always to have a snuffy old gentleman sitting the opposite side of the fire!" she would say. If she often wore herself out with her sympathy, she could at any rate feel that her friends had eased themselves of their troubles by pouring them upon her. With her usual vehemence she sometimes felt the worries more strongly than they did themselves, and perhaps expressed them with more intensity than the occasion required. She did not say more than she felt, for she was as truthful as the day, but the forcible expression of her feelings being natural to her, she was apt to pile up and reiterate her words.

"She was always so human," said one; "if one had done any wrong, one felt one could go to her, and she would understand."

Her kindness of heart naturally gave an opening to loquacious friends, who were a strain on her patience. "If ever my life is written, it

ought to be called ' The Hunting of the Snark,' "
she observed, and pertinaciously was the poor
Snark hunted.   " So-and-So came and stayed an
enormous time," is an entry often found in her
diary; or, " Mrs or Miss ———— came bothering
about something "; for with that confidential
friend, her journal, she allowed herself a refreshing
freedom of speech.   One of her intimates was
delighted to discover a weak point in her.   " I've
found out a fault," she triumphantly observed;
"you can't stand bores."

We are quite sure that though shrewd lookers-
on might read her feelings aright, the poor bore
himself would not be allowed to discover his
tediousness.   It was only to be expected that
one who took the keen delight she did in lively
conversation, should suffer proportionately from
prosy talk.   Her lively mind was restive under
it.   She felt as if she were being dragged heavily
along a dull road in a lumbering coach behind
slow horses, and longed, metaphorically, to spring
to the box, flick her whip, and be off at a
canter.

In her busy life such inflictions must have
been a real strain on her Christianity.

Her largeness of nature showed itself in
the matter of temper.   " I have seen her furiously
angry at cruelty or oppression," remarked one
who knew her well, " but cross, never."   She
just brushed aside trifles that would have ruffled

others, and walked on as if she had never noticed them.   Her heart, hospitable as it was, had no spare room for such mean guests.   There were certain subjects which always stirred her up— capital punishment, cruelty to animals, and the unequal treatment meted out by society to men and women, for sins against purity.

The employment of vivisection was a cause of great suffering to her, and she eagerly joined her friend, Miss Frances Power Cobbe, in her efforts to get the practice abolished.   She could not bring herself to believe in any legal safeguards or restrictions against the abuse of it.   Great was her joy when she caught so important a recruit for the Anti-Vivisection Society as the Archbishop of York.

Finding on one occasion that two pretty little dogs to which she had taken a fancy (belonging to an official at one of the Institutions which she visited) had mysteriously disappeared, her suspicions were aroused, and without losing a moment, she rushed off to find them, and would not rest till she had ascertained that they were free from all danger of an unhappy fate. When the new Laboratory was built at Oxford, she declared she could never go into the Parks again—though she found it impossible to keep her resolution.   Her sympathies with the sufferings of animals seriously affected her happiness.   She could not help making herself miserable over the treatment of the dogs, donkeys and horses which she thought were ill-used. " It is the only thing that tries my faith in Christianity," she would say, "and makes me long to leave the world." And if she could save a donkey from ill-usage by buying it, she would do so.

Some people seem to be born into the world with a special affinity for animals, and she was certainly one of them. Her dogs, Urisk, Bute, Toby, and Tatters, who succeeded each other in the snug berths she gave them, were to her like members of her family. You could scarcely imagine her walking along the street without one of them trotting beside her. Tatters entered the prisoners' cells with his mistress, with the confident air of having as good a right to do so as if he too had received his written permission from the Home Office. Every now and then he declined the low company offered him, and we often find in her diary the entry: "Went to the prison; Tat would not come."

And Tat was master of the situation.

Tatters earned his privileges, for she considered she owed her life to him. She had one day fainted away, and had fallen face downwards in such a position that she was sure she must have been suffocated but for him. He found her lying on the ground, and, frightened at the unwonted sight, ran to the top of the stairs, barking loudly to summon one of the servants to come to the aid of her mistress, which she was not slow to do.

She had a strong belief in the immortality of animals, and half in fun, half in earnest, would justify the vegetarian habits she practised for many years of her life, by asking, "How could I meet the ducks and chickens in a future state, whose bodies I have cut up in this?"

The beginning of her rejection of meat dates from the time of her return from Greece. There was a lamb on board to which she took a fancy, making a great pet and plaything of it. One day the little creature was nowhere to be found, but on the dinner-table stood a small joint to be eaten with mint-sauce. It gave Felicia such a shock that she could not bring herself to touch meat for years afterwards. Many will say it was weak-minded to give it up. But we wish to show her as she really was in her weakness and her strength.

When after one of her illnesses Sir Henry Acland insisted on her taking to meat again, she yielded, though it always went against the grain.

Her feeling of repulsion to it enhances her meritorious conduct on a certain occasion when visiting a poor dying boy. She was stooping over him, full of loving anxiety to soothe his last hours, and tenderly asked him if there were anything he would like.

"Pig's chitterlings, please, ma'am," were the words he faintly murmured.

She had not a notion what these mysterious "in'ards of a pig" might be, but she was determined that he should not be disappointed.

Off she set at once to a neighbouring pork-butcher's, the kind of shop she would cross the road to avoid, or manage not to see if she must needs pass it. The pig's chitterlings demanded, were elegantly wrapped up in newspaper and carried off to the sick boy.

Felicia was submissive to Sir Henry Acland's orders about giving up her vegetarianism, but she was not generally an easy patient to manage. It was a great trial to her energetic nature to stay quiet and rest—an essential in some of her illnesses, when she was under medical treatment for inflammation of the veins. Her doctors oscillated between admiration of her character and enjoyment of her society on the one hand, and aggravation at the impossibility of getting her to keep quite still on the other. "Now then, Miss Skene, don't go and kill yourself for that book!" they would entreat, as, quite absorbed in eager discussion of some volume, she suddenly changed her position and stretched out her arm to reach it.

She had much to sadden her in her life, but neither her own sorrows nor the painful tragedies she heard, and the wrecks of poor human nature she met with in her visits to the prison, could ever quench the buoyant spirit of fun that bubbled up in her. People used to feel that if only they could secure a seat next to her at a party, dulness was impossible. A good joke, whether against herself or any one else, would set her going again if she were flagging. She had her periods of depression, when her vital force was at a low ebb, and she was suffering from feeble action of the heart, from sleepless nights, or attacks of pain in the side. Then a droll story or funny saying would do her good like a medicine.

Her friend Mr Simeon—who has many amusing tales to tell of her—says, that once in her later years, when visiting her ward at the Infirmary, the sick man she was talking to interrupted her religious exhortations by the unexpected question, " How old might you be, ma'am ? "

" Seventy-one next birthday," was the answer.

" Then, don't you think, ma'am, you may be getting a bit childish ? " was the suggestion that sent her into fits of laughter. She would not have enjoyed a compliment half as much. Another of her acquaintances tried to hurry her on her downward course still more effectually.

" Haven't you heard I am dead ? " she asked a friend whom she met in the street. " Mr So-and-So has just been to my door with a face a yard long.

"'Dear me! Mr So-and-So, what on earth is the matter?' I asked.

"'I've just heard of your death,' he replied.

"'And so I suppose you have come to enquire about my funeral?' I answered."

When she was sure she could not be misunderstood, she would let herself go and revel in her fun.

"What would some people say if they heard me!" she would exclaim, as she laughed till she cried. "They think, 'There's that pious old lady, Miss Skene!' and they'd never dream I could be so wicked."

Two other characteristics of that largeness of nature of which we spoke at the beginning of this chapter, were hers in a marked degree— readiness to apologise where she thought she had been wrong, and generosity in giving.

One of the most vivid pictures of her in the memory of the writer is that of her tall, dignified figure, as she stood in the middle of the road by a pony-carriage in which two friends were sitting, that she might make a warm and thorough apology for words spoken by her that had unintentionally given pain. Her whole soul was in her expression and her voice as she reiterated her deep regret that she should have hurt her friend's feelings.

Sweet-tempered as she was, she was by no means one of those blindly-amiable people who

can only see the agreeable side of everybody.
She was shrewd about character, and could
be keenly annoyed. Being a person of strong
feelings and decided opinions, she could give
warm expression to them at times. But if she
felt that she had been warmer than the occasion
required, or given the slightest cause of com-
plaint, she never hesitated to make the *amende
honorable.*

" Wrote to apologise to So-and-So," is an entry
that appears now and then in her diary.

"To St Philip and St James. Went out
because of ' Be reconciled,' and found Mrs ————,
and went home with her to the door; back into
the church to finish prayers."

That was Felicia Skene all over! She was so
genuine all through. She never tampered with
her conscience, but went straight as an arrow
to the mark to which it pointed her. She had
all the humility of a great mind, and would no
more try to deceive herself as to her feelings
or conduct, than she would dream of deceiving
others.

Writing to her niece at the beginning of a
new year, she says :—

" You will be surprised to get a second letter
from me, but you must look upon it as a post-
script to my other, because I had posted it and
regretted that I had not said one thing which
has been very much upon my mind of late.

You know, at the close of a year one naturally looks back to see what one has to repent of, and in the year that is gone I blame myself very much for having been unkind and uncharitable in my judgments of others, and for having expressed them to some few of my special friends, amongst whom, as you know, you were yourself one to whom I was most unreserved. I went to a midnight service on New Year's Eve, and it was then especially that the conviction that I had been much to blame in this respect came so strongly upon me that I felt I should like to say it to both you and C——. You see, what I feel is, that really in this difficult world it is impossible for us to judge with anything like justice of one another, for so many things in the lives and consciences of others, which are unknown to us, may make them feel things to be right which do not seem so to other persons; and where we have every reason to believe that people would wish to act only conscientiously and rightly, it makes it worse to put an unkind construction on their conduct, as I have done, and still more to convey the same hard judgment to the minds of others. I am sure I have been very wrong in doing this, as I did with you and C—— last summer; for, of course, any uncharitableness kept in my own mind could only injure myself, but *told* out it becomes a great injury to those who were the object of it. I hope I may no more 'judge lest I be judged,' or 'condemn lest I be condemned,' and I earnestly trust that I may not be a cause of harm to others by what I have already done in this way. I cannot touch on this subject, however, without thanking you a thousand times for all the sympathy and tenderness and thought for me you always show me in every possible way; it is all more precious to me than I can tell, and I only feel I do not deserve it."

Perhaps the greatest proof of the nobility of her nature and the reality of her Christianity was shown in her forgiveness of a great wrong done to her. With her whole heart she determined to respond to the call made upon her conscience. Against the danger of an unforgiving spirit she prayed and struggled, striving to win the person who had wronged her, by acts of kindness repeated over and over again in the face of every discouragement and rebuff. She suffered much, but she rose from the trial strengthened and purified. In God's eyes we cannot but believe it was the highest of all her victories, for it involved the greatest sacrifice.

As to her generosity in giving, the difficulty was to restrain it within bounds. How, with her very moderate income, she could manage to rush to the rescue of all in need, was a wonder to her friends. True, many who were aware how constantly the poor and miserable made claims on her purse, and who did not know themselves which among the many needy it were wisest to help, often used to make her their almoner, and send her sums of money to expend for them.

She was able to earn money too by her indefatigable pen.   But still, without the strictest
self-denial, she could never have given away the
large sums she did.

Her contributions to the funds of St Edward's
School, Summertown—in which, for the sake of
her friend the Warden, she took a keen interest
—were of the most liberal kind.   For another
friend she drew on her capital to purchase an
annuity, and her prison diary is a continuous
record of presents of money, clothes, and other
gifts, which must have been a constant drain on
her resources.

There are some natures to which economy,
where others are concerned, seems an impossibility.   If she had been a millionaire, she would
probably have failed to keep a large balance at
the end of the year.   Some charitable scheme
would have been started, or benevolent institution have sprung out of the ground at her
bidding.

Lucky was the coachman who drove her, or
the servant who waited on her during a visit!
If she had a present to give—a doll for a child's
birthday, for instance—her choice gravitated in-
fallibly to the biggest and most expensive in the
shop.   She always wanted to pay everything for
everybody, and some of her visitors found they
had a hard struggle to prevent her from pre-
senting them with their railway tickets; and

where she brought her will to bear, it was not easy to overrule her.

That strong will of hers was always a difficult element in her nature for her to deal with. She had to bring her will to master her will. Looking back regretfully in her later days on an incident of her youth, she remarked sadly: "I was a wilful girl; my parents ought never to have given way to me."

But if she loved her own way, no one could charge her with allowing her strong will to make her overbearing to others, and her great-niece could write of her after her death, "She never became managing." Still she reserved a right to her own views, not to say prejudices. It was no easy task to convince her. After a whole battery of argument against some course of action had been expended on her, she would remark smilingly, " Yes, but I think I shall do it all the same."

Efforts to move her in certain directions had to be abandoned at last, as defeat was certain. Her friends might be slightly provoked for the moment, but they were far more amused ; and whatever she said or did was so essentially a part of her original and delightful personality, that they would not have had her different for the world. She certainly had her inconsistencies, as who has not? Indeed, we once heard her roundly described as a bundle of them. Perhaps

that charge might be brought against many
complex characters. There were so many sides
to her nature that one often appeared to contradict the other. Sometimes it was the shrewd,
at others the credulous, side of her that was
paramount; now the tender, then the severe,
when she would startle her friends by the uncompromising sentences she pronounced on
offenders. Perhaps, if we could plumb further
down into the depths of character, we should
find some underlying principle from which the
varieties and seeming contradictions alike sprang
—the same root below the surface, though above
it the branches might diverge widely. On her
purely intellectual side, if a similar inconsistency
were sometimes detected, it was probably because
she did not always allow her powers of reasoning
fair play, but allowed them to be overborne by
the feeling and imagination with which she was
so richly endowed. Where these did not interfere, you could trust her to give a sound opinion.
In a striking sermon preached about her after
her death, the preacher remarked that, " Though
she may have been every now and then too
sanguine, she gained, from some who watched
her keenly, a general reputation for good judgment."

Perhaps a devoted brother might be considered
a partial witness, but Mr William Skene was
so able and clear-sighted a man, that we cannot

help giving weight to his opinion, in spite of the
nearness of the relationship ; and he said of her,
" I think she is the wisest woman I have ever
seen."

It was her strong will-power that, humanly
speaking, kept her alive when feebler natures
might have succumbed. The vigorous mind
kept the body going. Severe headaches, heart
weakness, attacks of rheumatism—during one of
which a London physician told her it was very
unlikely she would ever walk again—all interrupted her work from time to time. But she
rose up again with fresh spirit and vitality to
triumph over the mistaken doctor, and to begin
the long walks once more. For the greater part
of her life she could accomplish eight or ten miles
a day with ease ; and afterwards, though she was
obliged to limit her favourite exercise, she would
not give it up. Her great dread always was that
she might be compelled to do so. But that trial
she was spared.

She had no love for driving, and her friends
found it was no good offering her a lift in their
carriages. As to tram-cars, you might meet
nearly all Oxford in them, but Miss Skene never,
one reason being that Tatters was not allowed as
a passenger. Railway travelling was the form of
locomotion she hated most.

Her great desire that she might be spared a
long period of enforced inaction at the close of

her life was granted her. There was so little
change in her daily chart of occupations during
her fifty years of Oxford life, that what she
began on her entry into the little house in New
Inn Hall Street was carried on till she left it for
the last time.

This was the general course of it :—

She began the day early, getting up at 6.30,
sometimes earlier. Seven o'clock found her constantly at the prison gates, that she might meet
the discharged prisoners and take them to the
Refuge if they would go, or to the station if a
journey were to be made, or to her house to
give them breakfast, "to comfort them," as she
often writes in her prison diary.

Then came the walk to an early service,
Morning Prayer, or the Holy Communion—at St
Thomas's, or St Philip and St James'. Then a
round with her dog in the Parks or Christ
Church meadows, in which latter place she had
at one time a four-footed friend, a certain
donkey, which always trotted up affectionately to
greet her. Breakfast was nominally at nine, but
was liable to be postponed to any moment
between that hour and eleven; for when she got
back to her house, she often found the hall full of
persons waiting to speak to her—tramps, discharged prisoners, poor clients of some description.
When at last they were cleared off, she was free
to sit down to the first of her two daily meals.

Then, if it were not one of her regular prison-visiting days, she would aim at a quiet time for literary work from eleven till the middle of the afternoon. Probably just as she had made a good start and her pen was skimming away through one of her flowing sentences and she felt thoroughly happy, tinkle went the bell, and a visitor was announced, come for business or sociability. Friendship truly has its penalties!

One ordinary interruption to work she did not have, for she never touched lunch. Neither that meal nor five-o'clock tea could she be prevailed upon to take; and she had no food till her six-o'clock dinner. During her vegetarian years that meal was light enough; and wine she disliked, nor did she require it, in her opinion.

By four o'clock she had put aside her writing or editing, and if visitors did not come to hinder her, would drop into St Mary Magdalene's for the short afternoon service. Then came her walks again, almost always on some errand of kindness or mercy.

In the evening undergraduates might drop in for a talk—a real enjoyment to herself as well as to them, for until the last seven or eight years of her life, when she was too tired, they always found a welcome—or she would take to her writing again, her large correspondence, her stories, or articles. And the small hours of morning, especially during her earlier years, would too often find her sitting up, pen in hand.

On her days for visiting the prisoners in the gaol, she would spend two or three hours in her rounds from one to another.

To get through the amount of work and exercise she accomplished, day after day, argues a splendid natural constitution. She strained it to the uttermost, and her diary became fuller, as time went on, of aches and pains of head and heart, of weariness and exhaustion. The only wonder was how it bore the strain as long as it did.

"She might have been spared longer if she had not worn herself out," said the doctor. But inaction would have made her miserable. Like a high-mettled horse, she must pull her heavy load to the last, no matter how great the strain, And if her life had much of labour and sorrow, it was also full of the joy as well as the pain of self-sacrifice.

As the memories of two of her friends, Mrs Humphry Ward and Miss Wordsworth of Lady Margaret Hall, dwell with special pleasure on one of the points mentioned in this chapter, her kindness to girls, whether to those living in the shelter of happy homes, or to the less fortunate, exposed to fierce trials and temptations in the world without, we will insert here the papers in which their impressions of Felicia Skene are recorded.

Mrs Humphry Ward writes :—

"My friendship with dear Miss Skene must have begun very early, though I cannot exactly remember how or when. But it was she who encouraged me to print my first published story, 'A Westmoreland Story,' which I wrote when I was seventeen or eighteen, and published by her help in the *Churchman's Magazine.*

"I remember getting a few pounds for it. How proud I was, and how pleased she was to have been able to help me! I think that even then I had read her book, 'Hidden Depths;' though I could understand, of course, very little of what such a subject meant to her. But I remember my general young impression was of a saint of goodness, humility, tenderness. I used to look at St Thomas's Church from the railway, with reverence, because she went there; and though I was already of a different way of thinking from her, and we sometimes used to argue religious questions, I never could pass the powerful, abstracted figure of Mr Chamberlain, the Rector of St Thomas's, in the street, without sympathy and a secret thrill, because of what I knew or imagined she felt towards him, as a holy man, and because of that hidden life that both represented for me. Once, *à propos* of her work among outcast women, she told me that she never locked the house door at night, so that any poor soul who wanted her at any hour might come in, and find refuge and help. That sank into my mind. Some of the things also that she would sometimes say about her work in prison,— how she had been reading and praying with a girl

who had murdered her child, or a woman condemned to death, — impressed me deeply.
When I read of 'Dinah Morris,' or of the
Bishop in 'Les Misérables,' I was reminded of
Miss Skene.   One felt that she lived for her
faith, that she would have shrunk from no sacrifice or pain to which it had called her, and that
the sacrifice would have been accepted smiling,
as though it were nothing.   That at least was
always my impression.

"Then some of my memories are quite
different.   I remember a girl of my acquaintance who had very little money to spend;
and one Commemoration, for a special reason,
this girl wanted to go to a particular ball.   But
she was already going to one ball, and she
knew she could not ask her parents to pay for
tickets for a second.   Miss Skene found this
out, and I suppose other matters too, for the
girl confided in her a good deal.   At any rate,
dear fairy Godmother! the morning before the
ball, the ticket arrived from her.   The recipient
hardly liked to take it, but Miss Skene
insisted, and she took the liveliest interest in
the ball dress.   Then on the day of the girl's
engagement, I remember her, when all was
settled, hurrying down to New Inn Hall Street,
to tell Miss Skene first of all.   And Miss Skene
bubbled over with delight in the whole business.
She had that gaiety, that childlikeness of heart,
which the noblest of the saints have had, which
the Catholics tell you is the unfailing characteristic
of the 'religious' life at its best.   In later days,
after my marriage, of course I often saw her,
but my recollections are not so clear as the

years become more crowded. She often talked
to me of her literary work, of the long stories
that she wrote for the *Quiver*, etc., and I used to
be struck with amazement at her patience, her
industry, her sweet humility about herself and
her gifts, the absence in her of the smallest
touch of jealousy or bitterness towards any one
in the world. Even where she disapproved she
loved. As far as I remember, she was interested
in 'Robert Elsmere.' At any rate it never
made the slightest breach between us, and I
think I must have a letter somewhere from her
about it. She had the most generous, tolerant
heart; while at the same time one felt she would
have been torn asunder for what she believed.

"The book she liked best of mine was 'Helbeck
of Bannisdale,' and her letter of praise, was a
great joy to me. After we left Oxford, she
and I did not often meet. But she was very
kind to my mother in her long and painful
illness, and my mother loved and reverenced her.
Wherever indeed there was suffering, wherever
she could help, there one was sure to find Miss
Skene. I shall often see her in memory, walking
along St Giles, as she was in later years, with
her slow and rather languid gait, her stoop
of growing infirmity, her dress so simple, old-
fashioned, yet dignified, her lined, irregular face,
her look, absent and shortsighted, till she
recognised a friend,—and through all, illumining
all, such spiritual and moral charm, the fragrance
of a beautiful soul.

"It is a deep regret to me that I did not even
know she had been ill, till I saw the announce-
ment of her death in the *Times*. I wish I could

have seen her again.   Others will testify to her
admirable prison and rescue work, her influence
in social reform, to the power and interest of
much of her writing.   I shall always think of her
as the beloved friend of those younger and weaker
than herself, as the pure, tender, consecrated
spirit, who made the Oxford of my young
days a nobler place for her presence within it."

Miss Wordsworth says :—

"You have asked me to give you my impressions of dear Miss Skene; but though she
has left a very strong impression on me, yet
I do not find the task an easy one.   The
kindliness of her voice, with its touch of Scottish
accent, is one of the things which lingers in
my memory.   It suited so well with her fine
tall frame and auburn hair, still auburn, though
tinged with silver, and that wonderfully loving
motherly expression of face, which I used to
think must have often won poor girls and
hardened women to better ways, even when
they were too rough to understand much of
religious teaching.   That 'continued comfort
in a face, the lineaments of gospel books,'
might have been written of her.
    "Our first meeting was when I made her
acquaintance, nearly thirty years ago, in order to
gain something from her experiences in 'rescue
work' before setting up a small Home in Great
Grimsby.   She let me have a glimpse of her
wonderfully devoted life, and see how her
influence penetrated some of the worst parts
of Oxford.   Ever since then Oxford · has

appeared to me in a sort of double aspect, the
bright, gay, clever, and on the whole, good
and well-meaning society which forms its upper
surface; and the dark, sad, sinful, sometimes
thoughtless, sometimes ignorant, but very often
deliberately evil, under-current of human life.

"It was very remarkable in dear Miss Skene's
character, that almost daily, even hourly, as
her contact with this evil was, it never affected
her wonderful natural purity and refinement.
You felt she was a lady, and something more
than a lady, be the topic what it would. It
may have been our lot to know women who,
with the best intentions, lost somewhat of their
delicacy of perception through constant
familiarity with what was coarse and hard,
but Miss Skene never offended in this way.
She was one of the most perfect gentlewomen
I ever knew. One always felt that she had
been brought up in the best of company, as
indeed she had been, and that as a child she
had sat on the knees of Walter Scott. One
saw reflected in her something of that innate
healthiness and purity of mind which makes
the 'Heart of Midlothian' differ *toto cœlo* from
some other books on painful themes. There
was a generous large-heartedness about her,
which had nothing petty or sectarian in it.
She was a true lover of human, and I think
I may add of canine, nature. One cannot think
of her apart from the pet dog, a rough Scotch
terrier, which was the constant companion of
her walks. If she had a failing, it was in being
too tender-hearted. The only time we ever
nearly quarrelled was on the subject of capital

punishment.   As neither of us ever succeeded in convincing the other, we had at last to 'agree to differ' in the matter.   To quote Walter Scott again, it was to us very much what that unlucky word, 'Benval' was to Jonathan Old-buck and Sir Arthur Wardour.

"She had a most charming vein of Scotch superstition, and told me at least one beautiful ghost-story, besides the one which you of course already know, of Scott appearing to her father, a little before the death of the latter, in his house in Oxford.   Of her deep personal piety, her kindness, sympathy, and generosity there is happily no need for me to speak : they were patent to all who knew her.   One always felt she would have given away the clothes off her back, and I should think she could never have made money, under any circumstances, ' stay by her.'

"I daresay some of her friends felt that it was a very happy thing for them and for others, that there was one Miss Skene, and only wished there could be more; but that it was perhaps as well that the majority of mankind should be rather more hard-hearted and matter-of-fact.   'It takes all sorts to make up a world,' and natures like hers will always be as inestimable as they are rare.   It is an addition to one's weight of moral indebtedness and responsibility to have known any one whose life was a daily realisation of the teaching of that 'Inasmuch' in one of our Lord's most solemn parables.   And on this side of the grave it will ever be impossible to measure or calculate the effects of such a life, or to appraise by any human standard the preciousness of such a character."

CHAPTER IX

RESCUE WORK

IT was natural that one who was so full of sympathy for all her fellow-creatures should take deeply to heart the sins and sorrows of her own sex, especially of those belonging to it whose condition and circumstances made them a prey to the worst temptations. No work is more painful and difficult than the rescue of poor women from the Slough of Despond into which they have fallen. None makes a greater demand on heart and head. None requires more faith, hope and charity, more patience, strength and decision, more tact, judgment and insight into character.

If there were anything lacking in the measure of these qualifications in the character of Felicia Skene—and who can supply them full-grown at once, like the goddess of wisdom from Jove's forehead?—time and experience fostered their growth. She had time enough to develop them, for she carried on her toilsome task for nearly fifty years. Wherever she met with girls and women who had yielded to the temptations in question—whether in her work at St Thomas's, in prison, or hospital—there in her pity and her love, she did all in her power to redeem them, though she never looked upon herself as a regular rescue-worker, or enrolled herself in any band of those who devote themselves to this branch of charity. There was pre-eminently one characteristic of her nature, indeed of the very essence of it, which fitted her for the work. She was herself capable of a great passion. Her own feelings had been deeply enough stirred during one period of her life to enable her to understand and deal with those cases where the sin was no cold and deliberate act, but committed through heat of passion. Though every feeling of her heart was controlled by "subjection to the obedience of Christ," she had suffered much in the struggle she had gone through, though she could learn to be thankful for it, because it had brought her nearer to Our Lord, and had enabled her to enter into what the difficulties of natures like her own must be, when unrestrained by a sense of duty and religious obligation. Many pathetic cases came to her knowledge, where the poor woman, fascinated and deceived by the man who had led her astray, clung to him with a passionate love that would not be gainsaid.

"I'll never give him up, no, never!" exclaimed a poor girl, dying of consumption in the hospital where Felicia visited her—a look of fierce determination on her beautiful face. And no argument or inducement suggested by this life or the next could move her. Her love for the man, unworthy though he was, was the highest thing she knew, and she clung to it. In other cases where the sin was cold and calculating, Felicia could be stern. Her strong will was brought to bear unflinchingly upon such. When a lady called on her to urge laxer measures than she approved, she writes : " I did not agree with So-and-So in the least. I think it is quite right to clear the streets of these bad women, and they get no more than they deserve." Hot was her indignation when a visitor of the " New Woman" order called on her to reproach her for interfering with the liberty of these unhappy creatures. The ideals of that kind of new woman-hood had no attraction for her, and she declined all suggestions made that she should lend her name and influence to the movement.

" She talked freely of subjects that even my poor girls would avoid!" she exclaimed.

Another of her qualifications for her work was her undaunted courage, her pluck, without which no good is ever accomplished, the presence or absence of it forming one of the great distinctions between human beings.

She might fail time after time ; she might be openly withstood or grossly taken in. She would not waste time in lamenting, but went on boldly to the next effort. " If you are deceived in nine cases, go on to the tenth," said St

Francis; and on this she acted. With her, the second of St Paul's three pre-eminent Christian graces was not forgotten, as it often is, and surely many of the poor girls she rescued were saved by hope. Granted that she was sometimes deceived, that she trusted in human nature too much, in how many instances did she not succeed through trust, where others would fail for lack of it? We must reckon our losses both ways. If after the manner of women she sometimes let her heart run away with her head, we must remember Pascal's saying, "The heart has its logic as well as the head," and logic of the former kind was often her guide to success.

Gradually and experimentally she worked out her principles, which were laid down in the articles and essays she wrote on this difficult subject. And it was a testimony to the high opinion held of her work that it used to be said, "If that is a very bad case, take it to Miss Skene."

In the early days when she first began trying to help her poor fallen sisters, far less was done by ladies to cope with the evil in question than at the present day. Felicia did not shrink from joining in Mr Chamberlain's crusade against the keepers of bad houses, or from entering them where she thought a personal effort could alone avail—though her whole soul must have recoiled from such abodes of degradation. On the one hand she had to brave insults and threats from the owner of the house; on the other, reluctance, too often, on the part of the victim herself, to be saved from her miserable life.

As in the days of the cholera, Felicia's street-door, guarded by a policeman, was kept unlocked at night, that she might be summoned to the aid of any girl in distress. If she had retired to rest, she would get up at once, execute a hasty toilette while the poor creature waited below, and then take her to some haven of refuge.

The only time when she was really angry with an old servant who lived with her, and was more apt to assume the part of mistress than of maid, was when that autocrat sent a girl peremptorily away, on the plea that her mistress was at dinner. Felicia felt it was a lost chance.

She did not, as a rule, go out into the streets in search of the girls. As long as her parents lived she could not well have done so. The exception to this was during a Mission in 1875, when a special effort was made on behalf of prevention and rescue. Felicia joined the party of good women who carried on their campaign in the streets at night.

Her usual efforts were made in connection with the Refuge. When it was found that the keepers of bad houses, if driven out of one

parish, moved on to another, two or three
excellent Oxford men consulted with Miss Skene
about establishing some house, to be kept open all
night, to which girls might go for safety, either
voluntarily or through the persuasion of others.
Here, under the care of a deaconess, they could
remain until they could be persuaded to enter
some Home or Penitentiary that would receive
them.

More easily said than done.

A treble difficulty confronted those who
would help them. They had to persuade the
girl to enter the Refuge, to get her to stay there,
and then to induce her to move on to an institution where the evil excitement of her past life
would be impossible, and where she would be
under a rule of strict discipline. It was characteristic of Felicia that, feeling strongly the need
of saving them at any price, even in spite of
themselves, she was ready to use any lawful
means, even to a little innocent bribery, to
prevail upon them to go in. She had received
permission to visit the disorderly women taken
to the old Spinning House, once a separate
building, afterwards merged in the old City Gaol
on Gloucester Green. Here they awaited trial
in the Vice-Chancellor's Court. Here she could
talk to them, pleading with them to abandon
their old habits and to come with her, when the
time of their detention was over, to the Refuge,

where the deaconess in charge would welcome
them and help them to make a new start in life,
and where she herself would visit and befriend
them. She could tell them of the many who
were thankful that they had yielded to her
persuasions and who, after going through a period
of probation in Refuge or Penitentiary, had taken
respectable situations or had married into happy
homes of their own. There were even cases,
which she may not have thought it of any avail
to mention to them in their present condition,
but which are interesting to record here, in which
the poor girls had ended by becoming Sisters of
Mercy, that they might help those still in the
pitiable circumstances in which they had once
lived themselves.

Sometimes Felicia's persuasions were all in vain,
and she had sorrowfully to give them up, hoping
that the inevitable sufferings that would over-
take them before their career ended, might move
them to yield at last from sheer misery.

If she managed to induce some girl to start
with her for the Refuge, it was by no means
certain they would reach their destination.
Sometimes her prisoner-of-war would give her
the slip by the way and make her escape. On
one occasion Felicia considered that she was
saved by her familiar spirit, the little terrier who
accompanied her on all her quests, and was as
well known in hospital, refuge, or penitentiary

as his mistress.   As she and a girl were on their
way to the Refuge, "Tatters" suddenly set up
a volley of violent barking at her young companion just as they reached a cross street.   So
angry was he that he seemed as if he would have
bitten her.   The girl afterwards told Miss Skene
that she had had every intention of running away
when they reached that turning, if the dog's
fierce barking had not stopped her.

If the young woman consented to stay at the
Refuge, Felicia's interest in her was unabating.
She would visit her, talk with her, win her
confidence, do her best to persuade her to enter
a Home, and keep up her interest in her afterwards by getting a place for her and corresponding with her.   How many she helped to
save from shipwreck none will know here.

If she were called up at night to some girl,
and on reaching the Refuge it was found to be
full, she would take her *protégée* to the house of
some poor woman of her acquaintance, pay for
the girl's lodging and breakfast, and, like the
good Samaritan, provide for her expenses if need
were, till a vacancy occurred.   It was often
enough hard work keeping the girls at the Refuge.
A restless fit would seize them, especially when
some excitement, like the St Giles' Fair, was
impending.   Finding, one September, that one or
two of them were trying to get their discharge
in time for it, Felicia hit upon the plan of a treat

for the whole party that would work off their wild spirits and keep them out of harm's way. She hired a brake, and she and they and the Sister in charge drove off together for a happy day at Abingdon. The feast she provided for them of ham and salad and other delicacies, and the dancing that followed, were not soon forgotten.

One night she was sitting by her window when she heard a voice crying out in evident distress, " Where, oh where does Miss Skene live? Will *no* one tell me where she lives ? " and a policeman, who must have been on a beat new to him, answering roughly, " I don't know, girl, I'm sure."

Immediately Felicia was down the stairs and in the street in pursuit of the girl. She found her in such a state of misery and despair that the poor creature said that if she could not find Miss Skene she had made up her mind to go and drown herself.

This was but one of several instances in which she saved poor women from suicide.

The relations of these unfortunates, too often their worst enemies, were frequently more painful to meet, because more hard and cruel, than the fallen women themselves.

Felicia's determination to save them if possible, at any risk to herself, sometimes exposed her to real danger. She tells the true story in one of

her Magazine articles of a wretched man in St
Thomas's parish, who had got the sister who
lived with him completely into his power, com-
pelling her to maintain herself and him by a
life of disgrace. She dared not attempt to
escape. But Felicia was not daunted. Ascer-
taining that he would be out one evening, she
set off for his house, and after seeing and talking
to the poor girl, at last extracted a promise from
her that she would try and make her escape
to the Refuge the next night, when her brother
would probably reel in, in a half tipsy state and
lie down on the floor to sleep, and she might slip
away unobserved. Just as the matter was
settled, a neighbour rushed in to say that the
man was lurking in a yard outside, threatening
to do for the lady. Taking the woman's arm,
and mustering all her courage, Felicia advanced
towards him and stood still for a moment, fixing
her eyes calmly and fearlessly on his face. The
ruffian was so astonished at her boldness that he
actually let her pass by him into the street,
which was full of people. A policeman who was
standing there told her he thought she was in
danger of her life, and wanted her to let him
arrest the man; but this she refused to allow. He
was arrested however shortly after, for a furious
assault on the neighbour who had helped Felicia to
escape. Their next meeting was in the gaol the
following morning, when she was going her rounds

among the prisoners. She had got permission to see him, despite the reluctance of the warder, who did not think it safe for her. During that visit and many subsequent ones, her courage and her kindness so moved him that he left the prison when his sentence was finished, a very different man from the one he had been when he entered it.

Still more repulsive to her was it to have to go and speak to a dreadful man of abandoned character, who had driven his three elder daughters to their ruin, and would treat his youngest child in the same way, if she could not be got away from him. There was no one else to undertake the interview, and Felicia had to steel herself for it. She was successful in getting the man to consent to give up the little girl; but how she dreaded and hated speaking to him, a letter to her niece reveals.

Her help and advice were often sought in difficult cases. If the police did not know what to do with a girl they would come to Felicia Skene, in the conviction that she would manage her if no one else could. The proctors too would come to consult with her. Highest of all, the Vice-Chancellor himself, Mr Jowett, appealed to her for advice and information.

" I was rather surprised,"[1] she says, " when he suddenly walked into my sitting-room one day and asked if I could spare time for some

"Some Episodes in a Long Life."—*Blackwood's Magazine.*

conversation with him on a subject that had
become important to him. . . . One of the duties
which devolved upon him with his new dignity
in the University (that of Vice-Chancellor) was
to preside over the Vice-Chancellor's Court,
when culprits were likely to be brought before
him for judgment, of a class which had never
previously come within his sphere of knowledge.
He had been told that, from various circumstances, the difficulties of dealing with those
persons were not unknown to me, and with his
usual straightforward simplicity he came to me
at once to learn anything he could on the question.   He walked in with a pleasant smile on his
round face, and quietly told me his object in
seeking me ; then he sat down, looking the
meekest of men, with his white locks crowning
the cherubic countenance which has been made
known to the public by endless photographs, and
also, I regret to say, by caricatures.   Our conversation on the matters which required elucida-
tion lasted for some time, while I simply told him
anything I thought could be useful to him,
without, of course, the least intention of imposing
my views upon him.   My dismay was therefore
very great when, on rising up to leave me, he
said, ' I am much obliged to you for your clear
instructions, and I shall do my best to obey your
orders closely.'   I protested against such an
interpretation of my simple statements, and
assured him that nothing was further from my
mind than the idea of instructing the Master of
Balliol, or giving any orders to the Vice-
Chancellor.   ' I am not so presumptuous,' I said.
' Nevertheless you have decidedly done so,' he

answered, smiling. 'You have given me full instructions, and you will find that I shall follow them implicitly.' He looked at the moment, with a merry smile on his good-humoured face, so exactly like a mischievous boy, that his preposterous charge against me seemed less absurd than it would otherwise have done. I met him often after that, when he always greeted me in the most kindly manner, and seemed to consider we had established a friendship between us, though I fear it might not have lasted long had any of the vital questions arisen, on which we should have entirely disagreed."

Dr Pusey was another distinguished man who appealed to her for information, knowing, as he says, her Christian interest in poor women, and her knowledge of Oxford. He had been asked to give evidence on the subject of lodgings for undergraduates before a Select Committee of the House of Commons, in reference to a Bill which Mr Ewart intended to bring before Parliament. The evidence which she enabled him to give was, he writes afterwards, evidently felt by the Committee, "though, he fears, only as something to wince at, by most." He thinks, however, it will "vibrate conscience," and ends, as in other notes to her, with the "God bless you," which must have been as a God-speed to her on her way.

Felicia lost no opportunity of learning all she could of the working of Institutions abroad for the recovery of girls and women who had lost their character. Either by correspondence, or by personal visits when she stayed in Paris, she ascertained the treatment adopted and the result of the system.

One of these visits to a Penitentiary, which gave her great satisfaction, will be referred to later.

There is one feature of her intercourse with these poor women that we will not omit before closing this chapter. Felicia Skene always maintained her dignity as a lady with them; she never allowed them to forget the difference in their social positions, or to take liberties with her. Though she would do anything to help them, she found it best, when she met them in her daily walks, not to greet them as acquaintances.

CHAPTER X

THEORIES AND METHODS

IN considering Felicia's work amongst fallen women, perhaps the most difficult class of all who need help, the question naturally arises, On what principles did she act? What system did she recommend? She who had so much

experience must have arrived at definite con-
clusions on the subject.

She gives the answer in several papers and
books she wrote, most clearly of all in a small
pamphlet called " Penitentiaries and Reformatories," published by Messrs Douglas and
Edmonston, as one of a series called " Odds
and Ends." It reached a second edition in
1866.

She sums up her conclusion in these words:
" It is by working on their affections alone
that there is the least chance of winning them."

That is the very gist of her discourse; and
she asserts, that instead of adopting this principle,
another has been substituted for it, with disastrous results, both to the characters of those
in authority in Homes and to those of the
fallen women themselves. The principle she
condemns is that "all moral effects are to be
produced by discipline alone."

That is the great point at issue.

To say that Felicia was never able to realise
the need of discipline for wrong-doers, is to
make too large a statement. She had too much
sense; and her prison diaries and other utterances are a sufficient refutation of the charge.
But it is perhaps true to say that she did not
always rightly balance love and discipline, or
rather did not see that discipline is but love
on its sterner side. The Penitentiaries which

she knew, outraged her sense of wisdom, justice and mercy. She took great pains to enquire into their methods, and her account of them is painful to the last degree. And her charge is a general one, for, "In describing one of these Homes," she writes, "and the system pursued in it we shall describe all, for they scarcely differ even in insignificant details." We can only hope that as the method was carried out by human beings, a little humanity did creep into it here and there to soften it.

Felicia makes two main charges. First, that discipline being considered the one thing needful, "Laws of the most narrow and rigid description are framed in an iron mould, to which the objects of charity must bend all their wants, necessities, and sufferings, without the smallest regard to the varieties of individual character or previous circumstance." Secondly, "the employment of a cumbrous and needless machinery, which exhausts the funds and paralyses in a great measure the energies and capabilities of the workers."

The second error led to a provoking waste of power; but the first was far more serious, rendering the so-called penitents miserable and rebellious and ruining all hopes of their reformation. The rules had become a sort of fetish to those who administered them, never to be relaxed in the interest of an individual. She quotes some of them to show how impossible and disastrous they are for general application. In some Homes there is one, for example, which if rigidly carried out, would simply quash the whole concern. They propose to receive none who do not give unmistakable signs of penitence.

This, she declares, is an impossibility; it is the object to be attained, through God's help, by the Penitentiaries. "Where, in the name of common sense," she asks, "are they to learn penitence, or catch so much as a glimpse of God's grace, in the horrible lives out of which they come?" And after touching on the miserable conditions, which have as a rule darkened their past lives, and the motives which drive them at last, through fear, disease, or disgust to seek the refuge offered them, ought we not, she enquires, to make it easy for them to come, to take them just as they are, and give them every inducement to remain? With all the eloquence she can muster, she urges gentle treatment and individual study and care. She recommends the appeal to some human feeling, not yet extinguished by sin, the love of parent or child; the cherishing of some spark of good that may be fanned into a flame. Too often, alas! the home has been the centre of evil, and some other motive must be urged. But instead of this, these generally wild, ignorant, lawless creatures are put at once under "a system of conventual rule and strict religious observance, which the best-disposed novice that ever sought to be trained as a nun will find hard to bear." Silence-times, punishment-rooms, solitary confinement, incarceration within the walls of the institution, instead of the freedom for air and exercise to which they have been accustomed in their wild life, hard labour, solemn classes for instruction, these are part of the heavy machinery that crushes life and hope out of them.

Felicia quotes a time-table of the daily round of duties gone through in one of these Homes, which bore the character of being one of the most lax. With the exception of the three half-hours allotted to breakfast, dinner and tea, the only time allowed for relaxation was the short interval between 12.30 and 1 o'clock, and that was to be divided between mid-day prayers and recreation. The whole of the rest of the day from 5 A.M. to 8.15 P.M. was filled up by work, Bible Classes and reading, private prayers, and Service in chapel.

This was all that was offered them in exchange for the baleful excitement of their past lives. And it was a system conducted, as Felicia declares, with little of the personal sympathy that might have made it endurable.

The instances she gives of the women's constant chafing or open rebellion under such treatment, are painful to read.

One girl she mentions, had entered a Peni-

tentiary to please a mother whom she really
loved. She tried to improve and to bear the
restraint imposed on her; but at last the confinement to the house and the sternness of the
rule grew perfectly unbearable to her, and she
made her escape into the fields. Conscience
however, soon began to work, and she turned
back to the Home, hoping to win approval for
having come to a better mind. But instead of
that, bread and water, the punishment-room, and
scolding awaited her.

"When Miss —— rated at me, she hardened
me—she did, for ever. I left as soon as I could
and I would rather die," she protested, "than go
into one of those places again."

"That girl," writes Felicia Skene, "has done
more to hinder her companions from entering
Penitentiaries, than the worst keepers of bad
houses have ever accomplished."

"I am now going to speak from the bottom of
my heart," said another, a poor, diseased outcast
in the tramp-ward of a workhouse, when she was
urged to return to a Penitentiary. "I would
rather go to jail for two months, than to the
'Home' for one day. Liberty's sweet, and it's a
black look-out to see a prison door shut upon
you; but, oh! it's better than the rules and
the silence-times and the curtsies to the ladies
every time you move, and being punished if you
forget."

And alas! that religion, which ought to have

been the comfort and refuge of these poor creatures, should have been manifested to them under a repelling aspect. There were some Penitentiaries too, in which in addition to the ordinary religious observances prescribed, Retreats were held annually for the inmates, when for one, two, or even three days, complete silence was enjoined; and the whole day, with scarcely any interruption, was spent in Chapel. The disastrous effect on one poor girl, and she a well-disposed one, is thus described:—

"She suddenly burst from the Chapel, where she was kneeling with her companions, and rushed into the courtyard, where she began shouting a ribald song at the top of her voice, and then laughed and screamed alternately till she fell into hysterics. She had no malicious intent in doing so, and was really sorry afterwards to have disturbed the ladies; but it was a simple reaction from a degree of mental strain, for which she, as well as the others, was totally unfit."

We may be thankful indeed that the severe system which Felicia Skene condemns has, generally speaking, been softened and modified. It is a question whether more changes in the direction she indicates are not still needed in some Penitentiaries. If so, the opinion of one whose practical experience gave her a right to be heard, may not be thrown away.

There is one passage in the tract so characteristic and so touchingly expressed that we cannot
forbear quoting it :

"When it pleased the God of all compassion
to seek the reformation of a whole world lying
in wickedness, there was but one agency employed, one only motive-power set in action
by Him to accomplish the mighty end.   That
agency was love—love so deep, so broad, so
high, that there were none too wicked or too
weak to find shelter for their wickedness in its
infinite tenderness and pity.   The worst of
sinners ministered to that Love manifest in the
flesh, and feared not to kiss His feet; the outcast children of the streets hung round Him
unreproved; the sick and sorrowful never
sought from Him in vain the healing virtue that
brought relief and comfort, though well He knew
their gratitude would be as fleeting as the
morning dew; the woman that was a sinner,
and the friend that denied Him, were the first
to whom He gave token of His return from
the grave to which their own sins and those of
others had consigned Him.   'I have given you
an example,' He said, when in all loving
humility He had performed His last act of
touching kindness to those who were about
to forsake Him; and He had indeed given
them an example all His life long of unwearied
efforts to save the lost, to reform the erring,
to raise the fallen by means of love alone, in
all gentleness, meekness, and tenderest compassion."

Felicia naturally received letters from friends and from strangers expressing opinions, favourable or the reverse, on the little pamphlet in which she had expressed her views so clearly and decidedly.

A clergyman wrote in strong disagreement, wishing that she would come and see for herself the Penitentiary in which he was interested, which he thought gave sufficient evidence of success. Thinking, as readers of her books often did, that he detected the masculine pen, he began his letter " Dear Sir."

" He asked me," she writes to her niece, " to go and stay for two days with him. I thought it would have been rather good fun to have accepted the invitation and seen his face of amazement when a lame female—(she was suffering from temporary lameness)—walked in, instead of the clergyman he expected."

Her old friend, Dean Ramsay, writes to her:

"EDINBURGH, *January* '68.

" DEAR FELICIA,—Many thanks for your kind letter and present of the tract from " Odds and Ends." You are a bold woman to write and publish such a *plain-speaking* opinion upon the too prevalent spirit under which good people mar so much of their well-intentioned efforts for the fallen and the ignorant. I fear you have too much truth in your statements, and I have no doubt the lesson given in the great

Parable of our Lord regarding the reception of returning Prodigals is forgotten, as in the sad case you adduce of the poor girl who had left to come back. Well! we can only do our best and say our wisest *as* the best and wisest appear to us. I should like to be able to write and hear from you now and then, when anything like this occurs.—Yours affectionately,

"E. B. RAMSAY."

She refers in another letter to Mr Gladstone having received the little book, but not having yet returned it : unfortunately there is no record of his opinion of it.

It is pleasant to turn from the gloomy picture she paints of English "Homes," to that of one she visited in Paris, two or three years after she wrote the little book from which we have quoted. The Reformatory of *St Michel* was all that she thought such a place should be. She made careful enquiries as to the system carried out in it; she heard all the particulars of its working; she was introduced to the six classes into which the penitents were divided; she talked to some of them herself; every detail of their dress, appearance and expression, was noted by her; and the result left in her mind was entire approval.

"Love, kindness, gentleness," these were the means of reformation employed, insisted the

L

Supérieure.[1] " If we attempted to win those wild untaught girls by hardness and severity, we should do no good amongst them at all; our one system of management is to try and win their affections, so that they may learn to trust and love us as their friends, and through us *le bon Dieu* who sent us to them."

Felicia was taken first to see the children and young girls, those who were sent to the Convent by *" la correction paternelle du Gouvernement."* They had been previously under the *surveillance* of the police, on account of a propensity for stealing, or other immoral practices. These children in their blue dresses and pretty little white caps were, Felicia says, as happy and healthy looking as any she ever saw. The only punishment inflicted for misconduct was the wearing of an ugly brown stuff cap, a dreaded badge of disgrace. One little girl was wearing it for biting a companion. Her stubbornness was melted at once by the sorrowful reproof of the Mother, and she dropped on her knees, " with an almost comical expression of remorse on her round face."

An elaborate system of rewards, classes of perseverance, little guilds and societies, whose members were decorated with medals, formed the stimulus to good conduct and proved

The quotations relating to the Reformatory of *St Michel* are from an article Miss Skene contributed to *Good Words*, in January 1870.

effectual; while occupation, air and exercise kept the girls well and happy.

From this department, she was taken to see the class of the *La Petite Persévérance* into which those children who wished to stay on after their time of detention was over, were drafted, and here she saw a fine display of medals and ribbons.

She was next introduced to the four classes into which the fallen women were divided. The first two were for the *filles du peuple;* and the members were of a low type, both as to birth and character. Their features and expressions showed this plainly enough; yet the pleasure they evinced if the nuns spoke to them, gave hope that they too would be won in the end by kind and friendly treatment.

Thence they passed to the great laundries, where busy hands were at work among the soap-suds, while eager tongues were keeping up a lively chatter. The girls she spoke to assured Felicia they were "quite happy and well content to remain under the guardianship of *Ma Mère.*"

She was next taken to the quarters for penitents of a higher social class. They were singing over their embroidery, and the impression they gave her was equally favourable; none the less so, because many of them looked sad and downcast, and were evidently keenly awake to the disgrace into which their sin had brought them. Here she found a compatriot, a Lancashire girl, who had been in the Convent for five years, and who told her that her great desire was to remain always in the Home and become a *Persévérante.*

As the fifty or sixty girls sang at the request of the *Supérieure,* the Litany that they had learnt from the nuns, with its

"*Agnus Dei, qui tollis peccata mundi,*
Da nobis pacem,"

Felicia thought she had never heard music more pathetically sung.

In the next department, that of the *Persévérantes,* whose members after going through severe tests of repentance are allowed to dedicate their lives to devotion and prayer and to remain in the Convent till death, she was struck by the serenity and contentment stamped on the faces. On asking one of the women how long she had been in the house, she was answered " forty years." During that time she had never left St Michel. Its garden walls, within which the children played and the penitents were allowed their two hours of exercise every day, were the boundary of her desires. She would never leave the Convent. "*On y est trop bien,*" she said.

Speaking of the *Persévérantes* the Mother

Superior remarked, "they seem to think they can never do enough to prove their gratitude and love."

Infirmary, dormitories, refectory, with their simple but pretty and refined appointments, all met with Felicia's warm approval. But what pleased her most was the spirit of love and liberty that prevailed. Somehow or other the nuns succeeded in carrying out their work, and managing their large community, with its varied and difficult elements, without any machinery of rules. It was a bold venture to make, but in their skilful hands, an evident success.

"Why should we scare them at the outset with anything of the kind?" asked the Mother. "They soon fall into our ways when once they have joined us—the general order of the house and the example of the others lead them on insensibly."

As to entrance into the Home, the penitent had only to come and ask to be admitted, and the Mother could always manage to make room. If they left and wished to return they would be welcomed back, even if they had fallen into sin again. "Do you suppose," she enquired, "that we should refuse them a refuge from the evil world? We should have better hope of them the second time than the first." None were ever sent away, unless they wished to go; and they were never bound to stay any specific time.

" How can they tell whether they will be able
to stay when they come?   It is an immense
change from their life, which, if it is full of evil,
is also full of gaiety and pleasure; and it is a
wonderful thing that they should deny themselves so far as to come here at all.   If we made
such a rule, the majority would surely go back
from us altogether.   No! we let them come for
a day, for a week, for a month, as they will,
when weariness, or satiety, or ill-health drives
them out of their wretched life; and when they
are here they learn, for the most part, to love
God, to hate sin, and to wish for pardon; and
then they gladly stay till we think it safe for
them to go out."

Felicia went away, feeling that she had found
her ideal Penitentiary.

Her visit to St Michel gave as much pleasure
to the good Sisters as to herself, and so pleased
were they with the article she wrote about their
work that the Mother Superior asked her
permission that it should be translated into
French.   She hoped it might produce a good
result in France, and begged that it might be
published with Felicia Skene's name; "*qui
donnera toujours plus de croyance à ce récit.*"

Before closing this chapter we should like
to refer to an article in the *Hospital* on
" Methods of Rescue Work," written by Felicia
when she was nearly at the end of her life.   She

is still convinced that the system pursued in Homes and Refuges, is open to her old charges; but lest she should seem unsympathetic or un-appreciative of the efforts of those who conduct them, she is careful to add:

" We must beg our readers to understand that we do not for a moment wish to depreciate the good work done by the admirable women who conduct these institutions, in all cases where there is a genuine desire to reform; or the kind treatment and devoted service they give to their unfortunate charges; our object is simply to propose a remedy for some of what we consider to be the mistakes of the system, with a view to their greater efficiency."

The remedy she goes on to suggest is that every Home should have a preliminary Refuge affiliated with it, to which women might come for shelter at any hour of the day or night, and which they might be at liberty to leave when-ever they pleased, whether in a month, a week, or even a day. The rules should be of the simplest order; no questions should be asked, and only quiet and decorous behaviour required. Every effort should be made to induce the inmates to lead better lives; and when good influences begin to work, then they may be prevailed upon to move on to the Home and there to go through the two years' training, which Miss Skene agrees with the conductors of such institutions in thinking a necessity for the attainment of real reform.

CHAPTER XI

" HIDDEN DEPTHS "

THE book in which Felicia Skene gave strongest
utterance to her views on the " Social evil,"
was her story called " Hidden Depths," written
out of the fulness of her large warm heart.   It
was a book with a purpose, and being what it is,
could not be otherwise than a painful one.   One
of the reviewers speaks of it " As the most
distressing we have ever read."

The purpose was to expose the " hidden
depths " of evil that underlie the smooth surface of
society, and which her efforts among the women
she tried to rescue from their wild life in the
streets, or whom she visited in the gaol, had
revealed to her knowledge.   She had pondered
over them until her heart was hot within her, and
at the last the fire kindled.   Especially was
her indignation aroused by the difference of treatment accorded by the world to the erring man,
and the erring woman.   The scenes she describes
were no fancy ones; but taken from her own
knowledge and experience.   The most terrible
incident of all, the deliberate murder of the
miserable infants placed in charge of a wretched
woman, to whom she gives the name of Mrs

Dorrell, is drawn from life. Felicia knew such a creature. It was to her house she had come, on some flimsy excuse, and it was there she had lingered till the ghastly deed she had plotted and prepared had resulted in the death of the babes. The woman was tried, but by pleading an *alibi*, since she was out of her house at the time, she escaped the extreme penalty of the law, as the case could not be clearly proved against her. Whether the characters in the book are real or fictitious they are alike drawn with bold strokes. If Felicia had merely used her talents to produce a work of art, she would have arranged her incidents more skilfully to give an attractive combination of light and shade. That was not her object; she wanted to produce a moral not an artistic effect, and therefore she relentlessly groups together the dark scenes and characters that move across her stage. Almost the only rays of light that relieve the gloom are those cast by the character of the heroine, and the clergyman with whom she carried on her works of mercy. Ernestine Courtenay is a noble woman. If she has a failing, it is that she is rather too perfect; but she is too spirited and courageous to be insipid in her goodness. Here and there the characters are somewhat overdrawn, the worldly, prosperous ecclesiastic, Dr Granby, for instance. The interview Ernestine has with him, clever as some

of the touches are, is open to the charge of
exaggeration, even taking into account the fact
that at the time when it was written, far less
effort was made than at present, to rescue poor
girls out of the snares into which they had been
drawn.   People were more inclined to let things
be, as if they were a matter of course.

As in all Felicia's stories, the characters of
a humble rank are far better depicted than
those of a higher one.   They have much more
individuality.   When she had to deal with men
and women of the educated class, her language
is often stilted; her power of expression runs
away with her; her language is too ornate and
too intense.   Such long sentences and well-
rounded phrases are not used in common talk.
We cannot call the language laboured as far as
the writer herself was concerned, for it was no
labour whatsoever to her to write thus.   The
sentences ran easily off her pen without any
effort; but the speakers would never have so
expressed themselves.   Her poor people, on
the other hand, are terse, racy and pointed.

It is remarkable that though the book deals
with subjects generally and naturally withheld
from the young, some of the reviews recommend
it not only for elder but for youthful readers.
Whether this advice is wise or not, it is certain
that the tone of it is so elevated and the morality
so sound, wickedness is made so repulsive and

goodness so beautiful, that it gives no opening to any tampering with conscience in matters of right and wrong. The sharp distinction between them is never blurred.

The letters she received about "Hidden Depths" must have been very gratifying to her. Strangers, some of them distinguished literary men, wrote to her to express their admiration of her courage in writing it, and of the book itself. We quote one from Mr S. C. Hall.

8 ESSEX VILLAS, ARGYLL ROAD,
CAMPDEN HILL, W.

"MADAM,—for I am sure I address a woman—I cannot resist an intense desire to write you a few lines of gratitude, for the most beautiful book you have published—a beauty that is holy!

"Mrs Hall joins me in this expression of deep feeling, but a man is perhaps better able than a woman to estimate the immense good you may do by these two volumes.

"May God aid you in extending a knowledge of what you have so admirably written! Surely the seed you have sown will bear abundant fruit. I am an old critic—worn out it may be. I have lived when there were giants on earth; and it is not easy to content me with modern fiction: the major part of it tends only to deprave the heart while corrupting the taste: but here is a Book, 'Hidden Depths,' that I can read with intense delight: a pure English style in composition, devoted to the highest and noblest purposes.

" I thank you for the enjoyment you have given me—and certainly Mrs Hall; but I thank you far more for the good work you have done for Humanity. It was a brave work to do. Your own conscience will not give you the only reward you are destined to receive for it.—Your faithful and grateful servant,   S. C. HALL."

Another writer, a well-known novelist, whose views on the most important subjects were diametrically opposed to Felicia's own, was greatly struck by the power of the tale. " I think," he writes, " that that situation in ' Hidden Depths,' where the ideally pure man is confronted by his dying victim, is one of the strongest I have ever known. I have often thought of putting it in a drama."

Its dramatic power struck other readers. A gentleman wrote to her from America, asking if she would allow him to dramatize it. Whether he did so or not, the book contained great possibilities for the stage.

Making due allowance for a little overfine language, " Hidden Depths " presents many beautiful examples of style.

" I have been reading ' Hidden Depths,' " remarked the late Professor Rolleston, when that book was arousing attention, " and I think it contains some of the finest specimens of English prose I know."

The Rev. W. B. Duggan, Vicar of St. Paul's,

Oxford, in his "In Memoriam Sermon" on Felicia Skene, refers to the book as one, "which, with the most earnest and most modern spiritual feeling, presents some of the constructive features of Greek tragedy."

The history of the book was a curious one. In spite of the admiration it excited among many whose opinion was well worth having, it had little sale, partly no doubt because of its subject. Many years after it first came out, a stranger called on her, asking whether she would sell him the copyright. The sum proposed being at that time an inducement to her, Felicia agreed to do so.

He thus describes the transaction and its result.

"ANNANDALE PIAKO, N. Z., 11th *March* 1901.

"ABOUT seventeen years ago, when I was unwell at Bournemouth, I sent to 'The Library' for a book. An old two-volume tale was brought to me, called 'Hidden Depths.' I read it, and was so much struck with its power, and the truth and beauty of its sentiments, that I wrote to the 'Publishers' for the name of the writer. This at first they declined to give; but after some further correspondence, Miss Skene wrote to me herself, that she was the authoress. I replied, telling her how much I admired the book; offering to buy the copyright for the purpose of printing it in a cheap form; as I thought it was a pity that a work of such unusual power should not be widely circulated. This was about the time of Mr Stead's disclosures in the *Pall Mall*.

"Miss Skene sold me the copyright for £50. I had some difficulty in getting a Publisher, but at length Messrs Hodder & Stoughton brought it out.

"Nearly 28,000 copies of this cheap Edition were sold in a very short time, and about 2000 given away to Societies for promoting the Welfare of Young Women. I have every reason to believe that the book did a great deal of good.

"From a financial point of view there was practically no profit; as the great object I had in view was to circulate the book as widely as possible, as a means of preventing evil.

"W. SHEPHERD ALLEN."

So "Hidden Depths" made its mark eventually; and attained the honour in addition, of being translated into several languages.

CHAPTER XII

CHANGES

So far as outward events went, Felicia's life at Oxford was not distinguished by any striking incidents or changes, beyond the usual births, deaths, and marriages, which mark and alter all family life.

What made it noteworthy was, that it was one of great and increasing achievement, both from her activities and from her personal character and influence. Her friendships, her literary work, her work among fallen girls, tramps and prisoners, made her a power in the place. Each branch of her labours was so remarkable, that we must consider them separately. Of some of them we have already spoken. Before entering upon the others we will touch upon a few family events which affected not only the inner current, but in some measure the outward course of her life.

One of the most important, and intensely interesting to one who took a keen feminine interest in matrimony, was the engagement of her elder niece, Miss Zoe Skene, to Dr Thomson, fellow of Queen's College. It was a marriage that gave Felicia hearty satisfaction, importing a new relation into the family who was to prove a constant friend and helper. The letters she wrote to Mrs Thomson abound in words of gratitude for his continual kindness to her. She writes warmly of the pleasure which his visits to Oxford with his children gave her; of the pride she took in his intellectual powers; of her thankfulness for his wise counsels to her in difficulties, and for the help he gave her on behalf of the unfortunates whom she took under her protection.

The appreciation was mutual, for the Archbishop, in after years, paid her the highest
compliment he could, by inviting her to make
Bishopthorpe her permanent home, a testimony
to the high opinion he held of her agreeable
company, her tact and sympathy. She could
not make up her mind to tear herself away
from her work and her own little home at
Oxford, but she was deeply touched by his kind
proposal.

When Miss Zoe Skene married, the parting, in
one way, could not have been an easier one. For
after a few months' absence in London, while her
husband held the living of All Souls, Langham
Place, they returned to Oxford, where Dr
Thomson held the post of Provost of Queen's
for six years.

It was an ideal arrangement for the two
families. Mrs Thomson was close by for
daily meetings; and being able to take
her younger sister Janie into society, she
could free Felicia for her out-door work,
and for the care of her father and mother at
home.

Mrs Thomson's children, too, became a fresh
pleasure and interest to aunt and great-grand-
parents, especially when in 1860 Mr James
Skene moved from the house in Beaumont
Street to one where there was a garden in which
the little ones could play.

Mrs. Shane of Rudasluw

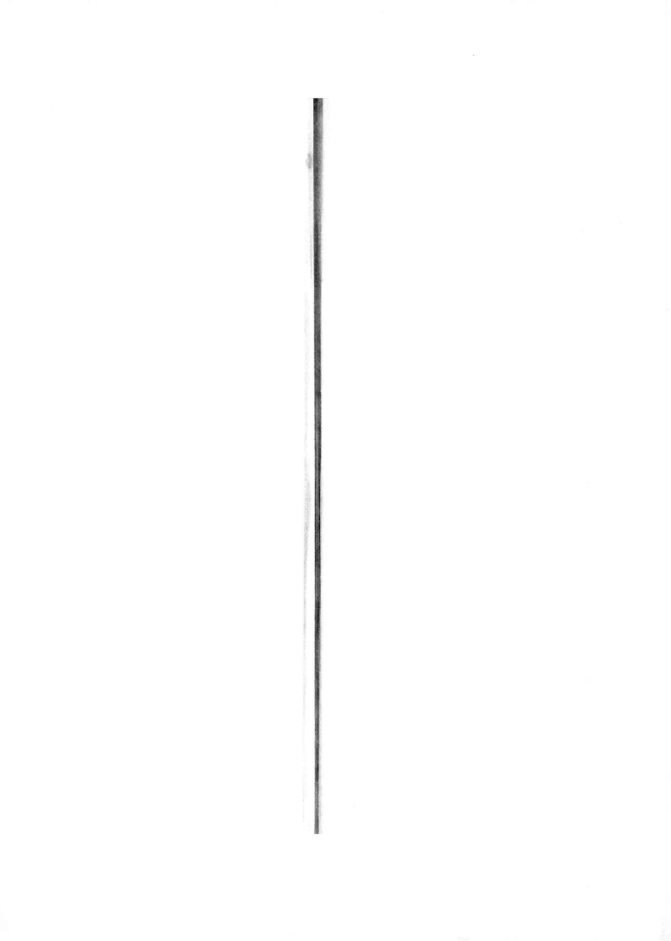

This was the charming old Frewen Hall, which had just been vacated by the Prince of Wales, who lived there during his residence at the University. When the Prince visited Oxford after his marriage, he brought his bride to the house that she might see the rooms he had stayed in, pointing out to her different objects with great interest.

His visit gave great pleasure to Mr and Mrs Skene, who were delighted to comply with his request to be shown the historical Bible of Charles I., kept among their family treasures.

In 1862 the first great sorrow in her own immediate family circle fell upon Felicia. Her mother, to whom she had always been particularly devoted, died; leaving the father more than ever dependent on his daughter.

It was a loss deeply felt.

The natural tie between mother and child was strengthened by the tender and intimate friendship that had existed between them, each sharing every thought and interest of the other.

The following year brought another separation, but this time of a more cheerful kind. Felicia's second niece, Janie, who like her sister won great admiration in Oxford society, became engaged to be married.

One exciting morning the postman's bag brought two letters of a flattering, but incompatible nature. Two lovers had written to

M

propose to her on the same day. Her choice
fell upon the Rev. Lloyd Stuart Bruce, afterwards Canon of York, a son of Sir John Bruce.
Though her new home was not to be at Oxford
like her sister's, and aunt and niece could not
often meet, Felicia kept up an almost maternal
interest in Mrs Bruce. Life was to bring the
bride, as the years went on, the cares of a large
family; and before her elder children were grown
up, she was to be taken from them after a long
and painful illness, preceding her aunt to the
unknown shore by nearly twenty years. So
long as her life lasted Felicia showered her love
and sympathy upon her, with every help in
trouble that it was in her power to bestow.

Felicia's three brothers, all men of marked
character and ability, each a student and an
author, were always a pride and delight
to her. The intercourse between them, though
often interrupted by long intervals, was kept
up by occasional visits and affectionate correspondence. She was most of all separated from
her youngest brother, as he had made his home
abroad. With the eldest, Mr George Skene,
the union was deepened by the bond of common
tastes and interests. Though a layman, he had
a great love for theological subjects, and during
the years when she edited the *Churchman's
Companion*, he contributed many papers to it.
Those on the " History of the Jews in the

Middle Ages," were much admired. Another
bond of interest was that of philanthropic work.
For when he gave up his Professorship at
Edinburgh, he devoted himself to trying to
better the condition, physical and spiritual, of
the poor at Old Town.

On one of the last occasions on which he
wrote to her, he speaks of the love which shone
through the letter he had just received from her,
as having been a perfect delight to him and of
"the entire sympathy that existed between
them."

But the brother who was most of all to
her was Mr William Skene, the Historiographer
Royal of Scotland, whose learning and ability
are too well known to be insisted on here. His
great desire always was that he might die on the
same day that she did. He was not left to
mourn her loss, for his death took place seven
years before her own. In character he was a
tower of strength to her and to all his family.
She regarded him as the ideal of all that man
should be. Those who knew him best say that
she has accurately described his fine character in
Walter Seton, the benevolent uncle in "A
Strange Inheritance." To the children of his
niece, Mrs Bruce, he was as a second father,
whose memory they deeply revere.

To him Felicia could refuse nothing, not even
her company at a place she particularly disliked,

Harrogate, when from time to time he visited it
for his health, and begged her to go with him.
Travelling by railway was always a trial to her
and made her ill, and the thought of leaving
Oxford and her work to walk up and down and
listen to the band among the gay visitors did
not offer an exhilarating prospect to her mind.
But then there was his company to make up for
it; and did he not speak of her "as the chief
comfort and happiness of his life?"

And when he referred to a former visit they
had made to the place together, how could she
say him nay?

"In 1879," he writes, "the doctor advised me
to go to Harrogate when that most delightful of
all companions, Miss Felicia M. F. Skene, joined
me and we celebrated my birthday there. Now
the doctor gives the same advice. I want to
know if there would be any reasonable prospect
of the same delightful companion spending the
month with me at Harrogate as she did before,
without causing her inconvenience or suffering,
and let us simply repeat what we did in 1879?"

No wonder she wrote to her niece,

"Please do not let Uncle William know a
word of what I have said about my feeling on
leaving home. I want him to have all the
pleasure I can give him without the slightest
drawback, and I shall always be glad I have
been able to be of use to him. At his age who can
say how long any of us can do anything for him?"

The event which brought the greatest outward change in Felicia's life was the death of her father, which took place two years almost to a day after that of his wife.

Something of what that grief was to her she indicates in a story written seven years after, called " Light out of Darkness," which came out in the *Churchman's Companion*. General Winston, the grandfather of the heroine, is said to be an excellent portrait of Mr James Skene of Rubislaw, both in appearance and in character.

As with most old people, the last weeks of his life seemed to have been lived in the past. His present surroundings appeared to have dropped away from him, and he was once more taking part in the stirring scenes of his youth and the early days of his married life. An allusion was made in the first chapter of this Memoir, to his conviction that Sir Walter Scott paid him a visit in actual bodily presence, at Frewen Hall. Mr Skene was then in his ninetieth year, and the poet had died thirty years before.

With Mr Blackwood's permission we quote Felicia's words :

" He was still well and strong in spite of his great age, and had the full use of his faculties with the exception of his memory which failed him only with regard to recent events. . . . One afternoon in the dark month of November, when he seemed quite well and peaceful, I had

left him alone for a few minutes sitting beside
the fire in his own room; his servant was within
call had he required him, but there was no one
actually present with him.   When I came back
to him, not having been more than a quarter-of-
an-hour absent, I found him with a look of radiant
happiness upon his fine old face. 'Oh, come
quick,' he exclaimed. 'I want to tell you of
such a delightful surprise I have had! Scott
has been here! dear Scott!   He told me he had
come from a great distance to pay me a visit, and
he has been sitting here with me talking of all
our old happy days together.   He said it was
long since we had met; but he is not in the least
changed; his face was just as cheerful and pleasant
as it used to be; I have so enjoyed being with
him.'   He went on for some time describing the
charming visit his dear old friend had paid him,
with a minuteness which was rather startling, and
then he asked me if I had not met Sir Walter
coming out of his room.   I told him I had not,
but I said no word to suggest that there was any
unreality in what he had seen.   How could I tell
what it had been? or how could any one express
an opinion on such an event?   I only know it
was a last ray of brightness from the setting sun
of my father's life. Very speedily after it had
thus gleamed upon him he followed his dear
friend to the unknown land, passing away gently
and serenely as a child falling asleep in its
mother's arms." [1]

The close of this account is very characteristic

[1] "Some Episodes in a Long Life."—*Blackwood's Magazine.* June,
1896.

From the Picture by   Sir HENRY RAEBURN, R.A

James Skene

[*To face p.* 182.

of the writer. Perhaps it was partly Felicia's
Scotch blood that always inclined her to the
belief in supernatural appearances. Anything
of the nature of a ghost story attracted her, and
she was easily persuaded in after years to become
a member of the Psychical Society. In this case
her father's certainty that Scott had been with
him in actual presence, had a stronger and more
touching significance than in other credited
apparitions, in view of the old friendship between
the two men.

Sometimes the old man would rouse himself to
give the word of command to the corps of Yeo-
manry he thought he was reviewing, and which
he had helped Scott to organise in the old days
at Edinburgh. But perhaps the most curious
instance of a return to the past was a sudden
outburst of grief for a child of his who had died
in the early years of his marriage.

Felicia Skene described the incident in the story
before alluded to, " Light out of Darkness," and as
the passage is interesting both from its adherence
to facts and from its being a good example of
her pathos, we give it here. She has changed
the relationship of the two actors in the scene,
for Wyntoun is the grandfather not the father
of Elsie, who represents Felicia herself.

" When Elsie came to his (her grandfather's)
side, she saw to her painful surprise that his head
was bowed on his hands, and that tears were

streaming down his cheeks. Elsie flung herself on her knees and clasped her arms round him.

" 'Darling grandpapa,' she exclaimed, 'what has happened? what is distressing you? do tell me; do not hide it from me.'

" Without lifting his head, he sobbed out, ' My poor little Mary !'

" 'Mary?'

" For a moment Elsie could not imagine whom he meant.

" 'Whom do you mean, grandpapa? I do not know the name.'

" 'Mary, my own child, my poor little girl who died before your father was born.'

" Then she remembered having heard that her grandfather's first child had been a daughter, who had died when but a few years old, and whom she had scarcely ever heard him mention, except on rare occasions, and then without any of the grief he was at present displaying, and which seemed unnatural with regard to the loss of an infant more than fifty years before.

" 'But that is so long ago, dearest grandpapa,' she said gently : 'surely you will not grieve over it now? Perhaps you were dreaming of her ; but you know your little child has been at rest for many years.'

" 'My pretty Mary,' he repeated, sobbing, without apparently noticing her words. 'To think I should have been called to see my sweet baby cold and dead ! I put her in her little coffin with my own hands, and held it on my knees in the carriage when we went to bury her—and there I was obliged to leave my own poor child in her lonely grave. Oh, my Mary,

my little Mary!' and from his dim blue eyes
the tears flowed fast, and the white head bowed
itself as if beneath a load of grief.

.   .   .   .   .   .

"Elsie tried to talk to him of other things, but
she could not even for a moment draw his
thoughts away from the little dead child who
had lain beneath the sunshine and the snows of
fifty years in her moss-grown grave. . . .   He
seemed hardly conscious that Elsie was speaking
to him on other subjects, and began to tell her
the history of the death and burial of this child
with the most minute details, as if all had
occurred quite recently.

"He described how she had died suddenly in
the night, at a seaside village, where she had
been sent with her nurse for change of air—for
she had been delicate from her birth, he said—
unable to speak or walk, but she always knew
him and looked happy if she heard his voice;
he detailed to Elsie with many tears, how she
smiled on him no more when he came that
morning to find her cold and motionless like
a white statue of alabaster, laid in her little
cradle—and then he told how he had not time
to take her to the family burial-place some days'
distant, but laid her to rest in the churchyard
of the beautiful village where she died.   He
explained to Elsie how the church stood on a
cliff overhanging the sea, so that the waves
sang a dirge for ever round the resting places
of the dead, and then he bade her bring him
a pencil and paper, and with the shaking hand
which had long before given up working at his
favourite art, he drew a sketch of the church-

yard and marked with a cross the place where his child reposed." [1]

With the loss of her father, there followed that of the charming home at Frewen Hall. Life had to be taken up alone under new conditions, with that sense of desolation which always comes with the realisation that the older generation with its protecting love has passed away.

In Felicia's great sorrow, Archbishop Thomson was one of her best comforters. No one could have shown more tender sympathy than he gave her.

A little house was found for her, some hundred yards round the corner from the old one. It was an ancient one, as she testifies in a letter written from Harrogate some years after, recording a curious discovery :

" My home is being set to rights while I am absent, and amongst other things the kitchen floor had to be renewed. When they took up the old boards they found that a horse had been buried there ! It must have lain there hundreds of years, for my house is I believe about two hundred years old."

The house stood in a street said to have been once known by the nickname of the Street of

---

[1] From "Light out of Darkness."— *Churchman's Companion,* August, 1871,

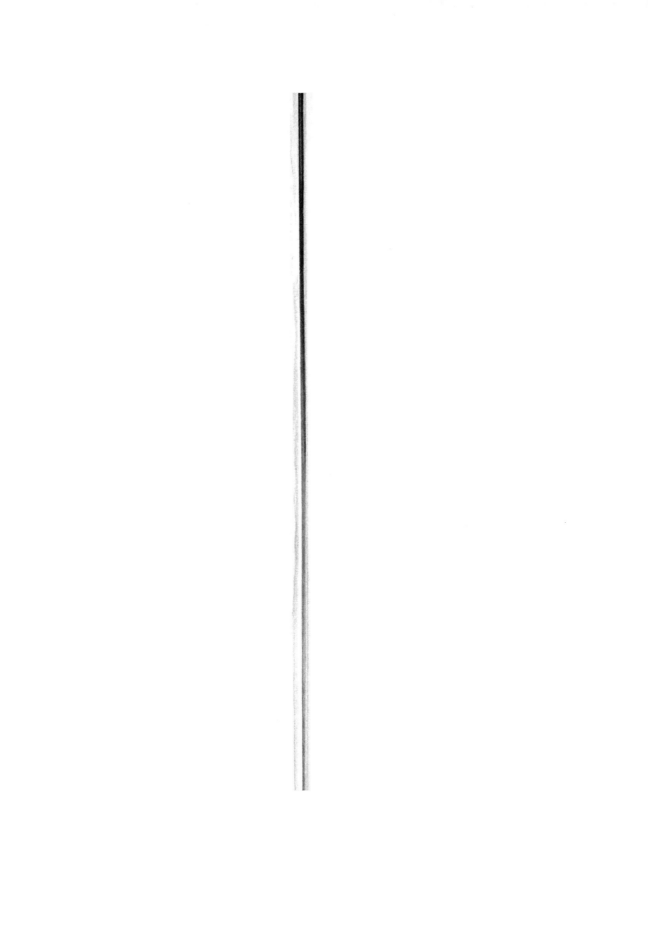

the Seven Deadly Sins. It has now risen to a more saintly title, being known as St Michael's Street. During most of the time of Felicia's residence there, it was called New Inn Hall Street.

If its walls could speak and tell the variety of persons they received while she lived there, the list would be somewhat startling. It might very well end with thief, like the list of professions often rattled off by children, but it might truthfully begin with all that was highest in character and attainments.

"You had better not leave your umbrella in the hall," she found it necessary to say to visitors sometimes, "for I have queer people coming to the house."

If she could not quite trust the strange acquaintances she made in her visits to the gaol, with the property of her friends, at least there was sufficient honour among thieves, to make them respect her own. For they never stole from her.

From one caller or another the bell was going all day, till she declared she had gone into the public line, and had become landlady of the Skene Arms.

No one who has ever enjoyed talks with her in that hospitable little house can pass it now without a sense of emptiness and loss.

CHAPTER XIII

PRISON VISITING

If any one were to enquire at Oxford why Miss Skene's name is held there in highest honour, nine out of ten persons would answer, on account of her work at the prison. And when we consider the difficulty of it, the success with which it was carried on, and the comparatively small number of the charitable who have the courage or the skill to undertake this branch of benevolence, we may consider the answer a natural one.

For the thousands of excellent women who devote their lives to the friendless and miserable who have never been within prison walls, there are but a mere handful who dare enter on the arduous and painful task of visiting those inside them. It was the work that tried Felicia most, and took more out of her than any other. Her whole soul went out in pity for those who, when once the prison-doors were closed on them, were, she averred, as completely forgotten by the world outside as if they were dead; and who when they came out would be recognised as gaol-birds, shunned by all, refused, as suspicious characters, the work they might apply for, till they were almost driven back on their old bad practices. The fact that they had deserved their punishment, that many of them were depraved and hardened, did not close the fount of her compassion but only made her feel that they needed her help the more.

In a long obituary notice of Felicia Skene, a writer in one of our best-known papers gives her this title to honour. "Her name," he says, " may appropriately be linked in association with the names of Elizabeth Fry and Sarah Martin."

There are many ladies at the present day who carry on the difficult work of visiting in gaols, but we believe that we are right in stating that Felicia was the first lady in England to receive official permission from the Government to become a regular visitor in one of the public prisons.

Her first introduction to prison-life began through her labours among fallen girls. She had visited them in the Spinning House when it formed part of the City Gaol on Gloucester Green. But her visits were not entirely con- fined to them; for from time to time she received permission to see other prisoners, and occasionally was admitted to the cells of those under sentence of death. The Archbishop of

York was able in one or two instances, to obtain this favour for her.

The old City Gaol exists no longer, and the ground on which it once stood, is covered with pens, filled with cattle on market-days. When it was abolished, its inmates were transferred to the County Gaol, standing by the one remaining tower of the old Castle in Queen's Street.

On 13th May 1878, Felicia Skene thus writes in her prison-diary, which she carried on to the close of her life:

"I received this day permission from the Commissioners to visit the female prisoners in the County Gaol, Oxford. By the wish of the Governor and the Chaplain it was settled that I was to go there regularly on two days in the week, Tuesdays and Fridays, at eleven o'clock, and also that I should be allowed to see the prisoners alone, without the presence of the matron. I have always regretted that I never kept any record of my visits to the old City Gaol now closed, where I have gone at intervals for more than twenty years, and I therefore mean to keep a register of the days on which I am able to go to the County Prison, although I am little likely to have even half the years to carry on the work there that I had in the older prison. Even if my life continues, my strength must fail."

She little thought that only half her course

of prison-work had run, and that another twenty years of it awaited her.

The venerable Castle used as the County Prison had had a varied record of good and ill. In its earliest days one of its towers had belonged to a church dedicated to St George. Alfred the Great had held his court in it, and Harold Harefort is said to have lived there. It had been battered in siege and rebuilt by a Norman baron. It had been invested by King Stephen's soldiers, while the Empress Maud was taking refuge there. Thence she had started on her adventurous flight on foot over the ice, in a storm of snow. In the reign of Henry III. it began its gloomy career as a prison. The fine old tower, flanked by a high grassy mound, is one of the picturesque sights of Oxford.

Here Felicia was to be a familiar sight, going in and out on her errands of mercy. Nothing but serious illness or absence from home could induce her to give up her bi-weekly visits; while if there were any particular reason for going to a prisoner, she would not wait for the right day, since, as one of the officers remarked, the prison gates would always fly open for her. She would not make her rounds then, as she had no right to do so, and never changed her day without asking permission of the Governor; but she was allowed to visit a particular case.

She certainly earned her privileges by a careful observance of rules.   The visitor's work is one requiring great tact and self-restraint.   Only by conscientious attention to all the regulations could ill-effects on the prisoners and friction with the authorities be avoided.

"She was more particular to keep the rules than many of the officers themselves," was the testimony borne to her by the present Governor who, speaking of the way in which she identified herself with their work and their interests, added, " She was quite one of ourselves."

One of the rules of prison life is that no information of what happens in the world outside, even in the prisoners' families, must be given to those who are undergoing their sentence.   And if Felicia thought there was anything that one of them really ought to know, the Governor might depend upon her asking his permission before she ventured to communicate it.   The necessity of silence was often a painful one to her, for she felt at times that if only she might tell a prisoner something she knew herself, she might have a better chance of influencing her.   But she was bound in honour to obey orders, and she kept faith with those who trusted her.

Her intercourse with some of the officials resulted in a real friendship between herself and them.   She discussed their difficult cases with them, giving them her advice and sympathy; she interested herself in their families; she kept up correspondence with them when they moved on to similar work in other prisons; indeed, her interest was pretty evenly divided between them and their charges.

When the head-jailor was dying, he would let no one go near him except herself, and always brightened up at the sight of her.

While most people would be touched with the woes of the prisoners, it is not every one who would be equally considerate of those whose duty it is to preside over their discipline.

When first she came to live at Oxford and paid visits to prisoners in the City Gaol, she had only done so through special permission from a Magistrate; the exception being in the case of the women in the Spinning House. When she desired to follow the prisoners to the County Gaol, the Governor applied formally to the Home Office for leave for her to become a regular visitor. Both he and the Chaplain testified warmly to the good effect which they were sure her visits would have on the female prisoners. "By all means," was the reply returned by Captain Stopford of that Department.

The condition to which she alludes in her diary, that she should see the prisoners alone, she felt to be essential. The presence of an

N

official, however kindly, would prevent confidence and quench the influence she hoped
to gain over them. To her alone they might
speak out; her visits they would learn to
recognise as the voluntary ones of a friend, not
as the duty-visits of a paid official. Leave for
these *tête-à-tête* interviews was soon obtained,
and Felicia was able to enter the cells alone,
and to have the door closed upon her.

Sometimes it was a dangerous experiment.
There was a woman in the punishment cell,
at one time, of so furious a temper that no one
dared go near her. Felicia Skene however,
would not shrink from the ordeal; and so
touched was the poor creature at finding that
a lady was not afraid to approach her, that she
laid her handkerchief on the dusty floor, in the
style of Sir Walter Raleigh, for her visitor to
stand on.

"I have seen prisoners who were quite stony-
hearted, utterly indifferent about their families,
break down under her influence," said a former
Matron at Oxford Gaol. And she summed up
her testimony by remarking: "I have never seen
any one in all my experience of visitors—and I
have known many—who had so much influence
and did so much good."

Knowing what a crucial moment it is in the
lives of prisoners when they leave the gaol—how
many are the snares awaiting them in their first

hour of freedom if they are reckless, how sorely
they stand in need of a friend if they wish to
make a fresh start—Felicia would be at the
gates to meet any woman on her discharge, as
early as seven o'clock in the morning.   Then
came the struggle to induce the released prisoner
to keep the promise extracted from her in
captivity, to go straight to the Refuge ; where
Sister Ruth, whose kindly rule generally had
excellent influence on the inmates, would
befriend her ; sending her on in due time to
some other Home, getting her a suitable situation, or restoring her to her friends if desirable.
Felicia's prison-diary is a chequered record of
success and failure, in that first walk from the
Castle gates.

Nearly the whole morning was spent at the
gaol, on her regular visiting days.   She
would go from one prisoner to another, trying
to establish friendly relations with them before
attempting to reach their hearts and consciences.
She would enquire after their families, promise
to visit them if possible and see to the children.
She was careful never to begin by a reference
to the crime for which they were undergoing
punishment, partly because she wished her visit
to be regarded as a friendly one, and also
because she would not put temptation in their
way to tell a lie about it.   If an infant was
brought to the prison by the mother, she would

arrange for its baptism if that had not taken place, often standing sponsor herself. It cannot be said that her god-children always did her credit in after life. She was walking along the road one day, when an ill-looking tramp marched up and confronted her, to her alarm. "I'm your godson," he remarked. Another grew up a terror to his family, and when in a drunken fit on one occasion, was with difficulty restrained from cutting the throats of his three children.

But at least she could do something for his offspring, for she got his permission to do what she liked with the poor little creatures, and saved them from a violent death by getting them into an Orphanage. The father, who professed to be a Protestant, was not likely to be particular about nice shades of theology; and on her failure to raise the funds to pay for them at a Church of England Home, was quite willing that she should place them at a less expensive one for Roman Catholics, which she did.

In her private interviews with prisoners she could generally get the truth out of them at last, though often we come to such remarks in her diary as, "Told nothing but lies." Here is a case in which she thought there were extenuating circumstances for untruthfulness. "Saw A. an old tramp; she and her husband have a month for stealing combs to sell; they both accuse themselves, to save the other. Nice old people! though they do tell lies."

One of her great efforts always was to persuade those women who had been living with men, to be married to them on leaving prison. It was no easy task. Sometimes neither of them was willing to go through what they considered an unnecessary ceremony; sometimes one would, but the other refused. Occasionally both parties were in gaol, on different sides of the building at the same time. When they left, the struggle to march them off to the Church or the Registrar's began. In her early visiting days Felicia chose the former; but afterwards, feeling that the presence of such low characters was a profanation to a sacred building, she generally escorted them to the Registrar's.

The wife of the clerk at St Thomas's has a vivid remembrance of one early wedding in particular, which took place in the church. The dreariness of the scene that cold, dull, winter morning made a great impression on her. The man was just out of gaol, and the woman with whom he had been living met him with their children at the door of the church.

The little ones had probably never seen the inside of one before, and stood in a cluster in the aisle, staring with dull eyes at the strange place, wondering what on earth the father and mother were about.

Felicia let no outward inducement be lacking to get such couples to agree to being legally united.   She would often provide the bride with a dress, sitting up all night in one instance, to finish making one for her; she would buy the ring and present it to the bridegroom.   After her death her niece found a parcel of cheap wedding rings among her possessions.   She would go to church with the pair, give the bride away herself, and then bring them back to breakfast at her house.

What that breakfast was may perhaps shock some strict teetotallers.   It consisted of a glass of gin and a twopenny bun.   If it was a bribe, she considered it a justifiable one in the circumstances, because likely to contribute to success in her righteous aim.   For Felicia was a woman of resource, and would leave no stone unturned.

Some of her experiences of prison characters were strange indeed.

There was a certain woman of rather superior class to the majority, a queer hysterical creature, whose foolish crime had made a good deal of sensation in Oxford.   Felicia saw her, and gained her confidence sufficiently for the prisoner to decide to leave her watch and trinkets in charge of her visitor, till she should be set at liberty. After a time the woman was moved on to Woking Gaol; and Felicia Skene, according to her

usual habit of trying to keep up communication with prisoners she had known, got leave from the Governor there to write to her. The woman suddenly and unaccountably took offence; and in a huff demanded that her trinkets should be given up at once. It was accordingly arranged that they should be handed over in due form to the family lawyer in presence of the Governor, and that a receipt should be given for them. Felicia went through the ceremony with more amusement than offence; and showed her good-will on the release of the prisoner, by trying to find her a situation.

After a time the woman wrote to her saying that she was destitute, and intended to commit suicide unless £5 were sent her at once.

Her kind friend forwarded her the money; but either the need was not so pressing as represented, or the sum sent was unnecessarily large, for the peculiar person wrote afterwards to say she had spent some of it in buying a bracelet in remembrance of Miss Skene.

An experience of a different and more touching kind was one she had while visiting a criminal sentenced to death for murder. The strain upon her feelings in this and similar interviews, especially considering how strong her views were against the infliction of capital punishment, may be imagined.

The man referred to had seemed to all to be

utterly hardened.   He was racked by a terrible cough, and Felicia obtained leave to take him a few grapes to moisten his throat.   As she handed them to him, he burst into tears exclaiming: "That's what my mother would have done for me."

A farmer, who had once ridden into Oxford to find out where Miss Skene lived, had been heard to remark, " If any one could save a person's soul, *she* could !" and as we think of that prison incident, his words recur to our mind.

In her anxiety to help prisoners in any way she could, she engaged and paid counsel to defend them in one or two cases in which she was convinced of their innocence.

She was full of sympathy for the children of criminals who had to suffer the disgrace brought upon them by the sins of their parents.

An instance of her interest on behalf of a poor little girl in these painful circumstances, is shown in the following letter to the present Bishop of Liverpool.

13 New Inn Hall Street,
Oxford, 10th *June* 1897.

" Dear Mr Chavasse,—I have always remembered with very great gratitude your exceeding kindness to me some years ago—when you raised sufficient money to enable me to place O—— S—— in an orphanage—the child of the unhappy man who was executed for the murder of his wife.   I write merely because I think it

will give you pleasure to know that the excellent
training she received, resulted in her being now a
perfectly respectable well-disposed young woman.
She has been confirmed and is a communicant,
and apparently truly religiously minded, so far as
her mental capacity goes, which has never been
great. She is in service, and seems to be giving
complete satisfaction to her employers.

"At the time when you helped me so generously,
I knew that if we did not provide for her, she
would certainly fall into the hands of her eldest
sister who was of a notorious bad character; that
poor woman is now dead, and there seems to be
no risk of evil influence for her now. She used
to be called 'Anna' at the orphanage, and I
have advised her to continue using that name, so
that I hope she will not be identified as the
daughter of the man who was hanged.

"With kind regards and many thanks for all
you did for her and for me.—I am sincerely
yours,   F. M. F. SKENE."

It would be a mistake to think that her views
on the treatment of criminals were always of the
soft and melting order. She could speak sternly
enough on occasion, both to and of the prisoner
whose crimes had brought just punishment upon
him. Not only her diary but her letters and
articles are proof enough of this, and they often
recommend severe measures as the truest kindness. Only when the extreme penalty was to
be paid, she considered pity and mercy should
have full sway till the painful end.

Her visits to the gaol would have been dreary indeed, if they had not been lightened by many gleams of hope.   Even where she seemed to fail at the time, her efforts may have borne fruit afterwards.

She does not enter in her diary into particulars of the talks she had with the prisoners, but she records some of them more fully in her " Scenes from a Silent World," of which we shall speak later.   No argument or persuasion that might possibly reach their consciences was omitted ; and if she felt sick at heart sometimes, at encountering hardness, indifference, and degradation among the wrecks of humanity, her faith and hope in God and in all in whom His likeness was not quite stamped out, upbore her amid disappointment and discouragement.

In an article she wrote on the " Work of Prison Visitors "[1] she sums up her conclusion in these words, " never till the grave itself has closed over the sinner, must they say of any man or woman, ' I give them up; I can do nothing for them ; I will attempt no more '; up to the very last let the charity that never faileth cling to them in hope."

Onlookers can sometimes judge better of the effect of work than the workers themselves ; and the testimonies of the officers of the prison, Governor, Chaplain, Warders, all agree in apprecia-

[1] From *The Helping Hand.*   A Quarterly Magazine.

tion of her labours. They thought these not
only valuable themselves, but helpful and inspiring in holding up a high standard of single-
minded devoted service.

Writing to the Prison Commissioners at the
close of his term of office, one of the Governors
remarked, that before leaving he should like to
mention Miss Skene's good work among the
prisoners, many of whom she had reclaimed from
a life of sin, while she had found situations for
them, " So that no woman needing help had ever
left the gates friendless, or without knowing
there was a helping hand held out by her."
He speaks of " her great wisdom and discretion," and of the quiet unostentatious way in
which her work had been done.

Another Governor, Colonel Isaacson, with
whom she formed a real friendship, writes of her
great influence. Among the wild characters
whom she tamed he mentions one woman in
particular, " who occasionally seemed to be almost
possessed ; but when at her worst, if Miss Skene
happened to be in the prison, she could calm her
instantly, and very quickly tears of repentance
were forthcoming. . . . She was simply beloved
by all who knew her."

One means of benefiting the prisoners came to
her through her musical talents. She could play
and sing at the Chapel Services. The sons of
one of the governors had been in the habit of

presiding at the harmonium. On one occasion
in the absence of both, she volunteered to take
their place. The Prison Commissioners were
applied to for permission for the time being.
They were also asked whether she might attend
the Chapel Services from time to time, when she
wished to do so. The position of the harmonium
would, they were informed, bring her into view
of the male prisoners, but not of the women; for
the instrument was placed on the men's side of
the wooden partition that divided the sexes.

Leave was granted at once.

Two days after, the Commissioners were
besieged with another request. The harmonium
was a bad one, might Miss Skene's offer of her
own instead, be accepted? Another grateful
consent followed. And ere long she found herself installed as permanent organist.

Twice every Sunday for years afterwards, till
feeble health compelled her to give up playing,
did she lead the music in the chapel. Whether
the prisoners sat where they could see her or not,
they liked to feel that she was there; one good
woman from the world outside had not forgotten
them. And the music if rough was loud and
hearty, for the prisoners enjoyed singing at the
top of their voices.

After Felicia Skene met with an accident and
broke her leg, she was obliged of course to give
up playing for a time; but in her zeal she returned

to her duties before she could walk comfortably, and had to be half carried up the winding stairs by which the women enter the chapel.

She not only played but came to the weekly practices—no small addition to her labours.

When she gave up her office as organist, she still made a point of attending the Services, coming to the Chapel once on Sundays.

With the Chaplains and occasional preachers, she soon got upon frank and friendly terms enough to venture to criticise their sermons every now and then, if she thought them unsuited to the audience. It was a special congregation and needed special treatment. It was a splendid opportunity, she felt, for getting hold of men and women who, when they were at liberty, had probably never attended a Church at all. She put herself in their place; she heard with their ears; and the result did not always satisfy her. The prisoners needed a certain stamp of clergyman as well as of sermon. A hard-working, East End type of parson, accustomed to deal with rough characters, would be the kind of man for the place. She tells a story of such a "right man in the right place," in one of her prison articles, in the serial,[1] from which we have before quoted. An elderly prisoner, sunk into the hopeless state likely to ensue from a life generally spent in workhouse or prison, had tried to starve

[1] *The Hospital.*

himself to death.   A strange clergyman came to
the Chapel and preached so earnestly, on the
theme that God helps those who help themselves, that the old man afterwards said to
the Governor, " Sir, that parson has come here
for me." On this remark being repeated to the
preacher, he visited the poor fellow, and the
result was the prisoner became in his own words,
" A new man," ready to take up the struggle of
life when he regained his freedom and carry it
on with renewed life and energy.   Sermons on
abstruse subjects or nice points of theology, were
as much above the heads of the hearers, as
Chinese metaphysics.

The Chapel Services were not always used by
the prisoners to edification.   In spite of every
precaution being taken to prevent communication between the men and the women, such as
wooden partitions and separate entrances, they
could find various means of imparting information to one another.   The hymns and responses
are very useful, as words of their own can be
substituted for those in prayer and hymn-book.
A bad cough, too, has its advantages for mutual
intercourse, and may be utilised as easily as the
knocks in spirit-rapping.   So, too, may be a
babe in arms.   A sly pinch producing a scream,
may inform the father on the other side of the
partition, of the presence of his wife and child.
The most ingenious employment of means for

the end required, was the use which Felicia Skene tells us was made of a large, highly-polished brass cross over the altar. Each man as he filed past to his seat was reflected in it, and a woman who sat in a certain spot, could see one after another as he walked by. The information gained was handed on to her fellow-prisoners. When the discovery was made how the knowledge was acquired, the cross was moved to a place where it could tell no secrets.

In spite of such disappointing experiences, it is a comfort to hear from the present Governor that the Services in Chapel are generally appreciated; that the prisoners like attending the short daily prayers which last only a quarter of an hour, and that a certain number of them come to the Holy Communion from time to time.

One of the most interesting objects in the Chapel, hung high above the wooden partition, so that the men on the other side, as well as the women, may be able to read it, is a tablet lately put up on which these words are inscribed : [1]

TO THE MEMORY OF

FELICIA MARY FRANCES SKENE,

WHO HELPED HER FRIENDS HERE AND EVERYWHERE TO

COME TO HIM WHO SAID,

"Him that cometh to Me, I will in no wise cast out."

---

[1] They were written by one of her great friends, Lady Sophia Palmer, whose residence in Oxford during the last few years of Felicia Skene's life, brought much happiness to her.

Another tablet is now being erected to Felicia Skene's memory in Christ Church Cathedral, which she attended regularly on Sunday afternoons during the last years of her life.

The two places of worship are widely different as to architecture, as to the congregations gathered in them, and the character of the Services held therein.

But that the memory of Felicia Skene should be held in reverence and affection in the plain little prison Chapel, is a more touching and remarkable thing than that it should be remembered in the beautiful Cathedral.

CHAPTER XIV

PRISON DIARIES AND LETTERS

A FEW extracts from Felicia Skene's prison diary, written, as we saw, from the time she began to visit in the County Gaol, will give the best idea of the characters she had to deal with and the way she tried to influence them.

"I took Anna H——," she writes, "and M. A. S——to the Refuge; the promenade through the streets was not agreeable, as they had large hats and short petticoats and talked very loud."

"Saw Sarah M—— who is still ready for the Refuge. The sisters H. and E. S——, who have been wavering, but I hope will go, and Mary S——, who informed me that if the Chaplain spoke to her again, she should insult him. I met him as I was going out, but I did not inform him of this pleasant plan of hers. She is very hopeless."

"Saw Anne S——, in great fear of being taken up again. I refused a present from her aunt this morning, of vegetables, lest it should seem a bribe to show the girl favour, and I asked the Matron to be present when I saw her, because she tells falsehoods."

"Saw Sarah S——, who has been sent back for stealing a cloak; she says she did not steal it, only took it; she has six weeks, which it were well if it were six years."

"Saw Jane W——, an old tramp whom I promised to help on her way on Thursday, when her time is finished, and who is an experienced old beggar."

"*Thursday 26th.*—Met J. W——, and gave her the choice of having a railway ticket to London, or half-a-crown and liberty to go her own way, —she chose the latter with enthusiasm, and pelted me with texts for a long way."

"*Tuesday 15th.*—I saw Francis S——, who has three months for keeping a bad house. She cried convulsively, but the chief cause of her grief was that she does not like gruel— she is utterly hardened. I could not get her to promise she would say even one prayer."

"I saw Mrs B——, committed for suicide, which was accomplished so far as her will was con-

cerned, but she was saved with difficulty. She
was driven to it by the ill-usage of her husband,
and is intensely to be pitied. . . . I also saw the
naughty little thief from Banbury, who is
much too sharp, . . and D——, who wishes to
know if I will give her money to get tipsy
with when she comes out, and I declined."

"*Friday* 13*th*.—I saw only Frances S——. I
want so much, if possible, really to move her
to lead a better life, when she goes out. At
present, she does not go beyond wishing to
be respectable and avoid the prison."

Often the cases she tried to help seemed so
hopeless from one cause or another, drink,
dulness and stupidity, or conceit and self-
complacency, that she must have been tempted
to give up in despair.

"Saw Mrs C——, who has been very bad,
and considers herself immaculate. Saw the
little Alice, whom I mean to try and teach
a little on each of my visits; she is absolutely
ignorant and exceedingly dense. Saw G——,
and settled to give her money to go to Reading
to try and get work, as I have failed to get
her into the Home for Inebriates.

"Saw Alice, who goes out on Friday. I fear she
is just what she was, a perfect little heathen. I
do not think I have succeeded in putting a single
idea into her head. I also saw H——, who
goes out to-morrow, and is quite satisfied with
herself. She talks as if she had merely been
paying a visit at a country-house. Saw B——,
an R. C., whom I hope to get married."

" *Tuesday 23rd.*—There has been a great disturbance about the letter-writing affair, in which H—— is implicated, and Mary W—— has been very deceitful. I spoke strongly to them both, and very differently from what I have done hitherto; and afterwards I feared I might have done harm. They have so little idea of right or wrong, that I believe they see no fault in what they have done, and thought me harsh."

" I saw P——, the comical old Roman Catholic. She goes out on Tuesday and I tried to speak to her of the sin of stealing, but she has views of her own on the subject.

" 'Well, ma'am, but I had nothing and they had plenty, and so I took something for myself.' She seemed to look upon it as 'natural selection.'

" Here is the last sight of the old woman.

" Old P—— came to-day for her breakfast and her fare to London. She was very comical. She told me she was as sharp as a razor, and then expressed her amazement that so charming a being should never have been married. Finally she began to speak French perfectly well. I sent her to London."

" Saw C——, who is utterly hopeless. She said, ' I talked so funny she could not help laughing,' because I asked her not to live with a man before she was married to him."

" Saw W——, a little less hardened than the last time; she quickly owned her guilt, which she steadily denied before. Minnie R——, as hard as a stone, but who does not, I think, dislike me, and that is something to be thankful

for.   Then I went to H—— in her cell, and she
made me foolishly happy by telling me of a
dream she had, when she saw me praying for her,
and Our Lord standing near all bright and
glorious, Who said, 'Wash her in the Blood
of the Lamb.'   She said she should never forget
it."

The next case is a heavy make-weight to the
more hopeful H——.

"Went to Mrs H——, who represented herself as a model of virtue, and has been a villain-
ous old wretch for years.   Saw Clara D——,
who was so insolent I had to send her away,
and Ethel P—— in such a temper that I sent
her out."

"Saw Clara D——, who promises to go back
to the Union and make an apology for the bad
behaviour which brought her to prison.   Saw
poor old L——, who always wants me."   The
next mention of L—— is "that she learnt half
the book of Genesis to please me."

"I took S—— away, to have her snatched
from me by a bad woman.   Saw B——, the
woman who starved her child, and Eliza G——,
who said it was her birthday of nineteen, (sic)
and she wanted me to help her to be good."

"Monday, 11th August.—The Chaplain is gone
for a month, and says he leaves me over the
women's prison, as 'Bishop.'   Saw W——, an
old humbug, and Laura T——, who stole a
prison sheet to make a chemise."

"30th April.—I saw C——, and made her
promise to apologise to the Governor (after she

had made a disturbance), and P——, who goes for trial to-morrow, and is most frightfully depraved. Saw T——, whose last words to me were, ' I won't never do right.' Saw L——, who was moved by all I said of Our Lord, I think."

"15th July.—Here follows a gratifying permission from the Governor.

" The Governor told me to-day that he wished me now to act according to my own discretion (with regard to a letter to a prisoner) in all such matters ; that I knew the rules and everything else almost as well as he did, and that I might say and do what I pleased, as he should never be angry at anything I did."

Here are two prisoners who were rather a contrast to one another.

" I saw Annie B——, a poor old country-woman sent in for taking a stick out of a hedge ; a most contented creature ; she said she came with the policeman quite like a lady, with a cushion to sit on and a footwarmer. Her husband had only fourpence in the world, and he gave her twopence, saying she would probably have nothing to eat in the prison."

"15th September.—I went to O—— in the punishment cell, who had smashed everything, but grew calm at once with me and put her handkerchief for me to set my feet on in the mess. She said she wanted to boil the cook in the copper to a pulp."

"23rd January.—Saw old B——, who gave me many blessings, and said the Lord and I were her only friends."

"*6th February.*—I was present at the marriage of Joseph C—— and Annie F—— at St Thomas's."

"Saw Polly F—— who has never said a prayer in all her life. I saw P——, who has two months, and is a most hopeless woman, saying she is an angel of goodness and all the virtues, and is sent to prison for spite. I saw D——, and gave her a breakfast; she at present means to do better. Saw D—— in the punishment cell where I got shut in,—and S——, and made her promise to give up her bad life. She said she promised me just as if I were Jesus Himself."

"I saw the poor violent Agnes, who says I may do what I like with her, and will go to the Refuge."

"*3rd October.*—I saw E. E—— to settle that she was to wait at the Refuge for the carrier to take her home. Ann M——, who is a most obstinate old creature, and declares she will not go to Nazareth House as the priest wished, but expects me to send her to Bristol. Saw Anna S——, who fully admits having stolen something to get a few shillings for a railway fare, and who is most heartily and truly ashamed and penitent. Saw Louisa B——, who is committed for the manslaughter of her child. She told me a very long story; the principal witness against her is her sister-in-law whom she has always hated. She told me they had several 'rounds' of a fight in the street, and described how, after having agreed to fight, they went home and put on suitable garments for the occasion. I have no doubt the child died from insufficient nourishment, and that she did not care about it, but I think it was more ignorance and carelessness than wilful neglect."

Another bellicose woman is mentioned, whose neighbour "heaved half a brick at her, and of course I returned it as was proper."

" Amy C—— has come back ; I hope to get her to the Refuge once more; also old Le G——, who declares her husband is a gentleman, and that she is a model of temperance and virtue. She has but one wish in the world and that is for a Bible."

"Saw a poor married woman named P——, committed for falling asleep tipsy on the road ; she is ill, and said she was only tired. She said to see me there was like an angel coming out of heaven."

" It was hopeless to insist on seeing Ethel P——, who goes out on Monday; we shall have her back no doubt very soon."

Many of the prisoners returned again and again to the gaol, with as great regularity as some people of another class visit German baths.

There is one entry about a woman who is described as very happy to be in prison ; which would make one smile, if it did not suggest melancholy thoughts as to what her home must have been like.

We have given many cases that seemed almost beyond the hope of reformation, upon which such melancholy comments are written

as "hard as a stone," "one might as well talk
to a brick wall," "utterly depraved," "a hopeless
case." It is refreshing to turn to one, which
though it appeared as bad as it could be, yielded
at last to the unwearied efforts of Felicia Skene
and Sister Ruth, the deaconess at the head of
the Refuge at St Thomas's. The story of
Millicent M—— is so remarkable and interesting,
that we give it here :

The girl had been imprisoned for theft at
Milbank, and when that gaol was abolished, she,
with many others, was sent on to Oxford to
finish her sentence. Felicia was pleased with
her ; she was a bright attractive girl, and there
seemed to be good hope that she might be
persuaded to go to the Refuge on leaving
prison. To the girl's story that it was her first
conviction and also an unjust one, as it was a
cousin of hers who had committed the theft,
Felicia gave entire credence. There seemed
a great deal that was promising about her.
She told her visitor that her mother was a
woman of much prayer, and that she had prayed
herself that some lady might come and help her,
and send her to a Home. When she was
transferred to the Refuge she informed Sister
Ruth that she had no relations except distant
ones, in England ; that her own people were out
in Africa, working in the mines, and that she
had not seen them for six years.

It took weeks to find out the truth. Millicent presently admitted to having an aunt in Wales, to whom Sister Ruth wrote to make enquiries. No answer came however. After a time a distracted letter from another woman arrived. "I think," it began, "that you have been writing to my sister about my daughter." And the description she gave of her was so exactly like Millicent, that there could be little doubt of the identity. Sister Ruth felt convinced that the letter was indeed from the girl's mother; and her previous suspicions of her charge were deepened by the woman's statement that it was her daughter's third conviction. She at once summoned Millicent into her presence and informed her that she had heard from her mother. The girl turned livid and her hands fell to her sides. Then she broke down utterly, and poured out the whole truth, declaring that after all God was stronger than the devil. She had been a servant, she said, at Cardiff, and had afterwards gone as assistant in a fancy wool-shop, where she was considerd very sharp and clever. She would take pieces of work to finish; sometimes she would put them back, at others she would give them away or dispose of them in some other manner. She was arrested at last for dishonesty, upon which her father, who was extremely angry with her, renounced her for ever. When she left the gaol she was sent to a Home for convicted prisoners. It seems to have been an unsuitable one; and instead of being the better for it, she was the worse. It exasperated her and brought out all the defiance of her nature. On leaving it, she determined to adopt stealing as her profession, and went from bad to worse. After a while she tried another Home. This time it was Mrs Meredith's Refuge for discharged prisoners. At her work in the laundries she made an unfortunate acquaintance. As there was not room in the Home for all the women employed there, some were lodged outside, and amongst these day-boarders was a professional thief-trainer. Soon Millicent decided to place herself under the tutelage of this woman, who taught young people from childhood onwards her wicked trade. Millicent learnt from her how to rob jewellers' shops. Being clever at music, she earned a little extra money by singing at music-halls.

Many of these professional trainers live in fine houses, and being associated with skilled burglars, make large fortunes. Millicent's trainer lived with a man whom she supported by her gains, and he it was who had the impudence to prosecute the girl for dishonesty. She and an accomplice had successfully robbed a shop in Regent's Street and had then quarrelled over the spoils. The man afraid that the end would be that Millicent would escape from her associate, carrying off the stolen treasures, had her arrested, and she was lodged in Milbank and thence transferred to Oxford Gaol. Here Felicia made acquaintance with her, and induced her to come to the Refuge, which was to prove in the end such a blessing to her.

Though Sister Ruth had succeeded in drawing the truth out of her as to her past life, she did not feel that any lasting impression had been made on her, and was anxious that home influences might be tried, if the father would consent to his daughter's return. So a letter was sent to him pleading for forgiveness and for a welcome home for Millicent. The result was only a harsh letter to Sister Ruth, saying that he would by no means allow the girl to return, after six years of the bad life she had led.

The Sister wrote again, but only to receive a second refusal. Millicent had tried to corrupt others before, and he would not risk an injury to her brothers and sisters. So she stayed on at the Refuge, under the charge of the kind friend who superintended it, visited by Miss Skene.

The winter months passed, the spring came, and with it a great spiritual change in Millicent's soul. It seemed to come quite suddenly, but surely the ground had been gradually prepared by the two good women who were caring and praying for her. She had gone with Sister Ruth to a week-day service at St Thomas's, where a clergyman was giving one of a course of sermons on Elijah and Elisha. This one was on Gehazi's theft, and the preacher's earnest words so went home to her heart, that the Sister, looking at her, thought she was going to faint. The change in her, begun at that moment, was carried on with all the fervour and sincerity of a strong nature. She poured out the confession of all her past ill-doings, in unmistakable penitence; setting her face as strongly towards good, as formerly towards evil. Great was the joy of her two friends; and Sister Ruth wisely determined to try and send her away to entirely new surroundings, where a fresh start might more easily be made. She wrote to a friend in America, who boldly determined to take her into her own service. The outfit was bought, the passage taken, and Millicent set sail from Liverpool, full of affection and gratitude to the Sister, to whom she clung as they bade good-bye.

Her new mistress, who had promised to keep the girl's past life a secret, met her and took her to her house.

Millicent turned out a first-rate servant; indeed she was so clever she would have done

anything well. The lady and her family grew
very fond of her, and the visitors who came to
the house were quite envious of their friend
for possessing such a treasure of an English
servant.

Millicent soon proved that the change in her
was more than skin-deep. It was the custom
among servants in the town where she lived, to
give card-parties to their friends on Sunday
afternoons. Millicent not only refused to attend
any, but when her turn came to give one, went
to her mistress and told her what had been going
on. Her next trouble was with her health.
She caught influenza and broke a blood-vessel in
coughing. She managed to struggle feebly
through her work; but soon after, Sister Ruth
received a telegram to inform her that Millicent
was coming to Liverpool;—could she be met?
The telegram was soon followed by a letter saying that consumption had set in, and the only
hope for her was in her native air. If she got
better, the mistress would be thankful that she
should return to her as soon as possible.
Millicent was brought back to the Refuge, where
the doctor confirmed the bad report. She was
carefully nursed, and the Sister tried to get
admittance for her to a Home at Ventnor.

As long as she stayed in the Refuge she did
all she could to influence the other girls there for
good. Her appeals to them were touching. Her

one aim was to try and make amends, as far as
might be, for the past. The clergyman who
came to the Refuge said that he never
realised the meaning of the Holy Communion so
much as at her bedside. She was very fond of
Felicia and enjoyed her visits, and could talk to
her and to Sister Ruth of all her past life.
Amongst other confidences, there was her own
love-story. A policeman in London, who had
come from her part of Wales, had tried to get at
her when she was connected with a gang of
burglars, that he might persuade her to become
an honest girl. She was pretty and clever, and
he admired her so much that if she would have
reformed he would have married her. He had
promised that when she came out of Milbank he
would take her to a respectable lodging. He
had too much cause afterwards to give up all
hope of her improvement, and they lost sight of
one another for some time.

Two years after she had last seen him she
wrote to him from America, and he answered,
telling her he was going to be married to some
one else. Millicent was miserable, and this
trouble probably helped to break down her health.
When she returned to England she wrote to him
again from the Refuge. The policeman kept
up his interest in her, and wrote a pleasant and
grateful letter to Sister Ruth, asking if there
were any hope of her recovery.

The Sister's great wish that Millicent should be allowed to return to her own home was fulfilled at last. Her mother was first allowed to come and see her at the Refuge; and a touching meeting it was, between her and her child.

After the mother's return, the father at last consented to have Millicent back again as soon as the fine weather returned. The long journey was successfully accomplished, and there Millicent stayed with her family, lingering on for a year, before her long illness ended in death.

Such a story as hers was enough to encourage Felicia to go on in hope.

She had other proofs too that her labours were not in vain. Discharged prisoners who had been melted by her kindness while in gaol and persuaded to turn over a new leaf on leaving it, would come and visit her afterwards, giving her reason to know that the change was a real one. There was one woman in particular, who had been regarded as hopeless by the prison officers. She was low and coarse in appearance and blasphemous in her speech.

Years afterwards she made a journey to Oxford, on purpose to see and thank the kind friend who had first touched her heart. Felicia at first failed to recognise her.

" She was then a woman with a pleasant

countenance, and very well dressed in dark and suitable clothing. . . . It was indeed the depraved criminal of the prison, who had never swerved from the path of rectitude on which she had entered when she left its doors."

CHAPTER XV

VARIED ACQUAINTANCES

IT is not surprising that in the course of her prison experiences, Felicia made acquaintances with some of the most peculiar beings that walk this earth.

Her knowledge of the class called Tramps was of a much less superficial kind than that of most persons, who are wont to put them roughly in the same category with the gipsies. From these, she says, they are entirely distinct. They are of no separate race, but members of the families of the ordinary dwellers in towns and villages, who are born with a natural hatred for any settled habitation and work of any kind. A general unity of taste and character runs, she tells us, between them all. They crave an unchartered freedom in every respect, whether of custom or morality. As to truth, you might as well try " to get that out of a crocodile as out of a tramp." The marriage-rite is of course in their eyes entirely superfluous. It is convenient to have a woman to tramp along with them, to help them cook, or carry, or invent the little fictions by which they draw pence from the pockets of the simple; but that is generally all that they require of their women-folk. If they quarrel they can just fight it out or part company. Sometimes they will change partners with another couple as easily as at a dance.

"'I say, old chap, I likes your 'ooman better nor mine here, let's swop. I'll throw in a bit of baccy with my wench, as yours is a bit younger.'

"'All right, I'm willing. I'm sick o' my 'ooman's tantrums, I'll try it on with yours.' And the transfer is made with the utmost ease, the ladies making no sort of objection.'[1]

Tramps are not, she asserts, dishonest as a rule, partly because of their abhorrence of a fixed residence in what they call the stone jug, in other words, prison. They have their good points—their *esprit de corps*, which makes them stand by one another if any of them get into a tight place, and their easy-going, good-humoured philosophy of life. Living from hand to mouth, they are quick-witted and often humorous.

The paper from which we have just quoted,

[1] From "The Ethics of the Tramp."—*Cornhill Magazine.* May 1898.

and a short tale which Felicia wrote in *Belgravia*, partly fictitious and partly true, give some admirable portraits of the class. The hero of the story called "The Autobiography of a Tramp,"[1] is drawn to the life. The portrait reminds us of one of Rembrandt's. She has caught the look, the language and the sentiments of her Bohemian pedestrian to perfection.

"With all his roughness he manages to attract us. There is a vein of genuine sentiment as well as humour in him. He has gone through a real romance, and he possesses a rich fund of fortitude and pluck. He will keep to the road as long as he can tramp it, without troubling about illness or old age, and as a last resort, he can always end his troubles by making 'a hole in the water like old Dad.'

"He was an adopted 'old Dad,' and not the tramp's own, but he was fond of him in his own way. 'I got on first-rate afterwards for a time,' he remarked. 'I used to show Dad's pipe and say it belonged to my dear father, who got drowned and left me a poor orphan, and I did not know how to get on, living without my father.' 'But that was not true, Dick.' 'Well, in course not,' said the tramp, raising his eyebrows in surprise, 'but we all tells lies. We couldn't get on without

[1] *Belgravia.* June, 1893.

it—not any of us.   No doubt you tells them yourself on occasions.—Wrong? I don't know what you mean.   How was I to get my living if I did not make up stories? The other fellows on the road said I was an uncommon good hand at it,' and Dick smiled with modest pride."

If Felicia had never written anything but those two papers, she would have proved she had the artist's touch.

She sometimes received some curious specimens of the epistolary art from acquaintances she had made in the prison.

Here are two of them :

"DUBLIN, 15th July '60.

"ILLUSTRIOUS MADAME, etc.—Praise for ever be to our incomprehensible Creator who seemingly appointed you to be the christionable friend of the liveing and dead.   I therefore through his infinite merits cease to despair of pardon, regarding my torrent of grief upon all Momentous occasions.   Particularly the idea of an endlys Eternity.   But the all-bountiful God etc pleaded in our behalf, so that we will not perish as our lot is in said confidence under the canopy of heaven.   And that the blessed view of Jesus etc, may be perpetually extended towards you and yours, dear Madam.   And upon all such real Christians, both dead and allive, for said meritorious acts of charity performed for love, honour and glory of God, and may he be pleased to destroy in me the spirit

of the world, and give me the strength to despise
its allurements until death. Dear Madame, I
was much pleased with my ever dear grandson's
writing, and I'm sorry to acknowledge that I
sprinkled it with an abundance of tears.

" Be so kind as to let the dearly beloved know
I'l write according to his affectionate request.
And be pleased also to remember me most
kindly to his dear afflicted grandma Walton,
etc etc I am Madam yours respectfully,

" ANNE C——."

" 16th April.

" To Miss KEANE.

"Miss——. Having resolved henceforth to abandon a life of wretchedness and
misery it is necessary, in order to carry into
effect my resolve, to solicit the aid of some
influential person.

" Now, Miss, as I have since my schooldays
had a sincere desire to be united in the Holy
bonds of Matrimony to a person who is the
choice of my Heart, and having obtained constant employ with the promise of assistance
from a few friends, I entreat you to lend your
hand in accomplishing this my great desire—
Namely, the joining together in Wedlock, me
and my intended bride. Finally should you
grant my request, You would do away with
a great deal of sin and degradation, and add
to your already numerous well-wishers. One
who is in truth, your most humble Obedient
Servant,   J. W."

"SHOULDER OF MUTTON INN,
HIGHOLT, ST THOMAS'S."

If Felicia Skene made some queer acquaintances in the prison, her visits there led to some
real friendships.   Among those formed with
the women-officers, none was more cordial than
that which subsisted between herself and Mrs
J., the Matron. Felicia knew that she would
always receive a warm welcome from her.

Writing to Mrs Thomson after one of her
pleasant visits to Bishopthorpe where she had
been pressed to stay longer, she says:

"I felt thankful that I had not been tempted,
when I went to the prison this morning, for
there was terrible need of me there.   The
Matron met me saying, 'Oh! I have such
a lot of work for you,' and she had been very
much troubled at having no one to turn to for
several difficult cases."

Not even the pleasure of her niece's company,
and the cheerful family party, and the beauty
of the Palace and its grounds—" Full of flowers
even at this early season, and the river running
under my bed-room window," can drive the
thought of her prisoners in their gloomy surroundings out of her head, as she goes over
the cases about which she is specially anxious.
The accounts received of them are eagerly
welcomed by her.

"Thank you so much," she writes to Mrs J.,
"for your nice long letter; I was so very glad
to hear all the details you gave me. I am

afraid you must have rather hard work just now, with an inexperienced assistant and so many women. I shall be so glad when I can get back to do the very little I can to help you. I think I can do something generally, at least, towards keeping the women in good humour; but, I fear, to you personally I am not of much use, excepting by my strong sympathy for all you feel in your responsible situation. I was very much pleased to hear that it is a prisoner who has played in my absence. I have written to Mr N—— and told him if he likes to continue the man as organist after I came back, he can do so by all means. I should come to the services all the same, as I like to join with you all in that, but I need not play unless I am really wanted. I hope you will see me walking in as usual on Thursday the 1st of November; the time seems very long till then."

Great was Felicia Skene's regret when Mrs J. left Oxford to take a new post at a large gaol in London. But interest in her friend's fresh surroundings and in all that concerned her, was kept up by letters. It was further enhanced by a visit she paid her at the prison at Wormwood Scrubs, where she was taken to see all that Mrs J. could show her of the place.

" I am very glad that you had not left the prison before I went there," she writes afterwards; "it was a great pleasure to me to see you again. Perhaps I shall hear of you sometimes from Major Griffiths; he is a very kind friend to me. He was here quite lately, when he gave me a beautiful little drawing he had painted for me."

She is so accustomed to consult Mrs J. over the prison cases that she must write and tell her all about them:

"We have C. D. in now, and so violent at times she seems almost out of her mind—a once respectable woman, for being drunk, and a woman with a man on the other side who want to get married. I hope to have it done outside. . . . I do miss you most dreadfully.

"I hope you are not quite forgetting me; I am half-afraid you are, as I wrote last and have never heard from you since. I get all the news about you that I can when they go to Wormwood Scrubs, and was very sorry to hear you had not been well. We go on much as usual. We have two bad cases—a man for killing his wife and a woman for killing her husband. I have seen the man twice and the woman of course often."

Amongst the prisoners with whom Mrs J. had to deal, Felicia was specially interested in one poor woman, whose affection for a little bird of which she had made a great pet in the prison, appealed to her particularly; for fond as she was of all creatures, birds had the greatest attraction of all for her.

"I was immensely interested in what you tell me of the poor convict and her little bird;

it is quite a touching story.   I wish so much
I could do anything to help her about it, for
it does seem hard that she should be parted
from it, and it may have a bad effect on her.
I would take care of it for her when she
leaves if you could bring or send it to me.
Perhaps you will let me know if it is possible
for me to help her about it in any way."

She reverts to the subject in her next letter.

13 New Inn Hall Street,
25th September 1893.

"My Dear Mrs J.,—I was most de-
lighted to receive your letter, it interested me
so much; it made me feel a great wish to be
able to go and work among those poor prisoners,
but I fear that is impossible, and I do not see
how the lady visitors can do much if they only
see any prisoner they ask for, and not alone!
How can they know who to ask for among so
many?   If these poor Arab women can talk
Greek or Italian I could speak to them.   I am
glad the poor woman's little bird is cared for,
though I would gladly have had it.   I think the
idea of the little tame bird being a comfort to
her is so pretty that I am quite inclined to put it
in a story—of course without any real names or
the least hint when it had happened or where.   I
should like to know a few more facts about it if
you could find out *how* the prisoner first came to
know the sparrow—did it fly in at the window,
or did it come to her first in the exercise-ground?
Also, I should like to know any particulars about
the woman—what her crime was which brought

her to prison, and anything you know about her history before. I should be so glad if you could tell me a little about it."

The end of the little bird was, as may be guessed, that he made his appearance in print. Felicia sent his history to a magazine, and the editor accepted it. He made a second, but an unwarranted appearance in another serial, for she writes :

"The story came out in another magazine of which I do not know the name. Some lady copied the story and published it with her own name."

The incidents related in it are quite true, and remarkable enough to be briefly recorded here :

There was a woman in a London gaol who, if we reckon up the various periods of the time she had spent in prison, had passed nearly eighteen years of her life there. She had a violent temper, which was constantly breaking out and bringing disgrace and punishment upon her. One day a small sparrow that had lost its tail, flew into her cell through the small, half-opened window near the ceiling. She fed it with some crumbs from her dinner, and determined she would keep it as a little companion. It was not surprising that she soon tamed it; the wonder was that it managed to tame her. It became the comfort of her prison-life, and the fear of being parted from it, if she had to be sent to the punishment-cell, was enough to restrain her from falling into her old fits of rage. It lived with her in her cell; it went about with her perched on her shoulder; it accompanied her to the exercising-ground, hopping after her as she marched round it. She took it to the singing-practice in the chapel, where she was a member of the choir. The only time at which she was not allowed to take it with her, was when she attended the services. She would then leave it in her cell, shutting the door carefully behind her. One day a warder, who had entered in her absence, unfortunately left it open and the bird flew out. When the woman returned, her fury knew no bounds, and she would certainly have been marched off to the dreaded cell if the officers had not felt sympathy with her in her loss.

On one of the warders going into the yard, what was her delight to see in the midst of a group of sparrows, the prisoner's pet, which she recognised at once from the fact that he was the only one that had no tail! She called him by the name his owner had given him, to which he always responded. As he refused to come at a stranger's summons, she sent for his mistress, and at the sound of her familiar voice he flew to her at once. The woman's rapture at finding him again was as great as her despair at losing him had been, and her storm of rage was lulled in a moment.

Hitherto she had met all the efforts of the

chaplain to get her to pay the slightest attention
to his words, with sullen indifference.   A new
plan struck him now—he would try and reach
her heart by means of the bird.   At his next
visit he made her read to him Our Saviour's
words about God's care even for the sparrows;
pressing the truth upon her that her heavenly
Father could care no less for her than for the
birds.   But no! the comfort was not for her, she
protested;   she had been too bad, she was a
wretched outcast.   For a long time she refused
to listen to his assurances; but slowly his words
made their way to her heart, and she began to
realise that the God who cares for each sparrow
that flies, watched and loved her, wicked as she
had been, with a like tender pity and compassion;
and her bird became to her a messenger of hope
and comfort, like the dove that went to and from
the patriarch in the deluge.

Mrs J. was by no means Felicia's only friend
among the prison officers.   To one of them, Miss
W., now holding a post as warder in Holloway
Gaol, she writes with affectionate regret at losing
her from Oxford :

" I was always so happy with you, and had
such perfect trust in you that you would always
do the best you could, both for me and for the
prisoners.   You are a great loss to me, and I
shall feel it every time I go there.   I found the

new matron very civil, and anxious, I think, to
be nice and good to me, but she feels rather lost
in our small prison, as she comes from Man-
chester, where she was one of thirty warders."

Miss Skene's prison-visiting and writings
brought her into contact with several interesting
men and women who have devoted their
attention to the same subject. The acquaintance
she made with the well-known writer on prison
subjects, Major Arthur Griffiths, was a great
pleasure to her. It began by her writing to
express her appreciation of his book, " Secrets of
the Prison-House." Her approval, he says in
his reply, gave him much gratification, and he
refers in return to one of her books. Though
writing to her as a stranger, he says:

"I know you well! I made it my business long
ago to find out who wrote the 'Scenes from a
Silent World,' as the book impressed me so greatly
when I read it. I learnt then that you were the
lady-visitor at Oxford Prison. The subject of
which you write, the 'Inequalities of Human
Justice,' is full of deep interest. As you will
have seen, I have touched upon it in my book,
pointing out how greatly sentences vary. You
would be doing a great service if you would take
up the question."

When Major Griffiths came to Oxford on one
of his visits to the gaol as Inspector, Felicia
Skene had the pleasure of meeting him and

having talks on the subjects that were of such
great interest to both.

As she was always eager to learn all she could
about other prisons, she was glad to accept an
invitation from him to visit, under his escort,
the one at Wormwood Scrubs.   Her diary
records a good day's work for an old lady of
seventy-four.

"I slept very little after two o'clock.   Prayers
at 5.30.   Up at 6.10.   Breakfast at 8.   Station.
Got in carriage alone.   Found Major Griffiths
on the platform; went in a hansom with him to
Wormwood Scrubs.   Taken by Mrs W., Matron,
and Mrs J. all over female prison.   Went
in Governor's office.   Then Major Griffiths
came again and took me through the male
prison.   Then we went to his beautiful house.
His niece entertained me till Mrs Griffiths and
her sister-in-law came.   General Russell came,
who had been invited to meet me.   They sent
the carriage back for me, and Major Griffiths
went with me to Paddington, and I got home,
thank God."

How favourable the impression was, that
Felicia Skene's character and work as a prison-
visitor made upon Major Griffiths, he records in
the following paper.   No one's testimony on the
latter point could be of greater value.

"I first became acquainted with Miss Skene
in 1894, shortly after the appearance of my
book, the 'Secrets of the Prison-House,' when

she wrote me a kindly and appreciative letter,
confessing herself the author of the 'Scenes from
a Silent World.' I had already ascertained this
fact, having been greatly struck by the articles
when they came out in *Blackwood*. I found
that 'F. Scougal' was Miss Skene, but I did not
know till later that she was the 'lady visitor' of
the Oxford Prison. I took advantage of my
next visit to Oxford to call on Miss Skene, and
from that time forth I had the honour and high
privilege of her friendship.

" I liked to meet her at the prison and tried to
so arrange it, knowing the days and hours at
which she visited, so that we might talk over the
more interesting of the inmates whose cases she
had in hand. Her influence with the unfortunate
women was great, and generally lasting. They
soon saw how deep and abounding was her
sympathy, how keenly she desired to lead them
back to the right path, gently and persuasively,
but with no sort of reproof or reproach. Her
efforts to reform were not limited to oral process.
She was indefatigable in giving active help
wherever possible. The aid that comes to the
prisoners on leaving the place of penalty is often
the most valuable in preserving them from new
lapses, and Miss Skene recognized this to the
full. Only those who have been much associated
with the poor creatures so often utterly friendless,
or worse, having to face fresh temptations from
the false friends by whom they have been led
astray, realise how much may be effected by the
helping hand that is offered on the day of release.
Miss Skene gave the best proof of her earnestness by seeking to secure the welfare of her

charges when they were once more free. She
watched over them continually, following them
if she could with good counsel and often
substantial aid wherever they went, and striving
to interest others in them.

"Miss Skene made no distinctions: her
ministrations were at the service of all, freely
and unceasingly. She did not despair of the old
offender, the almost hopeless case, persistent as
it might seem in wrong-doing, and more than
once succeeded in effecting aid. For the new
hands, the weaker vessels who had succumbed
for the first time, her kindliness, her tenderness
was infinite; and many who might have dropped
down further and further were pulled up and
saved on the brink of habitual crime by Miss
Skene. The pity was that she had not a wider
scope, a larger field of usefulness, and I can well
remember the eagerness with which she surveyed
the great prison of Wormwood Scrubs, to which
I escorted her, struck with the much larger
opportunities it would have afforded her. I
remember too how gladly she renewed her
acquaintance with the wardresses she had known
at Oxford, and whose services had been transferred to Wormwood Scrubs, and their outspoken
delight at meeting their dear Miss Skene. She
was beloved by the prison staff as much as by
those she tended; her arrival at the prison was
greeted with warm welcome, and she was on the
best terms with all, from the Governor downward. 'There is no one like Miss Skene,' was
the universal verdict; 'no one gave less trouble,
no one could have done more.'

" Her name will long be a precious memory at

Oxford Prison, and I venture to think that her self-sacrificing labours as shadowed forth in her book, and her fine generous character, have done much to stimulate and encourage others to follow in her footsteps. There is no part of modern prison management that shows more marked results than the system of visitation by ladies now generally adopted."

Adeline, Duchess of Bedford, was another acquaintance made, from a similar reason. The Duchess came to see her to ask for advice in her visits to discharged prisoners; and wrote to her afterwards, begging to be allowed to consult her sometimes about difficult cases.

Mr Tallack, Secretary of the Howard Association, she learnt to know through a correspondence in the *Times* on the subject of lady-visitors being allowed to see prisoners alone.

" One of the first letters quoted," writes Felicia to Mrs Thomson, " was from me, and the Home Office have been writing to our Governor here for the particulars of my appointment, but it is all in favour of lady-visitors, and there is an idea of appointing them to all prisons."

One of the correspondents, a visiting Justice in Norfolk, had written, strongly objecting to ladies having interviews with prisoners in the absence of any officers of the gaol. Felicia answered him, and Mr Tallack wrote on the same side, referring to her letter, and saying that her long and successful experience gave her a right to be heard, and that her services were highly appreciated by the local authorities, the prison officers, and the prisoners themselves. He came to see Felicia Skene at Oxford, and their occasional meetings were a pleasure to both.

He was the writer, after her death, of a long and interesting account of her philanthropic life and opinions, in the *Daily News*.

Another of her prison friendships was with the Rev. Father Parkinson.

" I think," he writes, " we were thrown together through our visits to the prison, and if I may say so much, we soon found that there was sufficient common ground between us to admit of our working together on it. I may say that from that time a cloud never came between us. If it did the culprit must have been myself. . . . The thought of the spotless simplicity and beauty of her character must always be a help for the improvement of one's own."

CHAPTER XVI

WRITINGS ON PRISON SUBJECTS

FELICIA SKENE entered on her task of prison-visiting with no light heart. She realised keenly how beset it is with difficulties, from the characters of those with whom the visitor has to

Q

deal. Ignorance, passion, the habitual practice
of deceit and cunning, a morbid strain in the
mind, a clouded moral-sense, evil environment,
heredity—each of these causes prepares pitfalls
for the visitor from which, humanly speaking,
only careful thought, ready tact and long
experience can deliver him. Felicia threw her
powerful mind into the perplexing subject, and
gradually worked out both in theory—and in
practice where the matter lay in her own hands—
the system she thought the best to pursue.

She gave utterance to her opinions in a series
of short essays in the *Hospital Magazine*, published from 1896 to 1899, from which we are
allowed to quote. The problems considered are
carefully thought out and expressed with much
literary skill. As she was limited to two columns,
she had to exercise a good deal of compression,
and so avoided the danger she did not always
escape in other of her writings, of too many
words. In point of style we see her at her best;
her arguments are clearly put, and the illustrations given with all her remarkable skill as a
narrator. In a series of about thirty articles, she
treats many thorny subjects, shirking no difficulties, but striving to grapple with them with
all the strength derived from long practice and
experience.

To mention some of the questions she treats,
there is an admirable set of papers on " Mistaken

Impressions of Prison Life ; " another series on
" The Ethics of Suicide," a third on the " Training
of Officials ; " a fourth on the " Treatment of
Juvenile Criminals ; " a fifth on " Criminal
Mania ; " and there are single papers on a variety
of topics such as " Short Sentences, " The Diet
of Prisoners," " Prison Reform," " Criminal Law
Reform," " Capital Punishment," " The Children
of Criminals," and other topics of a kindred
nature.

Those who only knew Miss Skene on one side
of her nature, admiring her solely as an incarnation of tender-heartedness and pity will be surprised that in many of these papers she strongly
condemns mere soft and sentimental views.   In
her advice to lady visitors she reminds them that
while giving hearty sympathy and efficient aid
to prisoners on their discharge, they must beware
of glossing over the criminality of the deed for
which the convicted have been undergoing
punishment.   She deals with the great difficulty
of getting the truth out of prisoners.   In insisting on the necessity of seeing each one alone,
either in her cell, or some room that may be
assigned to the visitor, she recommends the latter,
as a new sphere, as it were, invites freedom of
intercourse.   She thinks it advisable that if the
prison is a small one there should be only one
lady visitor, so that the same treatment of cases
may be consistently carried on.   Otherwise a new

visitor leads to new plans ; and confusion and
failure are the result.   In a large prison, where
many visitors are needed, each should have her
own group of prisoners.

In giving religious teaching, she was as clear
in her instructions how *not* to do it, as in her
advice how best it may be done.   She disapproves of the suggestion made by the Prison
Commissioner that ladies should give lectures
to select classes of prisoners.   " There is," she
says, "a certain *esprit de corps* among these
lawless women, who have been accustomed to
mock at religious topics, and to hold unconsciously atheistical beliefs ; and when they are
assembled together to listen to what they term
the 'lady's preachment,' they like to show
each other their absolute indifference to it,
and to jeer and scoff at all that is said by
means of signs and whispers."   No ! the only
plan is to have *tête-à-tête* interviews, and win
confidence, through interest in the prisoner's
personal history.   The fact that the lady comes
from the world outside and is an unpaid worker
is all in her favour.   Yet it is satisfactory to
find her testifying to the really good results
of the efforts made by the paid officials—
the governor, the chaplain, the matron and
warders,—to raise the moral and spiritual condition of the criminals, many of whom have,
to her own knowledge, left the gaol changed

characters, as they have proved in their after lives.

In a paper on " Prison-Training and Administration," she gives an interesting account of the teaching and probation to be gone through by the nurses. In another on " Reform in the Criminal Law," she expresses her entire approval of permission being given to prisoners to enter the witness-box and give evidence in their own defence; illustrating the advantage of it by cases which had come to her own knowledge.

She defends the prison system of diet, which she considers quite sufficiently good for men and women undergoing punishment. " Why," she asks, " should it be superior to what would be supplied in the workhouse, or in an honest working-man's cottage?" The great majority of prisoners generally leave gaol, she maintains, more robust than when they entered it. As to another point of accusation, the painful necessity of firing on escaped criminals, we must not forget that their efforts for freedom were too often begun by murdering their warders, or inflicting life-long injuries on them.

Short sentences she disapproves of, on the double ground that they afford neither protection to society, nor time for improvement for the prisoner, who is let loose after a short detention to carry on his old bad practices.

"I am glad Ruth C—— has got a long sentence," she writes to the matron, "as it will give us more time to influence her."

In her article on "Elastic Theories," she has a good deal to say about the danger of extending the plea of unsoundness of mind too freely; especially in the case of persons of good position, whose acts of dishonesty have often been politely and conveniently exonerated by the use of the term kleptomania. She has several papers on the subject of criminal mania, and on the great responsibility, often of life or death, laid on the medical profession in such instances. The subject is too large and too painful to enter upon fully here, and there are several others to which the same remark applies. Miss Skene's articles upon them are strongly and impressively written. In treating of what she says she must call "the present rage for self-destruction," she does not believe that, generally speaking, those who commit suicide are the least insane. As to the uneducated, it is impossible to persuade them that self-murder is a crime at all, as they maintain that their lives are their own, to do what they please with. The root of the evil is unbelief in a future state. "We come into the world," as a bad woman once said to her, "as the beasts do . . . and when we go out of it again, there is an end of us! There is nobody

but myself who has anything to do with settling
for me, living or dying.   Out we go, by the water,
the poison or the razor.   That's over in a moment
and all's done.   That's what I shall do, and that
is what every one of my friends and lovers will
do, and good-bye to everything!"   Misery,
revenge, cowardice, or even mortified vanity, are
quite sufficient incentives to the fatal deed.

She has a great deal to say on the subject
of "Juvenile Criminals."   She holds that
reformatories managed by masters only, are
not a success, and that women would be far
more likely to influence the characters of boys
for good.   She refers to the French system,
in which reformatories are superintended entirely by Sisters, who receive boys up to twelve
years of age at one of their three farm-schools.
At thirteen they are passed on to the second;
at sixteen to the third, where they remain
till they are about twenty years of age.   The
system seems quite successful in the hands
of the cheerful, animated French nuns; but
she thinks that our English Sisters are, as a
rule, too rigid in their methods to be suitable
mistresses for boys; but there are plenty of
other capable and well-trained women in our
own country, who would be likely to be successful.   She thinks, too, that it would be better
not to limit the age, after which boys can no
longer be received, to twelve years.

For the children of criminals she recommends separate schools, to which they can be sent on the conviction of their parents, where they can be sheltered and educated. She builds a castle-in-the-air of a large institution, the centre of which should receive infants who would thus be delivered from the danger of baby-farms, the horrors of which had been brought painfully before her own eyes; and there should be a wing for elder boys and another for girls. If they were sent to ordinary Homes and Orphan-ages, their unhappy parentage would be too likely to be discovered sooner or later by their companions, who would at once ostracise them. She quotes the case of a little girl, for whom a Home was found after much difficulty, and where she was only admitted on promising secrecy as to the terrible fact that her father had been executed. In about a week the child told a small friend she had made what her history had been, and the mistress at once felt it necessary to send the little girl away.

In her series of "Mistaken Impressions of Prison Life," she combats what she considers to be wrong ideas among the public, about the ordinary gaol-system. Two opposite charges had been made—that the solitary system shatters the nerves of prisoners and in the greater number of cases causes insanity; and that the association of greater and lesser criminals together leads to moral contamination.

To the first charge she answers, that the solitude is not of the strict kind generally imagined, since the prisoners can and do communicate with the authorities set over them. They see and can speak to the prison officers, and the chaplain can visit them in their cells and talk with them as much as he pleases. In many gaols there are appointed visitors from outside who are allowed to see them, under certain regulations.

To the second charge she replies, that in our country intercourse among the prisoners is carefully guarded against, and with much success in spite of their great ingenuity in occasionally conveying information to one another by various clever dodges. Except in chapel or at exercise, or when they are working together, each prisoner is confined to his own cell. When at work they are separated by a certain space and carefully watched to prevent communication with one another; and in their walks round the exercising-yard, the distance between one prisoner and another is too great to allow any conversation to be carried on.

On the question whether previous convictions should be taken into account on a trial for a fresh offence, she thinks they certainly ought. The first bitter taste of imprisonment may be enough to check a man at the beginning of an evil course, especially if he comes under good influences when in gaol; while an habitual criminal is a deadly peril to society, which ought to be protected by a longer sentence, such as would be given if his former crimes were taken into consideration.

As to hard labour, however idle prisoners may be when they are at liberty, they greatly prefer work to inaction when in gaol, and often feel aggrieved if deprived of it for the good of their health. A good deal of the labour carried on in the prison is far from disagreeable. The kind that she agrees with the prisoners in thinking thoroughly objectionable, is the unproductive toil of crank and treadwheel, a wearisome " grinding of the wind."

She is much in favour of a Government system of emigration, both for the relief of society in our own country, and for the advantage of the criminals themselves when they leave prison. She would send them to unreclaimed tracts of land in the Colonies, where they would be compelled to work for their own support, and be out of the way of the temptations to crime which they meet with in England.

The last paper of this series is on the subject about which she felt most strongly of all— Capital Punishment. She considered that it

was sanctioned by no Christian law and justified
by no human consideration; that it was no
deterrent to crime, since death was very little
dreaded, indeed often preferred to penal
servitude, as the frequency of suicide gave
proof; that it was brutalising in its effect on
the public, who gloated over all details of the
last painful scene; that mistakes as to guilt
are not unknown among judges and jurymen;
and that the same punishment in this life is thus
meted out to all alike though the guilt of their
crimes may be of varying degree; "while we
fling all alike out of our sight and knowledge
to a wholly unknown destiny, of which we
neither know the issue or the extent."

On this last great question Felicia did not
find many to agree with her. Most of her
friends thought that there was an answer to be
found to each of these arguments. But
occasionally she made a convert. One reviewer
of her "Scenes from a Silent World," in which
she repeats her views on this question, remarks
that she has made use of the strongest pleas he
has ever heard on the subject. A distinguished
English Dean, while praising the book as a
happy combination of pathos and humour, which
he prettily compares with "Minna and Brenda,
or a kingfisher on gloomy streams, or bright
flowers amid dark foliage," says, that he must
confess that her arguments against the penalty

of death have completely changed his views on the subject.

There are other prison topics with which Felicia Skene deals, but the reader will probably not care to hear more. From many of her opinions no doubt, those who from knowledge of the subject have a right to speak may differ. There might be plenty to say on the other side, but at least she states her own case clearly and forcibly, and can give reasons drawn from her experience in support of her views.

Though Felicia was never a platform orator, she wrote a prison paper on one occasion for a meeting on behalf of Friendless Girls at Salisbury. She did not read it herself, but Mrs Wordsworth undertook to do so for her, and she had the gratification afterwards of hearing that the Bishop pronounced it "a beautiful paper."

The same commendation was deserved of an article on "Prison Visiting," which came out in *Fraser's Magazine*.[1]

Every chance of learning about the management of prisons and prisoners abroad she eagerly embraced. When she visited Paris in 1871, she went to see *La Roquette*, where Archbishop Darboy, with five other good and notable men who had been seized as hostages by the Communists, were imprisoned, roughly treated, and

[1] December, 1880.

finally shot.   She described the particulars of
their   captivity   and   death   in   an   article
in *Macmillan's Magazine*, " La Roquette, 24th
May 1871," written in her usual graphic style.
A few pieces of straw from the coarse palliasse
on which the Archbishop slept, and which she
was allowed to carry away, were always prized
by her as relics of a saintly man.

The system of prison-visiting carried on in
Greece by " The Association in Christ," as the
Society is called, is in her eyes an ideal one.
Writing about it in an article in *Blackwood's
Magazine*, published in July 1892, she thus
describes the system :

" The noble Queen Olga, whose care for the
lowest and most degraded of her subjects is
the highest of her titles to honour, is the head
of this Association, and she is encouraged and
supported by the King in all her efforts.   She
visits the prisoners herself; she sends her theo-
logian, who had taught her own children, to
give religious instruction to the prisoners, in
addition to what they receive from the chaplains
at   the   gaol;   she   appoints   the   Managing
Committee of the Society; but above all, she
touches and influences the criminals for good
by her noble personal character, shown in her
intercourse with them.   No wonder they regard
her as an 'angel of goodness,' and that she is
almost worshipped in her adopted country."

A touching instance of the prisoners' love

for her was shown on the death of her
daughter, the Grand Duchess Paul of Russia,
when a Requiem Service was held in the chapel
of one of the prisons. All of the prisoners
attended it, and hardened as many of them
were, they gave unmistakable evidence of the
genuine sympathy they felt with their Queen
in her bereavement.

The members of the Association form no
Community, but live an ordinary family and
social life in their own homes. Four days of
the week they devote to their prison duties.
All proceedings of the Society are reported
each year to the Minister of the Interior.
Felicia's account of ἐν Χριστῷ Ἀδελφότητος is well
worth reading. The motto of the Association is
the appropriate one, " In prison, and ye came
unto Me."

Being very anxious to learn all she could
of the systems carried out in foreign gaols,
she was quite disappointed with a friend who
had visited South Africa without bringing her
any fresh information. " Did you not go and
see the prisons ? " she asked him reproachfully.

The stories she wrote about prisoners are
admirably told. The best are contained in
her " Scenes from a Silent World," of which
we shall speak in a later chapter. But from
time to time she published short tales in
magazines, drawn from her own knowledge of

those she visited in Oxford Gaol. There is one pathetic story called "A Released Prisoner,"[1] which many would find it difficult to read with dry eyes.

Her friend, Dean Ramsay, alludes to it in the following letter:

"23 AINSLIE PLACE,

"EDINBURGH, *9th January,* '68.

"MY DEAR FELICIA,—You will hardly be surprised at this accost from *so very old* a friend as I am. I thought from the initials that the article on the prisoner in the last No. of *Good Words* was yours, and I ascertained the fact from your brother. Besides the motive of a little communication with an old friend I wished to tell you how much I liked the article, and how much I was pleased with the manner in which you represent the prisoner not being directly appealed to till after his confidence had been won. I learn that there is more of truth than of fiction in the narrative, and I can easily believe it—I think the manner and time of adjusting such appeals to sinful characters is a great point, and I have perhaps more indirectly come upon the question in an article on 'District Visiting' in the *Sunday Magazine.* More than half the good of visiting is lost by want of tact and management.—I am, believe me, your affectionate and sincere E. B. RAMSAY.

"I hold out and preach and do a little, but time 'has told its tale.'"

[1] *Good Words.* December, 1867.

CHAPTER XVII

ANOTHER CHAPTER OF FAMILY HISTORY

THOSE who knew Felicia Skene only as a worker among the poor and needy, the prisoner and the outcast, might have imagined that it would be impossible that family claims should have their due share in her life; not that they would think that she was of the famous Mrs Jellaby type, however at one time she might have reproached herself for insufficient regard to family ties; but time and strength being limited quantities, they would feel it impossible that one person should do everything. But there are cases in which a large heart and wide sympathies seem to create time and strength, and so it was with her. And the more there were to love and help, the more her power of loving and helping grew. There was always oil enough in her cruse to fill every vessel that was brought to her; or, to change the figure, if a fresh person knocked at her hospitable heart and asked to be taken in, she never pleaded that it was full already, but just added another guest-chamber and received the new friend.

When the parents she loved so deeply were taken from her, and the older generation gradually passed away, she clung the more closely to her contemporaries in the family,—her brothers and sisters, and to their children and children's children; for the Skene family, even her own branch of it, spread out into a wide circle, and she took an interest in each and all. When her kinsman, Mr William Skene of Pitlour, came to spend some months of every year at Oxford, she was glad to welcome him and his family, and her diaries contain many references to the pleasant intercourse between them. If the nephews and nieces wished to come to Oxford, her house was open to receive them; if the children were ill she wanted to take them in and nurse them; if any one required change, advice or help, there was always a kind relation in a little house in St Michael's Street, ready to bestow them. And she was such excellent company that they were sure of a good laugh as well as a good talk with "Aunt Fifie." Many of the family were living abroad in Greece and in Sweden; but if ever they came to England, they knew where they would find a welcome. When Felicia's nephew by marriage, the husband of one of Madame de Rangabé's daughters, visited this country, he was sure the aunt at Oxford would like to see him in his military uniform, which he took to her house and donned for her admiration. The literary talents of M. Oscar von Heidenstam were a pride and pleasure to her, and she exhorted her friends to read his interesting life of " Louise Ulrique, Reine de Suède."

The De Rangabé family were endeared to her from the special love she felt for her sister Caroline. The pretty, bright girl whom we made acquaintance with at the beginning of this Memoir, full of fun and mischief, admired wherever she went, needed in her later years all the strength to be gained from " the merry heart that goes all the way ; " and no doubt that, as well as her faith and courage, helped to sustain her in her many sorrows. Her marriage had been a happy one, and her life at the different European capitals to which her husband's diplomatic duties took him, varied and interesting. She was proud of her distinguished husband, of her sons, of whom she had six, and of her four handsome daughters. The care of them all, their training and education, and the starting of the sons in their professional careers, all devolved upon her, as her husband's public duties engrossed his time and attention. But " the heart of her husband could safely trust in her," appreciating as he did her excellent judgment and great ability.

In Felicia Skene's sketch of her sister's life called " A Noble Life," which was published in the *Argosy*,[1] she gives an account of the heavy trials that fell on Madame de Rangabé, towards the close of her life.

[1] January, 1898.

The charge of such a large family would have been an arduous one in any case, and was made the more difficult from political jealousies and inadequate means. In the impoverished state of the country, her husband's property in land was much diminished in value, while his salary was not always paid; and knowing how great were the financial difficulties of Greece at that time, he refrained from pressing the matter on the Government.

Caroline de Rangabé took up the burden of life and bore it nobly for herself and her children. She never let her anxieties cloud her children's spirits, and her old fun was only softened into a gentle humour and harmless irony that made her company as delightful as ever. She did not mind what sacrifice of her own comfort she made, if only she could give every educational and social advantage to her sons and daughters.

With the breaking out of the Franco-German war, the real tragedy of her life began.

Monsieur de Rangabé had gone on an important diplomatic mission to Constantinople, leaving his wife and her younger children in the Greek Embassy at Paris. Two of her elder sons were with the Prussian army, which they had joined in order to get the best military training to be had, before entering the Greek army. They certainly did honour to their training, for

both of them received decorations in the field for
distinguished service.

Just before the siege of Paris, they were with
their regiments near Metz but on different sides
of it, and neither knew where the other was.
To the relief of their mother's anxiety, they
managed occasionally to send pencil notes to her
in Paris.

A painful situation for Madame de Rangabé
soon presented itself when a third son, who was
with her in the Embassy, and old enough to be
a support to his mother, was told by the
authorities that on the Prussian army besieging
Paris he would be ordered to serve in its defence.
The thought of her sons being brought face
to face in opposing forces was too terrible to
contemplate.

"I have heard," writes Felicia to Mrs Thomson,
"from poor Carry again. Aristide managed to
send her a most reserved, careful letter which told
her that he was alive on the 11th, but as he
is now in Prince Frederic Charles' army, he has
been in all these last battles since he wrote.
He had been suffering terrible hardships like all
the rest, but almost the worst part of the letter
is that she feels her own position in Paris to be
very critical. She says if the Prussians really
reach the walls of Paris, the populace will be so
exasperated that she thinks there will be special
danger for her and her house, because every
person in the street where she lives knows her

Prussian connections, also, she says, if they are besieged she will find it difficult to get food for so large a party. If, therefore, the Prussians seem to be drawing near (as the papers to-day show that they are), she will at once send the children to me, and I fully expect them next week, but it is said here that for her own safety she ought to come out of Paris, and I am sure she will not, as she knows now, that if safe, both Aristide and Emil are marching towards it. I feel very anxious about her altogether."

No wonder Felicia was full of anxiety. Though the De Rangabés did succeed in effecting their escape before the besieging army reached Paris, it was a very near thing indeed, for they only made their exit from the capital within a few hours of the closing of the gates. How one difficulty was removed, through Felicia's energetic action, so that a man suddenly appeared in Madame de Rangabé's salon and placed £100 on the table, saying, "on vous envoie cela de l'Angleterre," before he as rapidly disappeared, shall be described in her next letter.

" You will be surprised to hear that Carry and her six children are at this moment on their way here from Dover, and will be in this house in an hour or two.

" All her friends, myself among the number, urged her to leave Paris, which in every way was becoming wretched and dangerous for her with two sons in the enemy's ranks. I had a letter from her on Monday to say that she had decided to come away, as for one thing she could hardly get provisions for the children, or pay the tremendous prices asked; and much as she would have liked to remain, at least until she knew the fate of poor Aristide, she felt that if the siege commenced she would be in a dreadful position, shut up perhaps for months without money or almost food; but she wrote that in spite of the emergency she could not come away for the want of ready money. Her monthly allowance not being due, I at once telegraphed her a credit for £100, and the next day William sent her more. She got mine, and at once arranged to come, but it was some days before she could get out of Paris from the block on the railways. Last night, however, I had a telegram from Dover to say she was there for the night, and was to come on this morning, and I am writing this before she comes, as I shall have no time after. She has been suffering so much, and has still perhaps such a trial in the loss of Aristide before her, should it prove he has fallen, that it will be a real pleasure to try and make her comfortable, but you may fancy it is rather a business for me. I am going to have Carry, Eugene, Otho, Helena, and Chariclea in the house, the two boys having beds, but not meals out, and the Aclands take Zoë and Lilly. I have taken another servant (not sleeping in the house) to help my old woman, who is very willing but very muddle-headed, so that I have been acting housemaid myself in preparing for them, and shall, I think, do a great deal of the work myself all the time. I am dreadfully perplexed how they are all to sit round my dining-room table, which only holds *two* comfortably; but if they get the dinner after their experiences in Paris, poor things, I do not think they will care for the manner thereof."

But after all, the haven of refuge on reaching England was not to be at Oxford, "where the hoards were little, though the heart was great," for the Archbishop of York telegraphed to Madame de Rangabé, saying that he would receive the whole party at Bishopthorpe.

After the storm and stress of that painful time at Paris, Bishopthorpe proved a Palace of delight to all, to the children especially, who were rejoiced to make acquaintance with the new English cousins.

Writing afterwards about their visit to Mrs Thomson, Felicia says:

"Dearest Zoë,—I do not know how I am ever to be grateful enough to you and the Archbishop for all your wonderful kindnesses to Carry and her children. I am sure it was more than almost any one else in the world would have done, to have such a large party for six whole weeks; but it was a most unspeakable benefit to her just at this juncture, and I am sure you may feel you have done your duty by the war, and your relations too, most abundantly by such great kindness to her. She feels it, I know, most deeply, and every one belonging to her must be most grateful. She has so enjoyed herself with you.

"I do trust dear Ethel is better; she has excited quite a romantic attachment on the part of all the De Rangabés, especially Lilly and Otho. At a game in which they all had to wish for the thing they most desired, it was always that they might see Ethel and 'the others' again, but they will none of them ever forget all the kindness they met with at Bishopthorpe. How they did enjoy their box of Xmas presents from your children! I happened to be there when it arrived, and saw all their delight for days after."

When the De Rangabés left Bishopthorpe they went to Oxford; and though not under the same roof, the devoted sisters had plenty of opportunity of meeting.

"I give all my spare time to Carry," writes Felicia. "She has just moved from the house she had in Holywell Street to a villa in St Giles, called St Margaret's. She has it only by the week, and would not, I think, certainly be able to get it longer than to Lady-Day, but now that Paris has fallen she is looking forward to leaving England very soon. She is terribly anxious about Emil, not having heard a word about him since before the battle of Le Mans, in which he probably was. I think the moment it is possible for her to go where she could have a chance of seeing him and Aristide, she would start at once, probably going straight to Berlin. But dearest Zöe, my chief object in writing now is to beg you so much if you come to London in February to come down and see me, as I

From a Photo by   Most Rev. Dr. Thomson, Archbishop of York

can offer you the inducement of seeing Carry too for the last time before she crosses the Channel."

As soon as peace was proclaimed, and M. de Rengabé once more established at the Embassy, he sent for his family; and there, not very long after their return, Felicia went to pay them a visit. It was well for them that they had had a time of rest and quiet in England, to give them strength for a new calamity that was awaiting them. The younger of the two soldier sons, Emil, alluded to in the preceding letter, a fine, brave young fellow, was found one morning lying unconscious by the tent of his General, where he had been on guard. It was soon discovered that he had broken a blood-vessel on the lungs, and he was sent home as soon as possible to the Embassy. Here his mother nursed him devotedly till he had recovered sufficiently to be able to travel to Egypt, where it was hoped the climate would restore him. And he did improve at first, but he could not bear the separation from his mother. A sort of hunger for her seized him, and he wrote word that he hoped to be with her in a fortnight. Before that time had passed, he had died in a hospital at Alexandria.

Caroline's grief was profound. Emil had been the delight of her heart, and from that time her health began to give way. A fatal disease set

in, and for three years she struggled on in pain
and weakness, trying to keep up for the sake of
her family. No human sympathy could be all-
sufficient in such sorrows, but the conscious-
ness of her favourite sister's fellow-suffering
with her was something for Madame de
Rangabé to fall back upon.

"She holds me to my promise to come at any
moment she can have me,"

writes Felicia, ready to obey the summons whenever it came.

Another sorrow, and then another, and yet
another followed. Aristide, the elder son, fell
hopelessly ill, his health having been shattered
during the campaign; and the mother braced
herself to forget her own sufferings while nursing him.

While thus engaged, she received a telegram
saying that a third son had broken down from
over-work and was dangerously ill; and a bitter
grief it was to her that she was unable to go
and nurse him. As her husband was engaged
in his political duties, she could only send her
eldest daughter in her place. The poor boy
was being tended by German deaconesses, who,
strict in their rules, at first refused admittance
to his sister. But they could not resist her
pleadings, or send her alone to a hotel, and
at last yielded to her entreaties to be allowed

to come and attend on her brother. Happily he recovered, and they returned ere long to bring a little cheer into their mother's sad life. Her sufferings were increasing, and no hero on the battlefield showed more courage in bearing them than she did. She valiantly carried on her family and household duties, refusing opiates lest they should cloud her mind and make her less capable of fulfilling her task.

On the chance of a cure in which she did not herself believe, she consented at last to her husband's wish that she should go to Geneva to see a doctor, who was reported to be successful in treating the disease from which she suffered.

She set out on the long trying journey from Berlin with one of her daughters. When she reached her destination, and was being carried up the stairs of the hotel, she remarked that she did not believe she would leave it alive.

Her words proved true. But before the end came two more bereavements fell on her. Her young married daughter died in her first confinement, and then the news followed of Aristide's death.

Three weeks after the intelligence reached her, her own brave suffering life came to an end; and the words sent her as a last message from Felicia's old friend M. de Bouville, had their fulfilment: " *Dites-lui, ma chère, que le temps du repos est arrivé.*"

Felicia had longed to go to her, and had begged to be allowed to do so. But Caroline, in her unselfishness, wished to spare her and would not consent. It was a comfort to the bereaved sister to know that in her last night the dying woman's mind went back to the old home days and that she was continually calling for her Felicia, by the old familiar pet name. Writing some time afterwards to a friend in similar sorrow, Felicia Skene expresses something of what Madame de Rangabé's loss was to her:

"The time is short; we shall so soon have finished our little course, and gone to know what the loving mercy of our Saviour really is. I think we shall be so amazed when we come to know it in its fulness. Yesterday I had a little drawing sent me of the grave at Geneva of my dearest sister, Caroline de Rangabé, and a sprig from the pine-tree which shadows it. When I lost her, I seemed to lose half of myself; she had been my special friend as well as sister all my life long."

She had indeed loved this sister with a passionate devotion like that she had given to her mother. Only to one member of her family, her niece, Mrs Thomson, could she say afterwards as she often did, "*you* have filled up the place in my heart."

It was natural that the two nieces, who from

early childhood had been brought up in Felicia's own home, Mrs Thomson and Mrs Bruce and their children, should be in the innermost circle of her affections, especially the one of whom in her married life she was able to see the most—the elder of the two sisters. It would be difficult to exaggerate the strength of the tie that bound aunt and niece together. "When I lost my own mother," said Mrs Thomson, "she was set on trying to be a mother to me herself, and she succeeded."

Mrs Thomson's visits to her at Oxford and her own to Bishopthorpe, were times of refreshment to both. Except on these occasions, long letters were passing to and fro between them twice a week or even oftener, so that they could still enter into each other's daily lives, as in the old days in Beaumont Street and Frewen Hall. There seemed to be a sort of electric current of sympathy between them, so that anything affecting Mrs Thomson was flashed, as it were, along the wire to Felicia.

"Is it not a curious proof of how my love for you gives me an instinct of anything affecting you," she writes, "that for several days past, before I got your kind letter yesterday, I had been thinking of you so especially, and had such a longing for you and such a feeling as if you might be wanting me?

"Remember you promised (I think I made you *swear*) that you would send for me at any

moment if you ever felt I could be the least bit
of good. I would go to you at an instant's
notice any time, if you could ever wish for me
for anything.

"I would give all other obligations to the
winds whenever you sent for me, wherever it
might be, and rush away to you at an instant's
notice."

And with Felicia Skene, words never went
beyond feelings and acts.

Her visits to Bishopthorpe gave scope not
only to her family affections, but to the social
side of her nature, which thoroughly enjoyed the
change of mental atmosphere that the company
of other pleasant guests gave.

One of them, Lady Rose Weigall, writes to
Mrs Thomson of a pleasant meeting she had
with Felicia at the Archbishop's :

"You ask me for my impressions of your dear
aunt. They are very, very vivid, but I only
wish there were more of them.

"I met her at Bishopthorpe in the old days,
and I remember being struck with the extraordinary grace and charm there was about this
elderly lady, who had still all the vivacity of a
young person in thought and expression, combined with the dignity of her age. Her face had
still the beauty of extreme refinement, and she
gave the impression of a thorough *grande dame*.
Her conversation was brilliant and brimming
over with good-humoured fun, and I recollect,

during a drive with them, thinking that of all
the clever people one had met at Bishopthorpe, I
had never seen any one who brought out more
the Archbishop's own brilliant conversational
powers, and the delight it was to listen to two
such talkers !

"In latter years I saw her several times in her
delightful little house at Oxford; the pretty
drawing-room, with her books and pictures, and
her parrot, and herself in her simple grace, was
something to be remembered for life when one
had once seen it. But it is difficult to make any
one who has not seen it, realise its charm.

"There was such a sense of peace about it all,
and yet one felt at the same time that one was
in a centre of intellectual activity. Though her
good works, in Prison and Refuge, were enough
to fill up entirely the time of any ordinary
mortal, she found time not only for much literary
work, but also for keeping up her interest in all
around her, and in all the questions of the day.
Though her religious views were so pronounced
and definite, and the practice of her religion so
earnest and constant, she seemed always tolerant
of those who differed; and no doubt one secret
of her success in dealing with cases of sin and
sorrow lay in her large-heartedness. Her varied
experiences and her knowledge of the world,
instead of making her either cynical or frivolous
(as is sometimes the case) seemed to have added
to her intense religious earnestness a breadth of
sympathy, a comprehension of the feelings of
others, and a charity all too rare amongst very
earnest women. Then she had what is called the
'saving grace of humour' to a wonderful degree.

Some of her witty sayings linger in one's mind, with the very tone of her voice and twinkle of her eye; to repeat them to those who have not heard them with these accompaniments, would be to deprive them of half their charm; but to those who did hear them, they, and indeed every recollection connected with her, must be a precious and inspiring memory to the end of their days."

It was always difficult to get Felicia Skene to come to London; still it was accomplished occasionally, and a certain visit she paid to the Archbishop and Mrs Thomson, at a house they had taken in Queen's Gate, gave her a store of pleasures to look back upon. Plays and operas, picture-galleries and museums, were fitted into the time with great ingenuity. She gratified her love of animals by a visit to the Zoological Gardens. She re-kindled her enthusiasm for music by hearing Patti sing in *Dinorah*, and returned to Oxford with a fresh stock of artistic pleasures in her memory, on which to draw.

The Archbishop proved an excellent referee for information on various topics, and   letter to her niece, referring to such reques   playfully observes :

" I am afraid you will think me very troublesome, but if people will have distinguished individuals for their husbands, they must expect this sort of thing, and also they are sure to be bored if they have literary aunts."

When the Archbishop's health gave way, she takes the opportunity of writing him an affectionate letter :

" It is no exaggeration to say that illness falling upon you is one of the heaviest misfortunes that could come to me. You must not wonder if your untiring and most generous kindness to me in every possible way for so many years, has made you more dear to me than I could ever express outwardly, and I hope you will not think me intrusive in having written just these few inadequate words out of the great depth of all I have thought and felt."

After his last illness closed in death, she dwells with a sad pleasure on the thought of " his great kindness to her the previous summer, when he had taken her out alone with himself so many times, and given her her watch and chain."

What her sympathy was to her niece in her bereavement, may be better imagined than described. The letters in which it is expressed are too private and sacred to be quoted here.

S

CHAPTER XVIII

FRIENDSHIPS

WHEN we take into account the wealth of sympathy which Felicia Skene was endowed with, almost more than she knew how to regulate sometimes, it was a simple necessity of her nature that she should have nearly as many friends and followers as St Ursula, surrounded by her eleven thousand maidens; only in Felicia's case the attendants were of all ages and both sexes.

Of the subjects of most biographies it is generally said that they had a special love for children. It will therefore make a pleasing variety to remark that she had no out-of-the-way fondness for children in general, though she had her particular loves and friendships for certain of them, either for their own or for their parents' sakes, and that they were attracted to her in return.

The following round-robin addressed to one of her servants, shows how fully she was appreciated by one family of little folk.

"DEAR EMMA—

"We intreat you to use your influence with Miss Skene and out of real kindness to us,

obliging her to come to tea with us on Christmas
Eve at 5.30 o'clock. You can do so by not
setting her dinner, and when she asks for it,
telling her that there is some tea waiting for her
here, and she can have some meat with it if she
likes. And please send all the people that wish
her here.

" Yours truly,
Alice S.
Mary P. S.
Lœta S.
Walter.
Ralph."

After this follows a list of servants' signa-
tures.

" *P.S.*—You see every one in the house wishes
her to come, surely she cannot refuse so many."

No! she certainly could not. But the light
fare provided did not prove quite as satisfying to
her appetite as the compliment of the invitation
was to her feelings, for she writes:

" I ended by not getting any dinner, as the
little S.'s insisted on my going to look at their
Christmas-tree, which was just at my dinner-hour,
and I did not find their tea a good substitute."

If Felicia Skene had been condemned to live
the life of a hermit, or if, like poor Marie
Bashkirtseff, her affections had been driven in-
wards, her unemployed or misdirected sympathies
would have overwhelmed her. Perhaps in the

former case she would have adopted the plan of
Sterne, who said that if he were in the desert he
would love some cypress.

One of the most noteworthy of her friendships,
colouring the greater part of her life at Oxford
and adding largely to its happiness, was that
formed with the Rev. Algernon Simeon, for
many years Warden of St Edward's School.   It
was carried on uninterruptedly for about thirty
years, and all that it became to both of them it
is difficult adequately to describe.

Mr Simeon well remembers the first time he
saw her when he was an undergraduate.   He was
sitting in his room at Christ Church when he saw a
tall, striking-looking lady walking across the *quad.*
"Who is that?" he asked of the friend who was
with him.   "Don't you know who that is?   It
is the wonderful Miss Skene," was the answer.
And when soon after he made acquaintance with
her, he was not disposed to dispute the description.

Neither difference of age, or of opinion on any
subject, or change of place or circumstance, could
ever diminish their friendship.   It grew and
strengthened with every year of their lives.   As
Mr Simeon's lot was cast at Oxford, or close to it,
for many years, as undergraduate, as Curate of St
Thomas', and then as Warden of St Edward's, they
had abundant opportunities of intercourse which
they made the most of, for they met for walks

and talks nearly every day. When in the course
of time Mr Simeon married, as Felicia earnestly
wished him, as she wished everybody except herself to do, his marriage made not the slightest
difference in their intimacy. If she had ever felt
a natural fear that their relations could never be
quite the same after he had formed the most
sacred of all ties, she refused to give what she
regarded as a selfish misgiving, a moment's
harbour in her heart. And happily there was
not the slightest need. The old intimacy with
him expanded into a complete friendship *à trois;*
and Mrs Simeon soon enjoyed an equal share
with her husband of Felicia's affection; while
she cared for their children almost as if they were
her own. She was godmother to two of them,
but "Godmother" was the name by which they all
addressed her, and a fairy one she was to them.
If their parents were away she would walk over
to Summertown every day, to see that they were
well and happy.

In her usual whole-hearted way, she identified
herself with the life of the school, and the masters
might have truthfully remarked with the
Governor of the gaol, "she was quite one of us."

She gave the Warden not only her sympathy
but her practical assistance. In his absence in
the holidays she would interview parents, look
over his correspondence and answer his letters
for him. If any of the boys were ill she would

think nothing of sitting up all night with them; and was ever ready to amuse and cheer them with her vigorous presence and lively talk.

Many people find it difficult to talk to school-boys, but her natural tact—that quality which has been so well defined as "a refined sympathy" —stood her in good stead here as elsewhere. One of her great-nephews, who was at St Edward's, writes gratefully of her goodness to him :

"I shall never forget all the kind things she did for me in my school-days. We, as boys, used to go in to Oxford to see her very often, and then she would walk from Oxford back to school with us. Above everything she impressed upon us the need of truthfulness. She never failed to interest us the whole time, and looking back now I can only marvel at her wondrous patience with us for hours together."

When she had to break the sad news to her great-nephews of their mother's death, the same writer records with tender recollection how she afterwards left them alone "that they might talk to God about it."

It deeply impressed him.

It was a proof of the expansive nature of Felicia's sympathy that she included the servants as well as the children of her friends. When Mr Simeon's faithful old coachman—a great character —fell ill, she walked over to Summertown late at night in the cold and snow, that she might minister to him, returning to him early the next morning. And when his mind gave way and it was necessary to remove him to the asylum, she drove there with him, and constantly visited him afterwards. Almost at his last moments she was with the dying man, stooping down to kiss his forehead because she knew her gentle touch would soothe him. It was a great trial to her when at length Mr and Mrs Simeon left Oxford to go and live in Devonshire.

"I had the grief and pain," she writes to a friend just afterwards, "of seeing the Simeons vanish out of my life for ever. Of course I may, and no doubt shall, see them again from time to time, but the almost daily intercourse of St Edward's is for ever at an end."

But as far as close intercourse can be kept up by correspondence theirs certainly was. Budgets of letters, recording the incidents of their daily lives, passed to and fro, generally twice a week. With them she could cheer herself when depressed, by a chat on paper.

"I was so delighted to get your letter this morning," she writes on one occasion, "that in spite of my having written yesterday, I shall indulge myself in another. You see I have been rather heart-sinking lately, and you and A—— are like two rays of sunshine to me in the darkest mental weather. So your letter came as a brightener for to-day."

The name of Simeon must always have been pleasantly associated in Felicia's mind with friendship, for in her early days she had seen much of the present Dowager Lady Simeon; they had been extremely intimate, and kept up a frequent and affectionate correspondence. Up to the last, Lady Simeon went to see her whenever she could, at Oxford. The friendship descended to Lady Simeon's stepson and his wife, Mr and Mrs Edmund Simeon, whose residence first near and then in Oxford, enlivened Felicia's life considerably, and whose names are of constant recurrence in her letters and journals. They became a prominent and agreeable feature in her life, enlivening her with their visits when she was well, and taking as much care of her as was possible in the case of one who always hated to be made an invalid.

Another friendship of a different character, but of a very genuine and constant kind, was one formed with the late Lord Bute. It began in his undergraduate days, when she soon became on the most intimate terms with him. She gave him her opinion and advice, not only on the matters of personal concern in which he consulted her, but on various intellectual ones. Both were interested in ecclesiastical and theological subjects, and he constantly dropped into her hospitable little drawing-room in the evening for a talk. The time slipped away only too fast.

"Won't you be fined for being late?" she asked him one evening, as the clock struck a late hour.

"Yes! I pay my fine with distressing regularity," was his answer.

He particularly liked to hear all she could tell him about the Greek Church, with which her seven years at Athens had made her well acquainted. Many of his letters to her are on his favourite topic; and in one of the earliest, written from his yacht *Ladybird*, off Lerwick in Shetland, where he halted after a trip to Iceland, he gives an amusing account of the various Churches and Services he had been attending, with their different shades of theology — the Catholic Chapel in Faröe, the "unrelieved old Protestant worship in Iceland, of which creed," he says, "that island is a garden enclosed, or rather perhaps, a well shut up," and the Calvinistic Services with the sailors on board.

Other letters deal with more learned subjects.

In after years Felicia was often Lord Bute's literary helper and adviser. He sent her his MSS. to look over, telling her with regard to one of them that without her it could never have been done, and begging her to "look sharp to the translations," in one of those he sent her, of a Greek Liturgy.

The strongest proof he gave of his appreciation of her intellectual powers was his entrusting her with the task of overlooking, editing, and seeing through the press, a mass of papers left by the learned Canon Jenkins of Jesus College. The Canon had only published one volume; all the remainder was in MS. Lord Bute, thinking it would be well to bring out the rest, applied to Dr Jenkins' half-brother, who readily gave his consent, if a suitable person could be found to superintend the task. It was a work requiring some knowledge of the subject, a great deal of thought and close application. Lord Bute believed Felicia to be quite equal to it. The subject of the book was the History of the Church from the Ascension to the Second Council of Nice.

With all her other avocations the wonder was that Felicia could spare time and attention for such a task. Many people would either have declined it, or given up other work that they might devote themselves exclusively to it. But as usual with the busiest folk, the greater the demand on activity, the greater the supply. She accomplished her work, and she did it to Lord Bute's satisfaction. The book appeared under the title of "Passages in Church History." The friendship begun in Lord Bute's youthful days was carried on as long as Felicia lived. When he married, he was anxious that his old friend should learn to know his wife and children, and the acquaintance was a pleasure to all parties.

The following letters give an account of a visit she paid to Cardiff Castle, and of one she received from Lady Bute and her daughter when they were in Oxford:

"CARDIFF CASTLE, 7th September '87.

"Nothing can exceed their kindness," she writes, "and I find Lady Bute most charming. I am quite ashamed of the way in which they both give up their time, and I believe other engagements, simply to take me about and amuse me. I am going a long drive with Lady Bute this afternoon, and they have shown me the grounds and gardens and all their own rooms in the most friendly way; there is only Lady Bute's sister, Miss Howard, here besides the heaps of governesses, who do not, of course, appear; but one is a Greek, and they wanted me to see her, so I was taken to her. The children are charming, and the place of course is splendid. The room I slept in, Mary (my little maid who is with me) thinks just like a church; it is all marble floor, walls and painted and gilt dome with stained-glass windows. Mary is rather amazed at being waited upon by a footman, as you know lady's-maids always are, but she holds her own very well."

"34 ST MICHAEL ST.,
"OXFORD, 18th June 1899.

"DARLING ZOË,—I think it will interest you to hear of the day I spent on Friday. I have had a great many kind messages lately from

the Butes, as David[1] sees them often, and he
wanted me very much to go and stay with
them in London : that I refused absolutely,
saying I could never leave home, and then
there were plans of Lady Bute coming to see
me, which she says she had been trying to do
for a year past. I had heard no more about it,
however, till suddenly, late on Thursday, David
brought me a telegram in which she said she
was coming next day and telling him to send
my exact address, which he did. Next
morning, by first post, I got the enclosed.
Well ! you must know, as ill-luck would have
it, I was in the midst of spring-cleaning—no
carpets on the stairs—workmen and ladders and
buckets all about—and quite impossible to put
it all right ; only fortunately the carpet had
been put down in the drawing-room, but my
horror was as to their lunch ! The workmen
were in the dining-room, so that I could not
even have my own little breakfast there, and of
course the kitchen and the maids were all upset
too. I went off to David in despair to ask him
if he could give them lunch, and to my great relief found he had a note from Lady Bute to ask
him to lunch with her at the Mitre, and he said
we were all to go there together. They came
by the 11.8 train, and drove straight to my
house. I did not go to the station, but went
down to the door when they arrived, and explained the state of the hall and staircase, and
brought them to the drawing-room. They were
charming, as kind and nice as could be, and so

[1] Miss Skene's cousin, Sir David Hunter Blair (Father
Oswald).

pretty, both of them.[1] We sat and talked a
long time, and then, as Margaret had never seen
Oxford, I asked them if they would like to go
and see Christ Church before David joined us;
they said they would, so I sent for a carriage
and we went there, and fortunately I was able to
get the porter to get a man to show us the
rooms Lord Bute had as an undergraduate,
which interested them immensely. Then I took
them to the Cathedral, and the Hall, and the
Broad Walk, and when we went back to get
into the carriage David joined us; we went
then to the Mitre, where they had a fish
luncheon, as it was Friday. I sat with them,
not eating myself. Then we got the carriage
again and went to Magdalen and All Souls and
St John's, and finally to David's house that they
might see his chapel, and then we went to visit
Canon Kennard, who is R.C. Chaplain to all
R.C.'s in Oxford, and has a beautiful house and
chapel. David has always wanted me to know
him, and he was very pleasant and is coming to
call upon me. They had tea there, and then
David left us, and I went down with them to
the station and sat there with them till your
4.20 train came up, when they went away.
They seem to have enjoyed the day, and
Margaret made herself my attendant, making
me take her arm everywhere and helping me
in and out of the carriage. You may fancy I
was terribly tired when they were gone, as I
was never away from them all the day, but as
they came expressly to see me, I could not do
otherwise. There have been no end of friends

[1] Lady Bute was accompanied by her daughter.

coming to see me lately whom I have had to
be with.

"Lady Simeon (Kitty Colville) was here for
some days, and I had to be a great deal with
her; the Algernon Simeons are here for a
month. Last Sunday Miss Anson came early
to tell me Andrew Lang was at All Souls and
wanted to come and see me. I said I could
not be at home as I had an engagement with
Sophy Palmer, who was also here only for a day
or two, so she said I must go and sit in their
garden with him, which I did; and now to-day
I hear that Lady Mabel Howard is coming to
see me next week. I must say I shall be thankful when all this is over, for I am by no means
up to all this bustle."

The arrival at Oxford of the cousin alluded
to in this letter, Sir David Hunter Blair, led
to much intercourse between them. True, they
belonged to different communions, and she
could not agree with his views on many religious
subjects; but where she recognised devotion to
the same Divine Master, Whose steps she tried
to follow, there she could always hold out the
right hand of fellowship.

"In all that is deepest and most vital in the
Faith of our Lord," she writes in one of her
touching letters to him, "I am most thankful
to feel myself one with you."

The course of her long life had brought
her into contact with members of different

religious communions. In her early days in France, Scotland and Greece, she had been thrown with members of the Roman, the Presbyterian and the Greek Churches, and she had found friends to respect and admire among them all. And in our own Church her friendships included men and women of very different shades of opinion. If we must label those who profess fealty to " One Lord, One faith," we can only say that she deeply admired the fervour of spirit of the Evangelicals, and the high ideals and self-denying lives of those who are generally called High Church. The majority of her friends belonged to that party, and her sympathies lay principally with them, though an elaborate and minute ritual in worship fretted and worried her. She was never on the look-out to criticise and condemn what to many are the outward expressions of a reverent spirit; but where these externals forced themselves on her notice, or seemed to lack reality, they disturbed her calm, when her spirit would fain have risen above the things which are seen to the things which are unseen.

Those who knew and loved her would feel it a sort of profanation to identify her religious life with that of any party. More and more as time went on could she echo St Paul's words, " Grace be with *all* them who love our Lord Jesus Christ in sincerity." Her personal devotion to Him was the heart of her Christianity, and when her friends were with her they felt they were with one of His saints, whose life was hid with Him in God.

"Life is for all of us so full of distress and disappointments and regrets," she writes to her niece, "that a belief in the Love of our Saviour, which will in the end draw us all into peace and joy, is the only solid happiness we can know, the only support under the burdens that fall upon us one and all."

The only point of religious difference that really strained her friendship, was in regard to the tenet that she held to be an essential of Christianity, belief in the Divinity of our Lord. Though she could not bring herself to renounce an old friendship where this was denied, there was pain mingled with pleasure in the intercourse. Afraid at one time that a friend of hers was being led into error on the subject she writes sadly in her diary: "—— is disloyal to Our Saviour." Great was her distress on one occasion, when after a talk with an old friend, a fear seized her "that" as she writes, "I might have seemed to look upon ——'s denial of Our Lord's Deity as a less appalling and awful evil than I do . . . the only Life, the only Light, the only Truth, the only and Eternal Hope. He only has revealed God the Father to us. I do not understand any

Felicia Shove

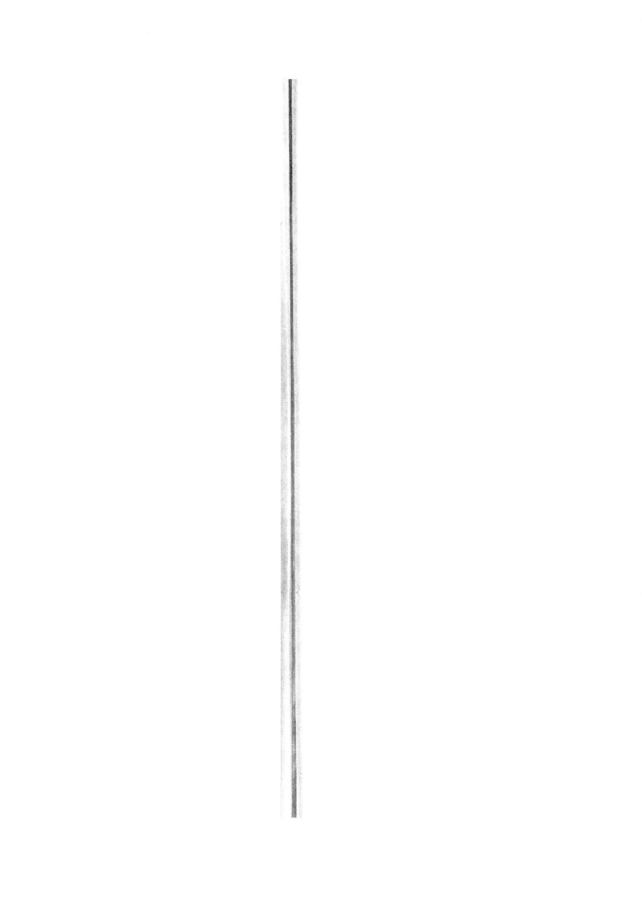

one believing in a Supreme Being, or at least a God of Love and Goodness except as revealed to us by Christ. . . . He Who said, ' I am the Truth,' is the one Divine Truth and Life Whom I hope in life and in death to worship and adore."

In that central Light did she see light and have fellowship with all who walked therein, by whatever names the world without might label them.

The sympathies of her mind were as strong as those of her heart. People liked to come and have a good discussion or argument with her, or to write to her about their intellectual or professional interests. Major, the Hon. Reginald Bertie, when with the International Force of Occupation in Crete in the autumn of 1898, wrote her letters of many sheets on the condition of the island. They show not only his warm regard for her, but the great respect he felt for her judgment and ability.

She might every now and then complain in the private pages of her diary that she had had rather too much of a good thing in the way of visitors, but she would not have liked it had they stayed away, and really enjoyed their pleasant invasions, such as the one she describes in the following passage from a letter:

" Here is a charming picture ! self having fallen

T

asleep in front of the fire; time 11.30. Enter
D——" (Mrs Edmund Simeon).

"I start up; before she had been a second
in the room, enter Mrs Mackarness and Daisy
Mackarness. Moving my chair to make room for
them I knock over my writing-table with the
inkglass full, and all my writing-materials, scent-
bottles, etc.—fearful smash—ink everywhere.
Before it could be even seen to, enter Ted"
(Mr Edmund Simeon) "followed by Miss B——,
who, after the rest scuttled away out of the
confusion, remained discussing the ' new woman';
self listening half-dazed, on account of heart
suffering from the start."

Her diary is indeed rather like a scene from
a play, from the constant entrances recorded,
far too many to enumerate. With Sir John
Conroy, always a great favourite of hers, she
could talk on the many subjects that were links
of interest between them with all the freedom of
an old friendship. When his mother, Lady Alicia
Conroy, died in 1885, he came to live in Oxford,
and they saw one another constantly. She used
to call him her grandson to his face, much to his
amusement. They were both full of humour,
and all subjects, gay and grave, were discussed
by them. Foreign interests and friends were
a great tie. When he was ill in 1897 she went
to see him every day, she being the only visitor
he cared to admit. During the last months
of her life she specially enjoyed intercourse

with him. He was full of sympathy with her in her failing health, and felt her death the more deeply because she was almost the last of those he cared for, whom he had known when he came as an undergraduate to Oxford. In those early days, he and his two great friends, the present Duke of Northumberland and the late Marquis of Bute, were amongst the undergraduates who dropped in most frequently to Felicia's house of an evening. The friendship between Sir John Conroy and Felicia Skene was not, as we cannot but trust, interrupted for long, for his call to the other life soon followed her own.

Her acquaintance with editors and publishers often led the way to real friendships, and she particularly appreciated the intercourse she had with Mr Blackwood, Mr David Douglas, and Mr George Bentley, to mention only two or three. It was characteristic of her Quixotic temperament that she was afraid sometimes that they were treating her too liberally, and even wrote to remonstrate.

Her philanthropic activities at the prison, the workhouse, the Radcliffe Infirmary, and the Eye Hospital, made a bond of interest with her fellow-workers, and inspired fresh friendships. Dr Doyne, the medical superintendent of the Eye Hospital, became not only her own doctor, but her personal friend. These friendships

were some compensation to her for certain
duties she would gladly have been spared—
attendance at committees and other meetings,
for she had no taste for the necessary but often
wearisome outward machinery of charity. To
her diary she sometimes confided the fact that
she had been " to a horrid meeting," or " looked
in at one, and feared she came out before she
ought." One of these compensating friendships
was with the Rev. L. R. Phelps of Oriel,
whom she met at the Charity Organization
Committees, and found in their private intercourse a congenial spirit. His impressions
of her in the following paper have the double
interest of showing her attitude towards " concerted action " in charity, and of their friendship
with one another.

"ORIEL COLLEGE, OXFORD.

" You ask me," he says, " to put on paper
some of my impressions of Miss Skene, and
I am glad to do so, not merely to gratify your
wish, but also because it revives many memories.
Let me make one or two remarks by way of
preface. My knowledge of Miss Skene did
not go much beyond acquaintance. We met
first of all at the ' Charity Organisation
Society '; later on we saw one another constantly at the Gaol, when I was helping in
the Chaplain's work, and I need not say that
I often called at her house, to talk over ' cases,'
or schemes for benefiting the poor, or new books,

or dead friends. Of the 'inner' history of her
life I knew very little, no more than hints
dropped now and again, or than could be
gathered from her character as to the forces
that shaped it. There will therefore be great
defects in anything I have to say; there are
sides of her life and character of which I know
nothing, and of which I shall leave others to
speak.

"Her judgment was a constant source of
surprise to me. I remember its being said
years ago in my hearing, that to be a good
judge of character, you must be either very
good or very bad yourself, the middling character makes mistakes. Now Miss Skene was
an extraordinarily good judge. It might be
said that she had very wide experience, but
experience is at least as apt to confuse and
weaken a judgment as to heighten it, and with
her, judgment was a swift instinct. Again, the
kind of case with which she had to do, it might
be thought, would lead to an indiscriminate,
hopeless pessimism, for constant contact with
evil is likely to exaggerate its proportions. Her
mind was wholly free from this form of weakness. Her judgment was clear, definite, and
well-balanced to the last. She would tell you
with regard to individuals exactly what you had
to expect: if she was by nature hopeful, her
hopefulness was of a reasoned kind, having
nothing in common with indolent optimism.
I remember—for in these things, a little egotism
must be pardoned—her noticing once that I
made little or no allusion to future punishment
when preaching in the Gaol, and in answer to

some commonplace explanation, she said with
some sternness, 'When you are my age you
will know that there is a class whom nothing
else will touch.' She never talked nonsense,
or used conventional language, or watered things
down in discussing people ; she gave you a
robust judgment and the grounds for it, and
she was almost infallible. As to action. Here
to the last she retained a noticeable distrust of
herself: she was before all things meek-spirited.
When I first knew it, her house in New Inn
Hall Street had been for years the Mecca of
every beggar in Oxford, and of every passing
tramp. She was by disposition generous,
splendidly generous, and her generosity had not
been chilled by repeated failure to do the good
she hoped. Failure led her to distrust her own
impulses, to look more and more to general
principles, and to study particular cases in the
light of them. And so she came to lean more
and more on concerted action and collective
wisdom.

"She was from the first a staunch and loyal
supporter of what was then an unpopular
body, the 'Charity Organisation Society,' and
she attended the meetings of its Committee for
years. At the meetings we always looked to
her and to her stores of experience for guidance
in the difficult work of helping the poor, and she
on her side, seemed to be always looking to us,
who represented the theory. It would be
difficult perhaps to say which leaned most upon
the other ; but the good understanding between
theory and practice, thought and action, head
and heart, was in her case never even threatened,

and was productive of much fruit. I may add
that few things did more to remove the prejudices
against the work of the Society than her support
of it, but this is unimportant. She was careful
to 'hear both sides,' but when she had made up
her mind, and she had the ability and the moral
purpose to do so promptly, she was unswerving
in her support of a principle. She had many
prejudices, many predilections, often bred of
impulse, but she was ready to sacrifice them all.

" In her literary judgments, and of these she had
a great many, she was always instructive. The
circumstances of her early life, which was spent
in the circle of Sir Walter Scott, and her acquaintance with Scott himself, inclined her to the
romantic school. She saw with her own eyes
and judged for herself; the conventions of
literature meant little for her. Of the form and
style of a book she would take comparatively
little heed (I say comparatively, for she was no
mean judge of style), but she went straight to
the heart of it, grasped its meaning and pronounced upon it. She always knew what she
had learnt from a book, and nothing that she
read was lost upon her. Add to this, she had a
keen sense of humour for the ridiculous, no less
than for the pathetic side of it, and an instinctive
appreciation of a tragic situation, or the develop-
ment of plot. For her, poetry was a criticism of
life, fiction was the study of a character in
carefully-devised surroundings. In both it was
the human element on which she instinctively
fastened. Her own writings, in their weakness as
well as in their strength, bear this out, for in them
the moral struggle is the one dominant interest.

"Of her special work others will speak at length:
I will give the impression that it made on me.
Her strength lay in the fact that she had very
strong feelings of her own, and a great sympathy
with passionate natures. She did not set up a
cold ideal of conduct, nor what is often so dis-
couraging, the perfection of the saintly character ;
those who came to her found a warm human
nature ; they knew at once that she could feel for
them. But in her case those feelings were dis-
ciplined by reason and religion, they were entirely
under control, and this gave her a tremendous
power in dealing with the victims of passion.
When you remember her keen insight, her vivid
imagination, her strong personal attachment to
all whom she strove to influence, you have, I
think, the secret of the spell she exercised over
them, for it was no less. She had no specific,
no prescription to suit all cases, but she gave
herself freely, her great gifts, her warm heart,
and she rarely failed to call out a corresponding
gratitude.

"I must draw to a close. As I write I seem
to see her once again threading her way through
a crowded street, paying no heed to the passers-
by, or to the incidents of the traffic, wrapt in her
own thoughts. So Dante, and Savonarola may
have stalked through the streets of Florence. Or
I see her sitting at her characteristic writing-table,
throwing off sheet after sheet of her vast correspondence. For she was one of those of whom
we rejoice to think that they did not give up to
family what was meant for mankind, and she
found in letter-writing a substitute for the intimacies of family life of which she always spoke

with a certain good-humoured raillery. Her letters, like her talk, bore the stamp of her two-fold character. They were bright and pointed, abounding in happy turns of phrase, in vivid description and narrative, but they were much more. To those with whom she corresponded she was an unfailing source of Faith, Hope, and Charity. She herself had a larger measure of all three than is often given to man, but above all she was inspiring, in the sense in which some great centre of heat produces a rich and varied vegetation on the soil above. No one could know her without being startled and raised, but above all kindled by the knowledge.

"*6th April*, 1901."

Whoever it might be whom she honoured with her friendship, would echo the words of one who wrote of her after her death,

"I am *proud* to think she could ever care as she did for me."

There is one difficult duty which friendship is often called on to perform, the writing of letters of condolence. There are few in which a delicate sympathy is more required, and they are a great test of the possession of it. It is not every one who can individualise a sorrow and avoid the commonplaces and generalities that would do just as well for one person in bereavement as for another.

Felicia had the discriminating touch, and could lay her gentle healing finger on the spot where

the pain was sharpest and most in need of sooth-
ing.   She knew how to express that appreciation
of the one who is gone, which always helps to
soothe and comfort the mourners, and to lift
their hearts to the thought of the larger, fuller
life into which they trust the departed has
entered.

We are allowed to quote two of them—the
first to Mrs Max Müller, who had sent Felicia
Skene the account of her daughter, Mrs Conybeare,
which came out in the Magazine of the Girls'
High School at Oxford; the other to her old and
valued friend, Miss Frances Power Cobbe.

"NEW INN HALL STREET,
"11th April 1894.

" MY DEAR MRS MAX MÜLLER,—I cannot easily
find words to tell you how grateful I am to you
for having allowed me to see and still more to
possess this just and appreciative notice of one
whose passing from this world must have taken
the sunshine out of life to all who knew and
loved her.   I had not seen it, and have been
deeply interested by it.   I heard much of her
formerly from the Aclands and Shirleys and
others to whom she was most dear, and my own
feeling with regard to her was peculiar, for I did not
know her personally, but I used to sit opposite
to her at the C.O.S., and used to admire her
beautiful countenance with its unmistakable revelation of the fine and noble spirit that lay behind
it.   I felt unspeakably for you and her father and

sister when I heard that in one moment such a
dear and lovely presence had gone from all mortal
sight, and I feel no less now, for I know that she
could only leave to you an undying regret. I do
not think that my niece Zoë ever saw this account,
and it will interest her too, very greatly.

"You must let me thank you again most warmly
for my charming drive on Saturday. I so
enjoyed it, and it seemed to revive me and make
me feel stronger,—Ever very sincerely yours,
　　　　　　　　　　" F. M. F. SKENE."

　　　　　　　　　　　" *February* 1880.

"DEAREST FANNY,—Your great unselfishness will
create one consolation for you now. You have
to bear the pain of separation which she is spared.
One must have gone first; had it been you, hers
would have been the anguish of loss you now
feel, and you are glad she is safe from it now, I
am very sure. As for her, I can fancy her smiling at the thought that it can be called a separation at all, so infinitesimally short and poor must
seem this fleeting life beside the endless existence
which has dawned upon her. I sometimes
wonder how we can trouble ourselves about
death at all, either for ourselves or others—the
inevitable end to which we were sealed in the
day we were born and all others with us. *Mors
janua vitæ;* you remember Goethe said, it cannot
be an evil because it is universal. Think of
getting out of all intellectual difficulties, of all
dimness of spiritual sight, of knowing even as we
are known, and of coming face to face with the
perfect Love, which I believe has been already

manifested. Think of understanding why it has
been best that the innocent should suffer; but
you have well thought of this; I will not weary
you more, except to beg you to believe that as
far as you can call me ' friend,' I yield to none in
anxious loving thought for you at this time and
always—Yours,   FELICIA."

Perhaps we cannot do better than close this
chapter on what formed one of the greatest
happinesses of Felicia Skene's life, with a letter
to the same friend, in which she speaks of the
inevitable limitations of even the highest human
intercourse here, and the hope of their final re-
moval in the life hereafter.

" You do not know how much I wish—in vain,
but still so longingly, that I could have been a
pleasure in your life, but you have been and done
all you could for me and I have been able to do
nothing for you, except in my solitude to speak
of you to our Father in Heaven.
" How I hope that in the higher, purer life it
may be part of the blessedness of immortality
that the thick cloud which seems here to veil
every human spirit from its fellow may be utterly
done away, and that we shall see down into each
other's nature as into a limpid pool, understand
each other fully, both as to the past of earth and
the present of eternity.
" It is so marvellous that here, however much
we may love one another, we are all such utter
strangers to each other. I do not believe that
any one could really make themselves known to a

fellow-creature if they were to try with the most
absolute sincerity and unreserve to lay bare their
inmost being—and no one can even attempt it;
there are thousands of barriers—conscience,
shame, love, humility, pride, and that incom-
municable secrecy of the individual spirit which
is and can be open to none save God—but in the
constitutions of that other life—it may not be
so."

CHAPTER XIX

AUTHORSHIP

ANOTHER of the great pleasures of Felicia's life lay
in her writing. Her outdoor activities, much as
they interested her, were not sufficient to her as
they are to many, because her mind and her
imagination were constantly at work about the
strange characters and histories she met with,
and where her thoughts were strongly aroused,
there she felt the need of expressing them. Each
subject suggested to her took definite shape in
her mind, and she did not feel happy till she had
thrown it on to paper. Writing as we have seen
was little labour and nearly all pleasure to her, and
the hours flew swiftly by on those rare occasions
when she was free from interruption and could en-
sconce herself in her big armchair, take up her pen

and throw off sheet after sheet of story or essay. " Wrote well," she occasionally inscribed with satisfaction in her diary ; but ten to one a visitor's step would be heard after the first page or two, and she had to lay down her task with as much resignation as she could muster. Her evening hours were the safest, but even they could not be relied on.

Stories long and short, books or articles on religious and philanthropic subjects, biographies, travels, essays on miscellaneous topics, were continually flowing from her pen.

Being a rapid writer, she did not refuse a good chance when it offered itself of producing work at the shortest notice.

In one of her letters to Mrs Thomson she says :

" I am rather hard pressed in the way of writing just now. I got an offer on the 28th of December to write a leading tale for the *Quiver*, to go on for twenty-seven weeks, I being bound to send in so much every week, and the first portion to be sent on the 5th of January. I had not one single word of it written, but it was far too good an offer to be refused ; so I bound myself in a regular legal document to furnish the required quantity every week, and I have accomplished five weeks out of the twenty-seven safely enough, but I find it very hard work."

On another occasion she writes :

" I have just finished a long translation of the 'Story of an Anarchist,' from the French, which is extremely clever. I found the translating nice work, and wish so much I could get some publisher to take me on their staff of translators, because honestly I think I have good qualifications for the work, in knowing French well, and having the habit of literary composition, also punctuality. I wrote this, which came to 138 huge pages of MS., in less than five weeks."

However rapid she was, she never allowed herself to become careless in style. Her danger was of just the opposite nature—that of being over-elaborate and Johnsonian in phrase and expression. That was why a three-volume novel was never her strong point. The space at her disposal gave her too much opportunity for exuberance of language as well as of imagination. Both were apt to run away with her. She needed the restraint of a framework of facts, to keep her fancy within the bounds of sobriety, and prevent it from soaring into the region of wild improbability; and a limitation of space, to restrict her to the few telling and powerful strokes, of which her pen was quite capable.

This may be partly the reason why her characters of a low rank socially are generally far better drawn than those of a higher. They were often borrowed from life, and therefore she is more or less bound down to facts, around which her imagination plays with its vivid force of realisation.

But the hero and heroine, *par excellence,* especially the heroine, being generally pure inventions, were clothed with every conceivable perfection, till they got out of the realm of reality altogether, and fail to arouse interest.

Her young girls are so exquisitely fair, so angelically good, so altogether unimpeachable, that we welcome with relief the arrival of some rough diamond of a character, or even the villain, though apt to be somewhat melodramatic in his villainy, as a refreshing change. No doubt it is easier for a writer to make a telling portrait of a rugged character than of a regular and faultless one, as an artist might paint a more speaking likeness of an Oliver Cromwell, with his warts and moles, than of the Apollo Belvidere.

We must also remember that when Felicia first began novel-writing, it was at a time when there was usually far less individuality in the typical heroes and heroines. Witness the novels of Sir Walter Scott, on which she was brought up. Who cares for the pairs of lovers in the "Waverleys" as they do for the spirited characters who aid or hinder the course of their true love?

As a rule, Felicia Skene wrote her novels with a purpose. Of one of these, "Hidden Depths," a book full of power, we have spoken elsewhere.

Of a similar kind was her " Through the Shadows," written with a religious intention. Nothing can be more elevated than its style, tone, and motive.

The plot is a remarkable one.

The agnostic and pessimistic hero, Lyndsay, overwhelmed with the sufferings of humanity and his own private griefs, determines to commit suicide, and is only stopped therefrom by an excellent middle-aged man named Stafford, whom he meets at a Swiss hotel. Stafford persuades Lyndsay to postpone his desperate act for a year. Through the influence of the elder man and his inhumanly-perfect niece, Vera, Lyndsay is restored to faith and hope, and dies, at the end of the book, on the very day formerly fixed for his suicide, while trying to rescue a man from drowning. He leaves Vera, while mourning his loss, to comfort herself with the conviction that the task she had set herself, to win him to Christianity through persuasion, argument and prayer, had not been in vain.

If it be objected that no human girl could have spent night after night as she did, even in winter, on the mountain-top in prayer for him, we must at least say in excuse, that we believe the writer was as exceptional in that way as the heroine; and that in the days of her youth and her health, Felicia would have been equal to doing the same thing. No one can read her

U

diary, with its continual evidence of the triumph
of the spirit over the flesh, without being
reminded of similar incidents in the lives of the
saints.

"A Strange Inheritance," published in 1886,
is a novel of much merit and more probability,
founded on a circumstance borrowed from the
family history of the writer. To her uncle by
marriage, one of the Macdonells of Glengarry,
was left the "strange inheritance" of an old
family burial-ground, the sole relic of a large
estate that would have been his but for a family
quarrel. In a half-ruined tower in the graveyard
lived the beautiful heroine, Marie, with her
father, an excitable half-mad being, who is hidden
away there lest he should be arrested for a murder
he was unjustly suspected of having committed
years before. The hero oscillates between love
for her and for another beautiful young lady;
and as two wives are an impossibility, Marie, who
would have been rather an inconvenient one,
dies, under tragic circumstances. The plot which
is a complicated one, is well worked out, and
some of the characters vigorously sketched. An
old shepherd who comes into it with his attractive Scots dialect, has been particularly admired.

There are two characters in the book taken
from life. Besides the hero's prototype, Macdonell of Glengarry, whose name is as romantic
as his appearance in the picture by Raeburn, of

From the Picture by   Sir HENRY RAEBURN, R.A.

COLONEL RANALDSON MACDONELL OF GLENGARRY.

[To face p. 306.

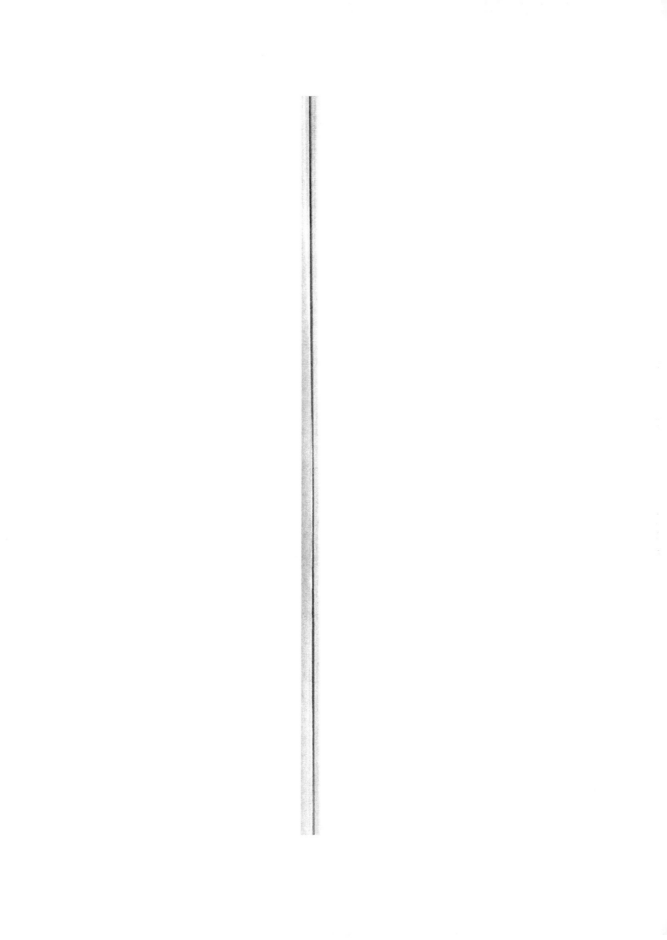

which we give a reproduction, is picturesque,
Felicia introduces her brother, Mr William
Skene, into the story, under the name of Walter
Seton. The likeness is acknowledged by those
who knew him, to be a true and accurate one.
Mr Skene was gratified by the compliment, and
declared that he must do his best to live up to
it; which from all accounts he certainly did. If
Seton errs a little on the side of too much
perfection, there is plenty of individuality in his
downright utterances.

In Felicia Skene's temperance story, of the
following year, "The Lesters," though the incidents related are all said to be true, the agony
is piled too high for artistic purposes, as in
"Hidden Depths"; and we can only say with
Macbeth after reading it,

"I have supped full with horrors."

In her short stories we think Felicia was far
more successful. They are generally admirably
told. The Greek ones—characters and incidents
of which are for the most part borrowed from
her own knowledge and experience while she
lived at Athens—are full of life and humour.
The same may be said of her tales about the
poor. She had so much skill as a narrator,
that she could make a good story out of the
slightest and most meagre incident, as a good
cook can serve up a dainty dish from mere odds

and ends. Take her little sketch in the *Quiver*
called " A Workhouse Episode." The whole
plot is, that a man in the Union refused to take
his share of the strawberries sent for the inmates
on one occasion, and accepted it on another.
Few writers could make much of that, but she
manages to rouse our interest so effectually,
that we feel we cannot put the tale down till
we have solved the mystery. Ghost stories
she loved both to hear and to tell, and two or
three came to her knowledge directly from those
who declared they had witnessed the apparition
themselves. They were all persons whose
truthfulness she had good reason to trust.

One of those she narrates, called " Light in
the Valley of the Shadow,"[1] is the more interesting, because she was herself with the dying man to
whom, as she relates, the ghost appeared. She
was visiting him in his cottage, and sitting by
his bedside at the moment. He had been a
man of respectable life, but had up to the time
of his illness been entirely absorbed in earthly
things. The loss of two of his children, a
lame boy named Joseph, and a little girl, and
his own sickness, had begun to rouse him to
more serious thoughts; and in the course of
Felicia's visits to him he talked to her freely
of his past life, giving every sign of faith and
repentance. It seemed likely that his illness

---

[1] The *Evangelist Monthly*. August, 1893.

would be a lingering one, but the end came
sooner than was expected. She was sitting with
him one day, when he suddenly gave a start, half-
sat up in the bed, and fixed his eyes on what
appeared to be a vacant corner of the room.

"'There's Joseph!' he exclaimed in a tone
of absolute conviction.

"There had been a slight noise in the street
below, and his friend imagined he thought it
was one of his elder sons arriving who had been
sent for, and therefore answered, 'James cannot
come, unfortunately; he must not leave his
work in London.'

"'I do not mean James,' he answered almost
impatiently. 'It is Joseph—my little lame Joe.
Do you not see him there?' He pointed to
the spot at which he had been gazing.

"'No; I see nothing.'

"He turned round to look up in amazement
when he got this answer; and as he did so, a
shade passed over his face; the keen questioning
eyes closed gently, one faint sigh passed his
pale lips, and he fell back lifeless on his pillow.

"It was impossible not to conclude that Joseph
had come to join him, and lead him away to
that unseen land, which was no longer an unknown country to the lame boy, released a year
before from the bonds and burdens of earth."

Still more remarkable was another ghost story
which came within her ken. Of the truth of
it she was absolutely convinced. As we
believe it has never been in print before, we

give it as related by her friend, Mr Algernon Simeon :

" It was in the height of summer, about noonday, that the children of St Thomas' Industrial School were playing in their yard after school - hours. A nun dressed quite differently from the St Thomas' Sisters appeared among them and watched their play. The children had the strictest orders never to speak to a stranger without permission, and being anxious to talk to her, one of them went to the Superior's room for the necessary leave. On returning however with the Superior, the strange nun had gone.

" The St Thomas' Sisterhood occupies land which once formed part of the Abbey of Osney, and the account of the children and simplicity of the witnesses make it difficult to doubt that the strange form was that of some deceased inmate of the old Osney Convent. Though a strict watch was kept, the figure was never seen again."

A book which is amongst the most remark- able of all that Felicia Skene ever wrote, is " Scenes from a Silent World." [1] The subject, life in prison, was one that brought out all her special gifts. It is beautifully written, and has neither a careless sentence nor a dull page in it. The stories she tells in it she knows to be true, and they are presented to the reader with extraordinary vividness. They are *tableaux*

[1] Messrs Blackwood. Edinburgh, 1889.

vivants in the literal meaning of the words.
The prisoners often tell their own tale to the
reader as they did to Felicia, in their characteristic racy language; and where they do not, she
makes their histories equally lifelike. Tragic
and terrible as some of the pages are, they are
relieved by the humour of the peculiar characters
often to be met with in the cells of prisons.

And the book abounds in pathos as well as
humour. She had the eye to perceive the better
side of the wild passionate impulses which had
driven some of the prisoners to commit crimes;
and the unexpected gleams of feeling that in
other cases relieved the blackness of their evil
deeds.

She tells many extraordinary tales that she
could vouch to be true; none more remarkable
than that of a certain handsome black-eyed
girl, whom she had visited in the Oxford prison,
and to whom she gives the title of No. 14. The
story of this young woman sounds more like
fiction than fact. Sir Walter Scott could have
made it the plot of a thrilling tale.

No 14 realised the truth in her own person,
that man is a fighting animal. Her earliest
pitch-battles had been with her step-mother;
the result of which was that she determined to
leave home, change her name, and live a life of
absolute freedom from all social and moral restrictions. She did this so effectually that she

found herself forced to pay visits to various prisons.

One of her last adventures took place in the room of the chief warder, where she had been summoned to receive a reprimand for breaking the prison rules. At a propitious moment, when the officer's back was turned, she made a sudden spring at the window, dashed the glass to shivers, forced herself through the bars, and at the risk of her life, dropped to the ground from a considerable height. She was stunned at first, but soon recovered, and managed to scale the walls with the agility of a cat, and to make her escape under cover of darkness. An acquaintance of hers to whose house she went, accommodated her with a suit of man's clothes in exchange for her convict's dress; and then, having cut her hair short and adopted every masculine characteristic she could assume, she carried out her *rôle* as a man for some time, until a new crime landed her once more in gaol, at Oxford, where she was identified as the missing female prisoner. Here she was visited by Felicia, to whom she became warmly attached, and who persuaded her, on leaving prison, to enter the Refuge. In both places her visitor's influence was strong upon her for good. Felicia Skene recognised in the girl, beneath all her lawlessness and recklessness, a deep and ardent capacity for loving. To this she appealed, striv-

ing to set before her the vision of the highest
love of all, which for her sake had laid down
even life itself.

She did not appeal in vain. When once the
thought of that loving Sacrifice had taken hold
of the woman's heart, nothing could be too
much for her to offer in return. She determined
to enter a Sisterhood. There her resolution was
tested by a strict novitiate; after going through
which, she became a full Sister, and wrote to
Felicia to say that she had not the smallest
wish ever to leave the Convent walls again.

This is the only story in the book that we
can indulge ourselves by repeating; but it contains others nearly, if not quite, as remarkable.

In many ways it was a bold book to write;
for Miss Skene keeps back none of her views
with regard to criminals, whether in agreement
with the general opinion or the reverse. She
throws down the gauntlet on the subject of
capital punishment, and her power of expression
enabled her to do her convictions full justice.

The greater part of the book had previously
appeared in *Blackwood's Magazine*, where it
attracted much attention. It was widely re-
viewed and much commended. She did not
publish it under her own name, but under a
nom de plume, Francis Scougal. When she did
not give her own, she generally turned to the
family history for the choice of one. Two

ancestors were laid under contribution, a Scougal and a Moir; the latter name representing her on the title-page of "Through the Shadows."

Her books, in spite of certain feminine traits, were generally supposed to be those of a man; and strangers would often write to her about them in letters beginning "Dear Sir," or "Rev. Sir." "The Divine Master" brought her one addressing her in the latter style, expressing hearty admiration of the book, and begging her to accept as a token of it, the present of a chair carved by her correspondent.

Felicia Skene's interest in human nature made the writing of biography in any form, whether of book or article, an attraction to her. The longest Memoir she published was that of Alexander Lycurgus, Archbishop of the Cyclades,[1] and her knowledge of Greek customs and the Greek Church made her fully competent to do so. The writing of it led to a little correspondence with Mr Gladstone, ever interested in any matter connected with Greece. Needless to say she kept and valued the letters she received from him, as well as the characteristic post-cards in his neat writing.

She was pleased and proud that he complied with a request she made him with regard to the book.

[1] The Life first appeared in the *Church Quarterly*, where it excited sufficient attention to be re-published separately by Messrs Blackwood in 1877.

"I have had another wonderfully kind letter from Mr Gladstone," she writes. "I told him I should like to dedicate the book to him, and he said that he could only receive it as an honour and pleasure."

The words of dedication are, we think, very happily chosen:

"To the Right Honourable William Ewart Gladstone, the first friend who welcomed Alexander Lycurgus to an English home, and the last to whom his thoughts turned with gratitude and affection in the hour of death, this record of his life is dedicated."

She speaks with equal gratitude in the letter from which we have quoted, of the kindness of Bishop Wordsworth of Lincoln, to whom she was indebted for the introduction to the book.

The short life she wrote of her cousin, Bishop Forbes of Brechin, was less interesting. The style is somewhat cut and dried; and there are no traces of the lively vein in which she usually wrote.

Far more attractive are the biographical sketches and articles she sent to various Magazines. The one on her ancestor, Lord Pitsligo, alluded to in an earlier chapter, is excellent. She was pleased with it herself.

"I should like you to see my new paper, 'Alexander Lord Pitsligo,' which is in the September number of *Temple Bar* (1894). I think it would be nice for you to have that, as he was a far-back relation of your own, and Charlie Trefusis now has his land," she writes to a niece.

Felicia Skene's cousin, the Hon. Charles Trefusis, we may mention by the way, was not only regarded by her with interest as the present owner of her Jacobite hero's estate, but because he had married one of the daughters of her great friend, Lady Jane Antrim, whose stay in Oxford with her pleasant family had led to a warm friendship with Felicia, and was a source of great interest and enjoyment to her. She was then far advanced in years, but so full of fun and life was she, that she seemed to meet her friend's daughters on equal terms. "One never realised how old she was," writes one of them, Lady Caroline Bertie.

Amongst her biographical articles we should place first and foremost one called " Sir Walter Scott's First Love," which came out in the *Century Magazine*.[1] It is written with peculiar charm. All the love and respect she had been brought up to feel for her father's great friend, shines out in it.

No one who reads the following delightful letter, which we are permitted to quote, could accuse her of exaggerating the fascination of the

[1] July 1899,

beautiful Williamina Stuart, who afterwards as the wife of Sir William Forbes, became Felicia's aunt. The letter is from Mrs Wilson, daughter of the late Dr Norman Macleod, and describes the ineffaceable impression which the charming lady made on the writer's grandmother, wife of Dr Norman Macleod, senior, who used to describe her as one of the most delightful, affectionate, and dignified of ladies, and was immensely impressed by the chivalrous courtesy and devotion of her husband.

He it was who came to Sir Walter Scott's aid in his financial difficulties, generously expending a large sum of money on his friend's behalf. It was consistent with the modesty and delicacy of his character to which Sir Walter alludes in these lines,

> " And thou, and I, and dear-loved Ray,
> And one whose name I may not say,
> For not Mimosa's tender tree
> Shrinks sooner from the touch than he."

that the kind act was performed anonymously.

Mrs Wilson's introductory description of her grandmother is so pretty, that we need not apologize for giving the whole of the letter.

" St Helen's, Murree,
" Punjaub, *8th June* 1898.

" Dear Miss Skene,—Mr Lang has told me of the interesting work you are engaged in doing, and that you are editing Lady Forbes' correspondence. He wishes me to tell you all I remember about my grandmother, Mrs Norman Macleod senior's, early friendship with and life-long love of her. There is not really much to tell, and yet it seems like sacrilege to say so, when I remember how much that little was to my dear old grandmother. I daresay many of us, as we go on in life, have found that amongst the number of our friends who have died, it may be a score of years ago or more, there are one or two who have a magic power to haunt our memory, and cast their spell upon us still, as if it were only yesterday that we saw and worshipped them.

"Lady Forbes had that place in my dear old grannie's heart. I think I must tell you a little about Mrs Macleod, before I tell you how she first met her beloved Lady For-bes, as she always pronounced her name in the old-fashioned Scotch way. She was ninety-four when she died about twenty years ago, but even at that age she had a wonderful freshness of feeling and power of loving people and nature, poetry and music, and all beautiful things. I remember being so touched by her saying to me when she was on her death-bed, 'Open the window and draw aside the curtains that I may feel the sunshine and hear those dear birds sing'; and then her love for the human beings about her came out, and she added, 'and give the day's paper to the servant girls, poor things. They have so much to do for me just now, and they need some cheering up themselves.' We used to love as children to be with her.

She would play her old Scotch airs to us, and
sing little bits of songs of which she had sometimes written the words herself, or repeat quaint
scraps of old-world poetry; and sometimes even
leave her corner in the sofa, to show us how the
minuet *ought* to be danced, moving her arms
and making her deep curtseys with a grace *we*
certainly could not emulate.   She had such a
number of stories to tell us, which had all a
halo of romance for us, and which we could
never hear too often; stories of her own childhood, and of how she had once heard her mother
and her aunt discussing the dancing-school they
went to in the Canongate of Edinburgh; of
the rush of horror that fell on her home when
her father announced that Louis XVI. had
been beheaded; of the general rejoicing then
when the news came of the battle of Waterloo;
of the wonderful history of a diamond ring she
always wore, and so on.   But far more important
to her was the story of the day on which she
first saw Lady Forbes.   Her father, Mr Max-
well, was Chamberlain to the Duke of Argyll,
and lived in a lonely part of Mull, near the
Bay into which the steamer—a rare visitor
from the outer world—sailed, landing its passengers by a small boat, which was rowed
out to meet it for this purpose.   Many strangers
who were travelling in the Highlands came
provided with letters of introduction to my
great-grandfather, but even without these, his
hospitality was extended to those in need of it.
Near the landing-place was an inn, intended
for the accommodation of travellers.   The inn,
however, was very small, and my grandmother

used to tell me how her hospitable mother
used to look through a telescope and count
how many passengers went to the inn! If
their numbers exceeded its powers of accommodation, then a servant was sent (I always wondered
at this point, if the servant was 'Black Sambo,'
about whom I also knew so much) with orders
to find out who the travellers were. Then my
great-grandmother or her husband would sally
forth to call on any one whom they thought
was in a strait, to offer them the hospitality of
their own home.

"On one occasion—the great occasion!—my
great-grandmother and her daughter noticed
that a poor lady was the only one of their
own sex amongst a party of men. They were
soon informed that this was Lady Forbes, who
was with her husband in an over-crowded inn.
'Agnes' was told to accompany her mother
to pay their respects to the lady. 'And glad
were we that we had gone,' said my grandmother, 'for we found the dear lady in a sad
plight; indeed she was weeping, for the landlord had just informed her husband that they
must share their room with another traveller,
and what was she to do? Glad they were
to come to my father's house, and there they
stayed for some days, and happy days were
they for me, for any one more beautiful than
Lady Forbes, I never saw. The very boatmen
who carried her on shore on that rough day,
said it was not a woman but an angel they
had borne in their arms. At the end of their
visit Lady Forbes asked my mother what her
intentions were concerning the education of

G. L. SANDERS.

SIR WILLIAM STUART FORBES OF PITSLIGO AND MONYMUSK,
SEVENTH BARONET.

[To face p. 320.

her daughter Agnes. My mother said her intentions were to send me to a boarding-school in Edinburgh to finish my education. "In that case," said Lady Forbes, "I hope you will allow me to be her *chaperon* while she is there. You can rely upon my fulfilling my duties towards her as if she were my own child." What was my joy when my mother agreed with grateful pleasure to the kind proposal, and what happiness was mine that winter when each holiday came round and it was spent with my beautiful Lady Forbes! Nothing could exceed the kindness shown by her to me in every way.'

"Lady Forbes' kindness was great, although on one occasion, as will happen, it was uncongenial! We have a letter at home, written by her, in the fine old 'Italian' handwriting, as it was called, with its thin and slanting sharply-pointed strokes. It is addressed to my grandmother, and is on the subject of a dancing-school ball which was to be given by Neil Gow, the celebrated piper and publisher of Scotch airs, at the end of the term, to the pupils belonging to his dancing-class, amongst whom was my grandmother. Lady Forbes informed my grandmother that she would prefer her not to go to this ball, but if she goes, she must, as her *chaperon*, insist on her not dancing with the other sex, but on her being content to look on, as she had not yet made her *début* and come out. My grandmother, who was passionately fond of dancing, was bitterly disappointed at this dictum, and elected to stay at home, in preference to the second-hand happiness of being a spectator of others' joy. It is all an old story now, with not many things in it, as I said, that seem worth repeating; but such as it is, it ever remained fresh in the memory, with that vividness with which we dwell on the little words and acts of those who have enthralled our imagination and our hearts. I remember once sitting beside my grandmother's bed, when she was near her end. The soul, the immortal part of her, seemed as if it were looking on at the decay of the body as a thing apart, and to mourn for it. I remember her bursting into tears and saying to me 'I am forgetting things now, I am forgetting everything.' I kissed her dear hand and said, 'Darling Grannie, there is some one you do not forget, and will always remember.' 'And who is that, dear?' 'Lady Forbes,'—— 'Lady Forbes? *Do* I forget? Shall I *ever* forget her?' And the old tale was repeated, and on the dying face was the old light of love.—Yours sincerely,

"R. C. WILSON."

If Felicia Skene could have been induced to write her autobiography, she might have given us a delightful book, of which her two papers of reminiscence in *Blackwood's Magazine*, "Glimpses of some Vanished Celebrities,"[1] and "Some Episodes in a Long Life,"[2] give sufficient proof. Mr Andrew Lang, with whom she had

[1] July, 1895.   [2] June, 1896.

George Forbes

a pleasant exchange of letters on historical
subjects, in which they did not always agree,
expresses his hope that she will soon give her
recollections a more substantial and permanent
form by writing a book of them, and expresses at
the same time his pleasure in having the good
fortune of making her acquaintance ; for he came
to see her at Oxford.   What an enjoyment would
it have been, to have overheard the conversation
between two such lively talkers !   Bright indeed
must have been the sparks when flint and steel
struck !

Her article on Lord Pitsligo, whom Mr Lang
compares in a letter to her, to General Gordon,
and pronounces to be equally too good for this
world, interested him much.

One of the great pleasures that her writings
brought her was that they often led to an
acquaintance with interesting and distinguished
men.

Amongst them was Dr George MacDonald.

"I quite envy you the prospect of making
acquaintance with Dr MacDonald," she writes
to a friend who was going to spend the winter
at Bordighera.   "I have the greatest possible
admiration for his writings.   I have read all that
I could ever get hold of, both in prose and poetry.
I never met him, but I once had some correspondence with him on one of the doctrines
brought forward in his books."

Flooded, as Dr MacDonald describes himself to be, by letters from strangers to which he finds it impossible to reply, he declares that one of hers, just received, must be an exception. " *That*, at least," he says, " is one that must be answered, simply because it is worth answering." The subject of his letter is the oft-discussed one of the meaning of the word *eternal* as used in the New Testament with regard to life, which he holds has no relation to time, duration, or anything of the sort. " That may follow as a consequence, not of the word eternal, but of the life itself. ' This is life eternal, that they might *know* Thee, the only true God.' "

As a proof of the value he feels for her opinion and of his interest in her letters, he begs her, when she has turned the subject over in her mind, to write to him again if she is so moved, and he will reply. Another letter from him follows before long, going more fully into the religious questions that interested both so deeply, and begging her to come and see him and Mrs MacDonald in London.

In a later letter he declines her self-denying proposal that he should not answer her letters, saying that he could not consent to such a suggestion :

" I consider it part of my work, and a great privilege and honour to answer such letters as yours. What else am I good for ? I feel inclined to say; though that might have a presumptuous interpretation. You *must* (with a heavy dash under it) come and see us."

If Felicia had been able to arrange a visit, few things could have given her greater pleasure than a talk with him.

Of her books written directly on the subject of religion, the one which made most mark was "The Divine Master," of which we have spoken before. Judging by the number of editions it went through it was the most popular, and it was considered by some to be the most remarkable of all her works. With the self-reproach of a truly humble mind, she realised painfully how far she was from living up to the ideal she had tried to set forth in it.

"Oh that book!" she exclaimed to a friend one day. "I think my Guardian Angel will hold it up before my eyes at the last day."

"The Shadow of Holy Week," written some years later, in 1883, made far less impression on the public than "The Divine Master," though it found many admirers, and is written in the same ardent spirit that inspires the earlier book. There is also little difference in their literary style, despite an interval between them of about thirty years.

The religious book on which she set most store, regarding it as her last legacy to the world, the final blow in the cause of that faith which she prized as the one thing worth living and dying for, was called " A Test of the Truth,"[1] published under the *nom de plume* of Oxoniensis. The beautiful lines she chose as the motto for the book, indicate its scope :

> "The sea of Faith
> Was once too, at the full, and round earth's shore
> Lay like the folds of a bright girdle, furled ;
> But now I only hear
> Its melancholy long withdrawing roar
> Retreating to the breath
> Of the night wind, down the vast edges drear
> And naked shingles of the world."

It is written in fervour of spirit, out of the fulness of her heart. Suffering keenly as she did from the inroads of " the scientific materialism, the rationalistic agnosticism and shallow supercilious scepticism " of the day, to quote her own words, she asserts her conviction that if only doubters are in earnest enough to recognise the importance of the subject in question, they may put the matter to the test if they will. Setting aside the strong internal evidence of the truth of the Bible, traceable in its own records, as well as that of the unique character of Jesus Christ, quite beyond the power of human invention, as she says, to imagine, she makes a fervent appeal that the doubter, " battling in the ocean of pain and mystery which surrounds him in this mortal life, should act like a man drowning in a stormy

[1] Elliot Stock. 1897.

sea," surrounded by "seething waters and pitiless
howling blasts, . . . who sends out his voice to the
unknown in a wild despairing cry for help . . .
though he knows not to whom it is addressed, or
if it could be heard of any that might answer."
Such a man, she says, is not a fool; neither is he
"who tests the possibility of Christ's existence by
a solemn direct appeal that He would manifest
Himself to him—if indeed He has any Being,
any Omnipotent power, such as He assumed for
Himself." To do this aright the doubter must
free himself from all contact with his fellow-men,
from earthly learning, and fallible teachers and
human wisdom, concentrating his whole being
upon the appeal. He must lay aside all that
might prevent "the contact with the fallible
human spirit, of that One Who alone claims
for Himself essential holiness and perfection,
acting on the promise, 'If any man will *do*
His will, he shall know of the doctrine whether
it be of God,' and Who promises to love and
manifest Himself to those who keep His com-
mandments."

Such an appeal, even if it had to be carried
on for a very lifetime, would not be made in
vain.

When she adds, "Fools or not, the experiment
has been made and not in vain," it is impossible
not to believe that she was writing out of her
own personal experience. None could say more

earnestly than she, "*With my whole heart*, have I sought Thee."

The book influenced readers differently. To some, in spite of its earnestness and sincerity, it did not bring conviction. To others it struck home with force. We are allowed to refer to one whose opinion will be received with general respect—the Rev. Henry Bevan, Rector of St Luke's, Chelsea. He writes :

" I have read the book with much interest and pleasure, and think it is excellent, and calculated to be of use to many troubled minds, at this present crisis of religious difficulty. It would make a suitable preface to Dr Hort's book, ' I am the Way, the Truth and the Life,' which carries on the line of argument indicated by the writer."

If Felicia had been a clergyman, she would probably, from her natural gift of eloquence, have won fame as a preacher. Indeed she did on one or two occasions preach by deputy with much success.

"Oh, dear ! there's that sermon to write," exclaimed a clerical friend to her one day, in a voice of fatigue and disinclination.

" I'll write it for you "; was her ready reply.

And so she did ; and her friend preached it not only on that, but on several occasions, and a striking one he declared it to be. It was on a subject which must often have come home to

Felicia Skene's mind in moments of pause after the fatigues or the discouragements of her work— Elijah's despondency as he lay under the juniper tree.

As would be expected of a person of her temperament, she showed as much courage and enterprise in her literary as in her charitable work. She would not let herself be discouraged or daunted. She aimed her literary arrows at a variety of Magazines, and when, as was often the case, they made an unwelcome return home again from one editor, she shot them off promptly to another; and almost invariably they hit the mark at last.

She was prompt to recognise any subject that would suit her pen, as in the case of the prisoner and the bird. Her own dreams—and remarkable dreams have been said by an authority on the subject to be a strong proof of imagination—came in usefully for the purpose on occasion. She was driving with a friend one day and related to her a striking one she had just had. When afterwards she happened to mention that she wanted money for some object —a charitable one we may feel sure—her friend remarked, "Why do you not make your dream earn some for you?" Felicia acted on the hint at once; and the story she despatched to a Magazine in consequence, brought her a welcome cheque for eight guineas.

Her sympathy and help to other writers, especially inexperienced ones, was always ready; though she might groan a little in private over the trouble they gave her. "Got a horrid MS. from——" she confides to that silent confidante, her diary, when an old friend sent her one to consider and advise upon. But though she would not welcome the MSS. she would do all she could to help the writers.

For nearly twenty years she was Editor of the *Churchman's Companion*, and did not spare herself the trouble of writing long letters to intending contributors if she thought they were worthy of encouragement. The necessity of hardening her heart, over the painful duty of returning impossible MSS., caused her kind soul much distress.

For some little time before her death she helped her friend, Mr Charles Wood, by looking over papers for the *Argosy*, when he was abroad.

When her great-nephews took to their pens, as many of them did with great success, her pride and delight in their writings was great.

"Cléon" (de Rangabé) she writes to Mrs Thomson, "sent me lately a beautiful book he has published, a poem in Greek, most splendidly illustrated, and which seems to be a success; and to-day he sends me another which has been translated into English in America, called

'Greece in the time of Homer.' The American translator gives an appendix with the history of the de Rangabés, whom he says are the most 'illustrious' family in Greece."

She was equally delighted at the literary success of another great-nephew.

" I think," she writes to Mrs Thomson, " Basil's last book[1] is a wonderful production, quite apart from his charming account of his own career as Prime Minister. The amount of knowledge and research which he shows in giving the history of Tonga is most remarkable."

Amongst the letters she kept and valued are some pleasant literary ones from her friend, Mrs Humphry Ward, who knew how keenly her old friend would interest herself in her work, and that to her she could describe, certain of being understood, the mode in which the scenes and characters took shape in her imagination.

" Your letter this morning," she writes, " has given me the keenest pleasure. I am so glad you like *Helbeck* and have been drawn to my two poor lovers. Their story came to me all in a moment, on an autumn day, in Westmoreland. I was visiting some friends near Kendal for a few hours. Something was said of an old Catholic house and family near by, and immediately afterwards I set out on my journey

[1] " The Diversions of a Prime Minister."

to Euston. By the time I got to London, Helbeck, Laura and Hubert Mason had risen out of the mist. I remember well what a happy day it was—one read nothing and saw nothing, only dreamed the hours away. Only a dimness hung over the end. But as soon as I began to work, that became clearer and clearer, and after the first chapter or two I never felt as if I could help or alter it in any way. You, as a story-teller, will understand this curious feeling of reality which, if one outrages it, just avenges itself by going away, and leaves you to work helplessly in the dark without it! None of my letters has pleased me more than yours, dear friend. It was very good of you to write it."

CHAPTER XX

CLOSING DAYS

WITH most people who attain to the well-nigh four-score years of life reached by Felicia Skene, there is a gradual slackening of work, the dropping off of one activity after another, before the tired worker lies down for his last rest. And it may be, as her doctor said, that if she could have made up her mind to act as others do in this respect, her days might have been considerably prolonged. But she would never have desired to give up any of her work; and knowing her as they did, her friends could not have wished it for her. To go on just as usual, with all her old pursuits, her unwearying service for God and man to the very last, and then to hear the sudden call to lay down her life of devotion here, to enter, as we trust, upon a higher one elsewhere, was just what she would have chosen, and we may be thankful it was granted to her.

For a long time it had been evident to all except perhaps herself, that the time of her rest was near. Those who saw her at intervals marked on each occasion the change in her aspect, the stooping feeble gait, the increasing pallor; and as they saw her creeping along the street on her old errands of kindness, could only feel that she would not be with them for long. As they marked the increasing spirituality of her countenance it would seem to them that she was only hovering on the confines of this life.

If the spiritual life within shone more brightly than ever through the frail and failing form, yet the human side was as strong and keen as it had always been. The friends who visited her found her as ready to talk and joke in her old pointed, vigorous way as in the old days. Talks grave and gay with such devoted friends as have already been mentioned in these pages, and

with others equally appreciative, such as the
Hon. Mrs William Lyttelton, Mrs and Miss
Mackarness, the President of Magdalen, and
Mrs Warren, were a refreshment and happiness
to her to the last.

She said she was in no hurry to leave this life,
still endeared to her by many sympathies. Rather,
she wished to live on in it that she might do
more work for God. She might sometimes
experience, when alone, the times of depression
which doctors tell us are often the accompani-
ment of the heart disease from which she suffered,
yet it might be said of her in the words of R. L.
Stevenson, that she had always tried to

> " Make this world our heritage,
>   A cheerful and a changeful page,"

and not only that, but a better and a more
kindly one. It is difficult to think that there
could have been many days in her life when
there was not some one in the world who was
the better for her being in it.

As her friends pass by her house now, how
often must the longing spring up in their minds,
" What would we give to stop at her door and
go up to her friendly room once more, and
receive her warm welcome, and have one more
talk with her ! "

She had never willingly left home, and the
journeys she had always disliked were more

dreaded by her latterly than ever. But if it were her **duty** to take one, she would not shirk it, thankful if she could get off sleeping away from her own home.

"I have not slept a night out of my own bed, but I have been twice to see K——" —her surviving sister—she thankfully records in her summary of 1897, at the end of her journal. "It remains to be seen what this year will bring, and whether I shall be permitted to live through it, and see another New Year ever." And then comes the frequent ending to those annual volumes, "*Fiat voluntas Tuas; ne derelinquas me, Jesu.*"

She was spared after that to see two more new years, little as those who noticed her increasing weakness would have anticipated it; and **up to** within a few days of her death, kept up her old habit of rising a little after six, that she **might** go to the Early Service she had been accustomed to attend. How, after her frequently disturbed nights from pain at the heart, she managed **to** get up so early and go out in all weathers, was a perfect marvel. "Bad night, could not sleep, up at 6.45 and to Early Service, pouring wet, answered all letters, went in cloisters, then to Broad Walk, very rough and windy, and to Cathedral Service, *pour mon malheur, je souffre beaucoup,*" is a specimen of entries made day after day.

As her charitable pursuits, whether in prison, hospital or workhouse, were kept on to the last, so was her literary work, both for herself and for the friends who often appealed to her for help and advice. In the beginning of her last year, 1899, she says, referring to an article she had sent to a Magazine, " I think it is the last payment I shall ever have for writing—I think I am written out." Yet only the month before she died, we find her writing, at the request of the editor of the same periodical, two more articles on a difficult subject connected with criminal life; while she was looking over MSS. for another editor, a great friend of hers, who was then abroad. Five manuscripts were examined and despatched by her the day week of her death. Her friends, who for a long time had been alarmed at her fragile state, watched and guarded her more carefully than she often knew, finding excuses when they could, for accompanying her in her walks, or escorting her to her home when they thought she needed their help.

" Took C—— to Balliol," she writes, " where John (Sir John Conroy) came; long dreary afternoon . . . at last John took me home," or, "John Conroy met me on the way to church, and told me he had followed me home on Saturday."

Sometimes her friends' anxiety would prompt them to send her doctor to pay her a visit.

" *Wednesday, 27th September*, 1899.—Up at
6.30. To St Philip and St James. Doubtful day.
Suddenly Dr Doyne came, whether sent or not,
I do not know, but he examined me . . . I think
he hinted ominously, and told me more than ever
to avoid strain."

That day was to end more brightly than it
began; for she was to have one more drive with
her friend, Mrs Miller of Shotover, into the
country and to enjoy its quiet and beauty.
Great was the pleasure she took in her friend's
garden, and in the little spinny into which they
wandered.

At her doctor's next visit the truth of her
state was still more plainly put before her.   A
letter to one of her greatest friends shows how
thankfully she received the news that the last
summons might come suddenly.

" Dr Doyne came to see me to-day, and I
have had it thoroughly out with him. He is
very kind, telling me my state quite plainly. Of
course my heart is very much worse, and I suffer
a good deal. I have been nearly fainting once or
twice lately, and at some unexpected moment I
shall faint and be instantly gone. A sudden
death is quite certain for me, and I told Dr
Doyne it was what I most earnestly wished; no
long illness, no nurses and friends troubling
themselves, but just a stoppage of breath and a
passing away to trouble no one."

It was characteristic of Felicia Skene that at

Y

the visit of the doctor described in this letter, the old undaunted spirit flashed out in her entreaty, as she eagerly grasped his hand, " Pray don't make me into an invalid."

" She begged hard," writes Dr Doyne, " to be allowed to have her meals ' like an ordinary mortal,' and when at last I said I would· see about it, she turned over on her side, saying, ' then now I can go to sleep.' "

She had never, as we have seen, been easy to manage in her earlier illnesses, and the difficulty did not become less in her later years.

" As a patient," Dr Doyne says, " she was hopeless ; a woman of iron determination and will, she could not bring herself under the subjugation of ' doctors' rules.' She believed firmly in the routine of life she had mapped out for herself, and any relaxation she would only yield to me as the personal solicitation of a friend, and not as the advice of a doctor ; and even then under the strongest possible protest. All this was intensified during her last illness ; quite a short time before her death she struggled down to the Cathedral in the wet, and barely got home by resting every few steps, but even then refused to be taken home in a cab. The night previous to that on which she died, she felt the cold in her bedroom from her open window, which she had not strength to close, and yet she would not even then disturb ' her little maid '—as she called her—to do it. I had incurred her real displeasure by insisting that 'her little maid' should light a fire in the bedroom the previous night.

I think the character of herself that most pleased her was one I gave her when she was especially difficult to manage during an attack of phlebitis; I said, 'Miss Skene, if you had been a bad woman, you would have been one of the worst.' She often used to repeat this, and laugh over it with the greatest satisfaction."

Perhaps it was in reference to this amusing remark of her doctor's that she speaks of herself in one of her letters to him as "your poor old evil-liver."

There might be grounds for her accusation of herself, in another letter, as "the most tiresome old patient any one was ever troubled with," but at any rate she appreciated her doctor's care of her, saying that, "for all these years he had shown her every conceivable kindness, and she could make him no return, but her deep gratitude and regard—giving him a thousand thanks for all his kindness."

No wonder he speaks of her as a "loyal and enthusiastic friend; indeed," he says, "the most severe criticism I could pass upon her is, that her extreme loyalty and keen partizanship for her friends might sometimes have carried her too far in their cause, so as to show scant justice to the 'other side.'"

Dr Doyne gives expression to what must have been a common feeling among all who knew her, when he says in one of his letters to her, " You will believe me when I say that I know no greater stimulus to do one's duty in this world, than to meet and talk with one whose whole life and work is made up of unselfish and true regard for the welfare of others."

Felicia Skene in her unselfishness might desire to spare her relations and friends what she thought might give them trouble, but it is needless to say how gladly they would have come to her at any moment.

Her last Sunday was spent in the usual way; up at 6.15 to attend the service which had ever brought comfort and joy to her; twice to her familiar haunt, the prison chapel; then to the Cathedral, from which a friend walked home with her. She felt ill the next day but managed to get to St Thomas' Church and to the prison, followed by her anxious and faithful servant. Wednesday saw her for the last time at the Cathedral, where she had to be helped to her seat. The rest of the day was passed resting in her drawing-room in the arm-chair, which she valued because it had belonged to her parents. She was able to see two friends who visited her, and they were almost the last from outside with whom she talked; for the next

From a Photo by   Miss E. VENABLES.

day she saw no one except Dr Doyne, and
retired early to her room. Her servant who,
despite her orders, was sitting up with her as
on the previous night, in an adjoining room,
was with her at the last, when in the early morning of Friday 6th October, 1899, the call came,
and her happy spirit, released from the burden
of the flesh, passed into the presence of Him
Whom she had loved and served so faithfully.

If the words of the prayer offered in our
Baptismal Service for those received into Christ's
Church on earth ever find fulfilment, surely
they were richly answered in the life of this
noble woman. "Steadfast in faith, joyful
through hope, and rooted in charity," could any
description of the life of a Christian more fitly
portray hers?

The frail body was laid to rest in the churchyard of St Thomas's. The church was crowded
with relations and friends, with men distinguished as heads of colleges, professors and
high officials both of the University, of the
prison, and of the many charitable institutions
at which she had been so well known.

But if her spirit hovered over the spot where
so many assembled to show their love and
reverence for her, we cannot but think it would
have been most of all touched by the presence
of some of the poor and the erring whom she had
tried to help and to raise, and who now formed

part of the mixed congregation that gathered round her grave. Among the flowers sent were some with an inscription that would have pleased her, scrawled in an uneducated hand, " From Anne S—— to the one I love."

Words are not needed in such a case to say what all were feeling about the loss sustained by Oxford.

When on the following Sunday one of the clergy was preaching on a text which he said he felt to be peculiarly appropriate to the life of Felicia Skene, " As unknown and yet well-known; as dying and behold we live; as chastened and not killed; as sorrowful yet alway rejoicing; as poor yet making many rich," he made use of a beautiful expression, which sums up the inspiration of her life:

" She lived in the Vision of an unconquerable Hope."

A BEAUTIFUL brass tablet has lately been placed in Christ
Church Cathedral, in memory of FELICIA SKENE. The
inscription was written by her friend, the President of
Magdalen :—

IN · PIAM · MEMORIAM

FELICIÆ · MARIÆ · FRANCISCÆ · SKENE

AQUIS · SEXTIIS · NATÆ · A.D · X · KAL · JUN · A.S · MDCCCXXI

MORTE · PEREMTÆ · APUD · OXONIAM · PRIDIE · NON · OCT

A.S · MDCCCXCIX

FILIÆ · JACOBI · SKENE · DE · RUBISLAW

QUÆ · QUUM · PUERILES · ANNOS · EDINÆ · DEGISSET · MOX
ATHENIS · E · BOREALIBUS · IN · IPSAM · URBEM · CECROPIS · PRO-
FECTA · FLORES · INTER · GRÆCOS · ÆTATIS · SUÆ · FLOREM
EXPLICAVIT · POSTEA · UBI · CASUS · PARENTES · OXONIAM
ADDUXISSET · IISDEM · MORTEM · OCCUMBENTIBUS · IPSA · RE-
MANSIT · IAMQUE · SUÆ · POTESTATIS · FACTA · FEMINA · FEMINIS
OXONIENSIBUS · ITA · SE · DEDIT · UT · PER · MULTOS · ANNOS
ESURIENTIBUS · MANDUCARE · BIBERE · SITIENTIBUS · DARET
INFIRMAS · VISITARET · INNUMERAS · IN · CARCERE · CLAUSAS
ASSIDUE · ADVENIRET.

VERBI · DIVINI · NON · IMMEMOR.

IMPRESSIONS OF FELICIA SKENE

BY LADY SOPHIA PALMER

IT was from August 1895 that I really knew Miss Skene. Before that I had been acquainted with her through Lady Jane Antrim, but had only realised the beauty and greatness of her character and the richness of her gifts, as one does treasures disclosed by genius in picture, music, or in poem, the first time one hears or sees. Living with the thoughts and harmonies gradually initiates, and so it is with souls. Her loving kindness, freshness of mind and keen interest in, and enjoyment of this life; of music, literature, art, radiated from her wherever she was. Her work, especially in the Prison, but also in the Infirmary, the Workhouse and, outside these, in helping the needy in souls and bodies was known of, though never from herself, throughout Oxford; and, as years passed, more widely still, from its effects, and the centre which she became of wisdom and experience. But, as I said, I only realised more and more what she was from 1895.

Looking back, her goodness to me fills me with wonder. Her life was brimming over with interests, affections, work; her working day began

345

at six to end at ten. Yet full as was each hour, more or less tired as she always was, with breaking health, over seventy years of age, amid ceaseless demands upon all that she had and was, she made room for me, when, as it happened, I was wanted in Oxford during that August, 1895. Having hitherto been there on delightful visits with my parents, latterly with my father only, it was not quite easy to return alone. This Miss Skene understood without a word, and every day she came to my lodgings to carry me off as her companion on her rounds, or to sit in some College garden. That was for a month, and in the somewhat slacker time of the Vacation; but I was recalled in October, and all through the year that followed, she never failed me. Then I was more wanted elsewhere and could only put in at Oxford for Sundays, and during each August, and part of September, when, as it happened, one job was over and before the next had begun, and still she made time and nourished me with her friendship. The difference this made is inexpressible; one could not, would not, have asked for such help—but she knew without a word. Many of a different make might not miss continuity, their very own people, friends and work, life and spontaneity; but perhaps because we were made in such things rather alike, she fully knew. And her interest in people and life in its deepest, widest sense, in thought and experience, made our walks and long hot hours in College Gardens very refreshing. And her instinct for love and admiration was like water to a thirsty traveller, as my whole past life had been lived in an atmosphere of widest appreciation and sympathies, and in communion with a mind in which experience had begotten reverence for law, and its application by self-discipline, as the only security for individuality without deformity, and true liberty; not to crush individuality or to hinder liberty: for to him the end of law was freedom. And into all this Miss Skene entered—we were at one.

She was never weary of my heroes, nor I of hers. At first we had our *salons* chiefly in the Warden's Garden at All Souls—but latterly in Balliol because she was more tired; it was nearer her home and close to St Mary Magdalene's Church. In Vacation, when worshippers were scarce, she usually went there to Evensong "to meet," she said, "Him who is there as third or fourth." So in the College Gardens we had our *salons*, those hot afternoons which were the times I could not be with my invalid aunt. Miss Skene introduced me to her family and friends and they became mine; Sir Walter Scott and many another of the interesting and great people who had enriched her life. We shared those who had crossed both our lives, and she welcomed with eager interest such of my own people and friends whom she had not known—some to whom one owes more than one can ever repay in this world or the next. I remember she accepted from me Lord Tennyson, with Mr Browning thrown in, as *perhaps* a fair exchange for Sir Walter Scott!

We both delighted in human nature; and this point in common it was, I think, which made her wish that had I intended to settle for life in Oxford, I should take up her Prison and other work, whenever she should be obliged to give it up. Once when I objected that anyhow I should have been unable, having had no training to fit me, and that especially I felt I could not do her Rescue Work, she answered that she had never had any training other than that which had also been mine; education by intercourse with every kind of mind to interpret books, and books to interpret men. She declared that the less artificial training one had the better. "You, like me, have no cut and dried theories," said Miss Skene; "nor preconceived ideas as to people to hinder you—be thankful for that if you wish to help others. Take each as you find him; that is the only way to be of any use, or to learn yourself. Knowledge of human nature can only come from experience, enlightened and enabled by selfless sympathy—a sympathy I mean which feels with, not only for, another, and that only the Divine Master can give." She paused, and her face, tragedy itself, suddenly lit up in a flame of Salvation as she added, "*in* all their affliction He was afflicted."

As to Rescue Work she repeatedly assured me that it had come to her to do incidentally through her relationship with men and women of all classes in the jostle of life, and particularly through the Prison—helping in Missions, Workhouse and Infirmary. More and more the help needed from her had been in respect to those special forms of temptation and evil which have come to be classified as Rescue Work;

just as, unfortunately, the evils of drunkenness have absorbed the name of intemperance. She told me also that, in her case, she believed her usefulness in Oxford, as to these matters, had been chiefly due to her not having been seen on platforms, or considered as a Worker with a capital W, belonging to any Society, but, "just a woman who tries to help others in whatever trouble or sin they may be."

Publicity she shunned; advertisement she abhorred. There was no self-will or self-esteem in her, she was absolutely humble; and so absorbed in her Divine Master, and her fellow humans, that Self was lost. Not that she was not always herself—vigorous in mind, soul and heart—but there was in her that Sacramental Grace of exceeding sweetness, humility, patience and sympathy; that insight, and capacity for ever learning from the Holy Spirit, which makes the difference in the virtue as a balm, medicine, refreshment and inspiration between love which has ripened into the Fruits of the Spirit, and the raw material, however strong and deep. Love is always love; but even love needs sanctification to keep pure, to be efficacious.

And Miss Skene, by what love had become in her, is one of those who have borne, to me, irresistible witness to the fact of Sacramental Grace. It is in her living union with her Lord that she lived and lives, and by her life and its character, she helped to impress on me the lesson that Communion with God by Sacrament, worship and prayer, whether more or less difficult, congenial, or the reverse, as natures vary; must be attained by attaining, for the

Christian life to be lived in active expression
with real life-giving effect to others. Also, and
still more important, with truth and safety to
the worker. That for this, by this, the Christian's life must be well nourished, patiently,
ploddingly nourished, and kept in constant touch
with the Divine; and thereby also constantly
corrected in proportions and tendencies, kept
in line with Living Truth, instead of falling
behind or sterilizing into passing expressions.

Wherever I went with her or to meet her, to
the Prison, or wherever it might be, in accidental
talk her inner life showed itself as the secret of
her wonderful work and influence. She only
spoke of what she was trying to do because she
said it helped her to think and talk with me; and
perhaps my interest did help her. But there was
no egotism in her, and the utmost sense of delicacy
and reserve. She never once made one shrink,
or gave pain by that sort of bluntness which
seems too often the fate of people as immersed
in the sin of the world as was Miss Skene.

A gift which certainly kept her sane (and with
such an imagination and sympathy as hers, this
was of no small value), was her keen and rich
sense of humour; and she often said to me she
could not have gone on year after year as she
did, but for the spontaneity ensured her by her
independent life, and as part of that life she
owed much, she felt, to her literary work. Inside
she was as fresh and young as a child. At times
this impressed me the more when something
humorous struck our fancy, and suddenly the
tragedy would lift from her face and the child
in her would reassert itself; she who the moment

before had shown her soul travailing in pain for the sins of the world.

Each year the Waters of the Spirit in which she lived and worked had risen higher and higher round her. The Waters which, red with sacrifice, passed through Kedron to heal and qualify the lives of men, until their dead waters become fountains of the Spirit. Sacrifice, suffering, identification with sinners, all were in her; yet making her mind, heart and soul always more loving, more hopeful, clean and humble, and fresh as that of a little child. So she also was of those who helped to teach one that true appreciation of evil never defiles, only cleanses. But all this costs—the peace of fruition is in another world, the travail is in this.

Sometimes, when latterly her sight had almost gone and she did not see me from a distance, the separation of initiation struck me written on her face. She looked like a Sibyl with a message to a people deaf and blind. Then we met, and her face lit up into a radiance of happiness and love, which made her young again. She walked latterly feebly and very slowly, but it was the progress of a Queen. How proud I felt as her companion—when people of all classes saluted her, unseeing though she was. Never a postman, cabman, ostler, policeman, did we pass, but she received her salute; working men and women, beggars and tramps, all knew her; the citizens honoured her, and no wonder. They recognised a life, with all its gifts and resources, spent without reserve for the use of her fellows.[1]

[1] She said to Canon Gore, almost the last time he met her, "I'm like the Martyrs' Memorial! Every one knows me, and nobody's interested in me."

Her income was very small, but by most frugal living and unwearied literary work, she had her cruse always full and flowing to fill again for others.

Her literary taste, in criticism of style, was excellent; her own art seemed too consciously dominated by her moral purpose; to some loss, I thought. And this characteristic affected her judgment as to all literature. Instead of her exquisite moral sense only inspiring and purifying her literary judgment, I think it trammelled her mental action, fossilized it almost, in a way which was emphatically not the case in her daily, personal dealings with people and situations. I mean, she seemed to me in her own writings to consider what effect would be produced, rather than to write freely, as she would act and speak, in immediate, moment to moment, touch with the guiding Spirit. I may be quite wrong in this, but I was often puzzled by the difference between her freedom in acted thought, and trammeldom in written expression; though, of course, the relatively less fleeting character of literature, and the apparently much wider reach of its influence, would always give one awe of the responsibility this entails.

The last year she was here, she went back more than ever to Greece and her younger days; and she constantly gave me prayers and thoughts from the Greek Liturgy. With all her affection and absolute loyalty to the English Church, her æsthetic sympathies were, to the end, with the Greek. She often told me that had she not returned to England she should have joined the Greek Church, but being absolutely satisfied as to the validity of Anglican orders, she thankfully lived in, and was nourished by, the Sacraments of the Church of England in the country of her service.

She had, to the end, several dear friends, members of the Roman Communion, notably Lord Bute and Father Oswald (Sir David Hunter Blair); and all who care for Miss Skene must appreciate the great pleasure Father Oswald's affection and constant kindness brought her, just perhaps when she wanted it, the last two or three years she was in Oxford, when his special work there began. But despite these and other Roman Catholic friends and correspondents, she never had for herself any doubt as to the Church of England.

There is only one point upon which she repeatedly expressed her regret, and begged me, should occasion offer, to use her experience with her name, as one who knew sin and sinners in men and women, boys and girls, of all classes. While she expressed herself vehemently against the bondage of the Confessional established by law in the Church of Rome, she had the wit to recognise that this could never have come to pass without the fact of sin, the needs of human nature, the desires for repentance which, surging up again and again in the ocean of time, create a demand for such help. Of course she fully realised that the help of God through man had been often misused, perhaps misinterpreted; had often in the helper's hands become tools for harm, and to many under the law of the Confessional its use had been that of a mechanical charm, or a mere act of outward conformity. But nevertheless she

z

deplored that, from whatever cause, the Gospel of the Confessional should have been largely lost to mankind, and its truth and grace in the English Church obscured by party support and party objections.

She preferred this loss, great as she held it to be, to any alternative of confession to man as in any sense a condition for communicating or for confirmation; or to its being taught, or implied, that necessarily a man or woman is better, or more spiritual for its use. But, she asked, why should this be the alternative? and she longed for the Bishops to face the matter boldly, despite all the prejudice (not wholly unreasonable nor unaccountable surely) and honest, however ignorant, misconception and misrepresentation of the subject. In face too of the hypocritical element which joins the body of honest opposition.

"While sin lasts there will always be this question," she said. "When the Church languishes, it will languish; when the Church really lives and works, this difficulty will persist"; and she pointed to the Salvation Army, to Moody and Sankey's work, to Wesley's, Whitfield's, and all mission work.

"My dear, they all practise confession, can't help it, and I confess I fail to see that the situation is saved by irresponsible, untrained men and women being father and mother confessors— more fit because lacking ordination I suppose!" [1]

[1] It is hardly necessary to say that Miss Skene fully recognised the difference between such Confession on Conversion, in public to the Assembly; or to individual men or women whose sole qualification would, I suppose, be described as being "called by the Spirit"; and the Confessional throughout the Catholic and

No, what I deplore and object to is that in the Church of England we do not honestly face it out now. There it is—it can't be prevented; if it were only the clergy to deal with, there might be a chance, but it is the fact that the need is never absent, that laity will have it—will have as members of the Church of England what their Prayer Book teaches them, their Church offers them—will ask what their consciences hunt them to seek—that makes it absurd to shun and ignore the subject. Absurd? Wrong! Face it out; own to the fact and regulate it. Don't leave it open to ignorant young men to hear confessions and give advice. It's as bad for the young clergy as for those who go to them. Let the Bishops face it, I say, with properly licensed clergy of unquestioned character and age, and

Apostolic Church, whatever difference there may be as to the details of its use. But she held that all who really fought with evil and had wide and deep knowledge of it, must agree as to the necessity of going to the very roots of sin; and she recognised Confession as a help to this. Also she held that the struggle with the poison of sin in some cases, and in some characters, needs the special treatment and help supplied by Confession. On the other hand, she was very jealous of every system of Confession. She had at one time availed herself of it, and depended on it to a considerable extent. From this view, she became entirely emancipated; and she had for many years ceased to "go to Confession," as the practice is called. She not only felt that she did not need it, but more; that it would be a hindrance to her, an encumbrance rather, in that intercourse with her Divine Master, in which she lived, and in which He seemed to be always speaking to her; and her realization of this it was which made her so jealous of any system which might bar such intercourse. She actually dissuaded from the use of Confession to man, when her opinion was asked by those who were considering the matter theoretically, or merely on some external suggestion; and she urged the utmost caution in its use, when the enquiry had a practical origin, and arose from a sense of personal need. She expressed herself freely to me, being satisfied that I entirely agreed with her as to the responsibility of the individual for him or herself to God; and that forgiveness for sin, and the cleansing of one's being, depend on Him only and are to be had by repentance and faith through our Lord Jesus Christ.

open confession in Church.   Of course there will
always be abuses of the best things; but where
there is a real want and an authorised channel
to meet that want, you only lessen safeguards,
and increase risks, by refusing honestly to face
facts, and regulate what you have no right or
power to prevent."

I remember when I was editing my Father's
Memorials, and reading to her the proofs as I
corrected them, she understood how I shrank
from his self - sacrifice in revealing some
of his inner history, and particularly as regards
Confession, and what he felt he owed to its help
in the struggles of his early manhood. And
when I told her that he had insisted on giving it
to the world; " I owe it to my God," he said.
" What helped me might help another, and if he
be but one—I owe it to my God!" She told me
how thankful she was that such a man as he
should have left his experience on record. She
felt the limitations and drawbacks of all human
agencies, but she also fully recognised them as
consecrated and empowered by the Incarnation
—indeed part of the mystery of revelation by
limitation, Thought by Word.

The Incarnation was the keynote of her life,
and wherever her work for the Divine Master
brought her into connection with His disciples,
naturally, she eagerly claimed their friendship,
and appreciated their work, to whatever school of
thought they might belong. Loyalty to Him
was the touchstone with her, and from living as
she did, in ever closer communion with Him,
jealously searching her life by the Spirit, she
opened out more and more (if I may say so with-

out impertinence of one so infinitely beyond one's reach) to the revelations by death and life and by all creation, to the greatness of the love of God, and the infinite variety of the manifestations of that Love, in His relationship with men.

She made me promise to go to her, if possible, when her time should come to die; but I was in Italy when the end so quickly came.

I heard first of her death from Sir John Conroy, who was to her almost like a son. He had met her on Saturday, the 30th September, on her way to the Cathedral for Evensong.

" It was deluging," he wrote, "and I met Miss Skene in Tom Quad, with the cape of her mackintosh blown over her head, and the rain driving against her arms. I pulled down the cape and went with her to the porch of the Cathedral, and there we walked backwards and forwards for half-an-hour. She seemed much as she had been when you were here—very feeble, but I noticed no change. . . . She was rather less well on Monday and worse on Tuesday, but she insisted on going to the Prison and the Cathedral, though she had great difficulty in getting home, and had to stop and rest seven or eight times. On Thursday she was sitting up in the drawing-room. . . . I do not think there was any actual suffering at the end, though she was very ill—heart and slight bronchitis; all was over on Friday morning early."

Over, or begun?

I think of her in her sitting-room saying good-bye to me one Christmas time as I was leaving for Hatfield, to join my own people who were there. I had said I felt for her, leaving her alone

for Christmas. "Alone!" she cried. "No! that
one day in the year I take for myself, and after
the Blessed Sacrament I shut myself up here,
see no one, and loneliness is over. My people
are with me, and I touch the cup of happiness
which I shall drink into, when I am with them
again, in the life of the world to come."

Her face was transfigured (as many must have
seen it) when she was listening in Christ Church
Cathedral to some anthem in which she was
delighted.   SOPHIA M. PALMER.

July 1901.

A RECOLLECTION OF FELICIA SKENE

BY CHARLES W. WOOD

MY friendship with Miss Skene dated from
the later years of her life. Though I lost much
by not meeting her in earlier days, when her
remarkable gifts of mind and person attracted so
much attention, I also gained in knowing her only
when the harvest of her rich nature had ripened,
and all that was best and noblest had become
as it were established and confirmed; existed not
only in the heart invisible, but was manifest in
the kindly gaze of her large blue eyes and the
singular sweetness of her expression.

Her charm was not at all the placidity that is
sometimes due to want of character. She was
a pillar of strength in time of trouble; a well-

spring of sympathy abundant and inexhaustible. Her individuality was very marked; nor have I ever met with any one at all like her. The ordinary failings of humanity seemed to have passed her by. One looked in vain for the small blemishes that beset men and women of our every-day life. The hasty word, severe judgment, fretful interval, selfish moment — she appeared to know nothing of all such weaknesses. Human nature is fallible, and none are perfect, therefore she could not have escaped the lot of mortals; but if I were asked to point out a fault in Felicia Skene I could not do so.

Rarely have I seen any one in whom there was so little of the finite, so much of the heavenly; self-sacrificing, self-forgetting, counting herself as of no moment, living for others; her great aim to do good; to confer happiness if possible upon those in whom she was interested; but at least to leave them better than she found them, richer for the knowledge of her.

Not that she esteemed herself holier than others. Her religion was too deep and true, her conception of the Divine Perfection too exalted not to feel intensely how great the interval between the very best on earth and the lowliest in heaven. A more spiritual mind could not exist, therefore she was filled with humility. I doubt if she ever even thought of herself, or ever glanced at the measureless distance separating her from the erring men and women she visited in prison. "Not I, but the grace of God which is in me," she would have said if questioned. And her life's motto might have been: "Bear ye one another's burdens and so fulfil the law of Christ," for that was the end and aim she placed before her and kept steadily in view year after year; never pausing, or ceasing, or looking backward, never taking a day's interval or a day's rest. Suffering for many years from a serious heart-trouble, her life seemed to have been almost supernaturally prolonged. A single year of such constant activity might well have been too much even for one in full health and strength; but she lived on in spite of all human prophecies that she was bringing her days to a premature close, and in spite of all physical reasons that this should be so. Like Ignatius Loyola, of whom the doctors after death and examination said: "He ought by all the physical laws of which we are cognisant, to have died twenty years ago. We cannot tell what supernatural power has upheld him, but supernatural it was"—so the same might have been said of Felicia Skene.

Whatever gifts she possessed, and they were many and varied, in her Memoir it should above all things be brought out in strongest colours that she was deeply, earnestly devout. The unseen world seemed almost as close and real to her as the visible. She was of the material that saints and martyrs are made; in the days of Smithfield would have gone to the stake as bravely as Cranmer; rejoicing in being counted worthy to suffer; and on her face would have appeared that strange reflection of Heaven's light, as far as it may be found on human countenance. I have myself seen there that beautiful light, but in quiet moments, when there was present no question of stake or martyrdom, no crowd of spectators, or unusually stirred emotions, or any element of sensation whatever. There were other times and moments of religious fervour and ecstasy when, under the influence of a new thought or possibility, the eloquence of a preacher, or the strains of devotional music—"the pealing anthem swelling the note of praise"—her expression would approach nearer to our conception of the angelic choir than we should deem possible in one not yet translated to the higher life. But I have more often observed it when there was no extraneous influence, no exaltation to account for it, when we sat within the four walls of her little sitting-room, and none were present but we two, whilst she described perhaps a visit to the prison, some sad character she had tried in vain to influence, and the hopelessness of repentance ever reaching the fallen soul. Then would follow her own sad exclamation, and a depth of compassion would fill her eyes, overwhelmed with the terrible possibility: "What shall be in the end thereof?" And she would add: "My only consolation is that God does not judge as we do; His mercies are infinite; Abraham left off asking before God left off granting." It is for all this never-failing, more than human love and sympathy, that the life of Felicia Skene should be widely known and, as far as possible, imitated.

There are too few like her. Possessing faith that could remove mountains, she was a fervent witness to the Truth. To know her well, was to be convinced of all the realities of the life beyond. Many a time she must have strengthened the feeble knees, and brought hope and consolation to desponding hearts.

Disappointment never discouraged her patient continuance in well-doing. She never grew weary. One would say to her: "This cannot go on. It is shortening your life. Will you not consent to do less?" And she would reply: "I have put my hand to the plough, and if I am to pretend to follow in the footsteps of my Master, I must not fall short of the very utmost. As long as I am needed, strength will be given; I never doubt that. When it is God's will, then and only then I shall be taken." And though she reached the age of seventy-six, she might have lived many years longer had she been willing to take an occasional rest; ease from her shoulder the burdens of others she so constantly bore. Religion was the key-note of her life. She held that it must be found in the heart, and in later years lamented the "advanced" party in the Church as bringing with it a sword, not peace. In earlier days, influenced by the ornate ritual of the Greek Church, she had to some extent accepted many of its views, even to acknowledging merit in the use of Confession. This her maturer judgment entirely rejected. She lived to see that Confession was a practice that too often brought about the very evils it was supposed to remedy, and must never be permitted to obtain foothold in our Church of England. It is quite conceivable that in those earlier years the florid Greek rites appealed to her vivid imagination; but even when I first knew her all love for the mere ceremonial had passed away, and she thought only of the spiritual.

If in the exuberance of youth—when Heaven and the things pertaining to it seem so very far off—religious influence was less marked, still it must have been there as the foundation of her character; ready to bear fruit in Heaven's own time. And as mortals are made perfect through suffering, so suffering and trouble came to her. Felicia Skene was capable of the deepest emotions of a strong and passionate nature; and there is no doubt that she was tried in the refiner's fire and came out as gold seven times purified. Yet hers was never the religion of the cloister. No one could look at her remarkable brow and not see that her sympathies were capable of endless expansion. She was not one who was *only* religious; was the very last to hold the world in contempt, or affect to lightly esteem its honours. In her anxiety for the eternal interests she never despised or undervalued the earthly. To do so would have been to deny the traditions of her race. Nothing delighted her more than the temporal success of her friends; to hear of the promotion of a relative, or that some unexpected piece of good fortune had fallen to them. She took keen interest in the marriage of a friend, and where she thought it for their happiness, would leave no stone unturned to bring about a desired union. To the last she was young in mind and heart, fresh in feeling, maintaining an extraordinary amount of active and lively zeal in everything that concerned those about her. No one ever thought of her as old. She was never old. Too often, as a rule, sympathies weaken with age, the mind loses its grasp upon the world, the grasshopper becomes a burden, the days of the sere and yellow leaf have come, and nothing is as it was. With Felicia Skene it was never so. She was full of life and responsiveness up to her last day on earth; never failed or faded, but died in full harness, as she had lived.

That last day had been one of great activity; anxious care for others. Some extra pain at the heart had necessitated a visit from her doctor —whom she would only see on the rarest occasions—and his subsequent order: "This cannot be neglected. There must be a change, and you must do less in future. It is imperative." "Then to-morrow," replied Miss Skene, "we will see what part of my work can best be laid down." But for her there was to be no partial laying aside and no to-morrow. She retired at her usual hour, and quietly in her sleep, none knew when, even as none suspected the end was near, the end came. For her it was not the ending but the beginning of life. She had entered into the glories eye hath not seen nor ear heard. "If there are many mansions in that world," wrote a friend lately to one she much loved, "how can I ever hope to see her again?" And the friend replied: "About the many mansions I don't think it matters a bit, because if we get in at all we shall be all right. Her perfection of holiness and the increase of it which doubtless will have taken place, will not lessen her power of meeting any other soul which has any light of God upon it. You could meet her in soul even here, and we also, to our infinite ennobling, and you will meet her closer yet. What I cannot conceive is her happiness if we were shut out; but—well, we mustn't get shut out, you know!"

These words strike a dominant note in her nature. Heaven itself would scarcely be Heaven if her beloved on earth were never to meet her on the eternal shores. And yet her life was so far above the lives even of the consistently good, that if there are different spheres, and different degrees, and different awards, it is difficult to imagine how she can be found in any realm attainable to ordinary men and women.

Her self-denial could only be realised by her most intimate friends. She was of those few and rare natures who do unmeasured good, "expecting nothing in return."

Few were more intimate with her than the writer; few knew her better; few observed her more closely and keenly. To none did she speak out more openly her heart and mind. No thoughts were withheld; there were no "reservations," which so often disturb the smooth-flowing current of friendship. It was only another proof of her clear, confiding trust. Never was a more candid soul and spirit; a purity that, having nothing to conceal, charmed you by its delightful frankness: one of the rarest qualities in mankind. She amazed you by the rapidity with which she identified herself with your life and interests, making them her own; the way in which if you once took possession of her heart she kept you there for ever, and poured out in return all the treasures of love and sympathy

in which she abounded.   One of her most
touching traits was her own intense gratitude
for the smallest service it might be in one's
power to render.   Rare occasions indeed when
the tables were turned and she was the recipient,
not bestower of favours.   With an income that
her charities made more and more limited, she
yet gave away so largely[1] that she was supposed
to be wealthy.   For the sake of others she
had so lessened her fortune that at the time
of her death she had scarcely more than
sufficient yearly income to meet the requirements of her modest household: the two
servants who had been long with her and
worshipped her.   All she earned by her graphic
pen was immediately given away.   And as it
often happens in this world that to the generous
and charitable an object will never be wanting,
so Felicia Skene's list of those whom she
substantially helped on their way through life
was a singularly long one, comprising all ranks
of society: from those whom she "comforted
in prison," to friends and relations who "basked
in the smiles of royalty," and whose duties
at foreign courts were perhaps more distinguished than rewarded.   One could only
marvel, sometimes remonstrate, at her excessive
generosity, the absolute disregard of her own
personal claims.   It was impossible to make
the slightest impression upon her; she would
only smile and perhaps shake her head; never
seeming to realise that she ever performed what
is called "a good action."   It was all done

[1] It is perhaps necessary to point out that Miss Skene, with all
her charity, gave with great discrimination, since charity un-
wisely directed is the cause of much of the evil in the world.

so simply, so unconsciously, in so matter-
of-fact a manner, that the person benefited,
being present, would have felt they were
granting rather than receiving a kindness. I
have seen her sign away half her income for
ever for the sake of others with as much
calmness as though she were answering an
invitation to a friend's house. "Let me do
what I can as long as I am here," she once
replied to a remonstrance. "My wants are few;
I have all I need. To them this sum will make
all the difference in life. It is not the much
I give which troubles me, it is the little. My
one anxiety is how to get more to give more.
To attain that I would work night and day
if it were possible. But after my day's work
I am so tired that I can only go to bed—and
it is often hard work to get there," she would
laughingly add.

So, year after year, she endured immense
physical fatigue, which should have worn her
out long before the end came.

I can never forget our first meeting, for which
I had gone down to Oxford from London.
After a little searching I found the small,
quaint, old-fashioned house in New Inn Hall
Street. The door was opened by one of the
two Scotch servants already alluded to, and
who were so like each other that I would
laughingly call them the Sisters Dromio, and
never learned to know them apart. She was
a singularly silent woman with a narrow,
pleasant Scotch face. No word did she utter,
but her lips and eyes half smiled as she made
way for me to enter. Already she seemed to

look upon me as a privileged being, admitted
to the *sanctum sanctorum* of her beloved
mistress.   The house was as quaint within as
without.   In humble hands it would have been
a mere uninteresting cottage of the years gone
by; but Felicia Skene had thrown over it all
the quiet charm of her relics and possessions.
Each room seemed steeped in her special atmosphere, and the cottage was transformed.
Flowers and plants bloomed in a recess and on
the staircase: flowers more often than not sent
by devoted friends, frequently conspicuous
amongst them her own favourite arum lily.
It was a type of herself, though she knew it not:
great and majestic amongst flowers as she amidst
women.   A short flight of stairs led to the drawing-room, in the centre of which she stood, a tall,
commanding figure.   Her presence seemed to fill
the room, which appeared too small for her.   In
that first moment nothing was more evident than
her dignified carriage.   Her grey hair, verging
towards white, was abundant in its rich massive
coils.   She half sprang forward in eager welcome,
and her very hand-clasp, the tone of her true
voice, the earnest gaze of her eyes, told me at
once that her nature was rare and generous and
large-souled.   We spent the day and evening
together and part of the next day, and before
the end of that first visit it is not too much
to say that we knew each other intimately and
had become life-friends.   She possessed the rare
merit of meeting you more than half-way; of
making herself known to you by that rare frankness of which I have spoken; the whiteness of a
soul that has no *arrière pensée ;* by bestowing no

half-hearted confidences; by telling you of herself and leading you on to self-revelations in return. Highly intellectual, her conversation was often deep and sparkling. She was an excellent talker, keen, witty, and to the point; and still rarer merit, a good listener. There were few subjects into which she could not throw all her mental vitality and strong interest.

Even in that first interview I was amazed at the versatility of her mind, the enormous number of interests bound up in her life, the numerous people who wrote to her about their own plans and concerns, expecting immediate sympathy and invariably receiving it. Sometimes it almost seemed that the more unreasonable the demand, the more certainly would it be granted. All her intellectual faculties had been diligently drawn out and cultivated by her father, from whom indeed they were inherited. James Skene of Rubislaw was a man of learning and wide accomplishments, master of many subjects, combined with refined tastes and great sensitiveness. We know that he was Scott's intimate friend, and to state that fact is to grant him at once a patent of nobility. She, Felicia Skene, had sat as a child on Scott's knee, listened to the stories he was so fond of repeating to children, noted the tones of that rich, subdued voice, the kindliness that transformed that rugged countenance to one of actual beauty. All through life she never forgot the great Sir Walter, or the impression he made upon her and her sisters; and when towards seventy years of age she specially wrote out for me a chapter of reminiscences about him, she told me that his

2A

venerable figure, the glance of his eye, the tone of his voice, the Scotch accent which gave additional force to his already forcible words, every incident she described—all was as vividly before her as when sixty years ago she had felt his kindly arms about her.

Many and many a talk we had concerning Scott. On one occasion, when twilight was creeping through the small panes of her large old-fashioned window in Oxford, she told me for the first time, but not for the last, her father's one ghost story. How Sir Walter had appeared to him on the eve of his death, just as he had been wont to see him in life in the years gone by, and had announced that his hour was come. He died, in fact, the next morning. Told as it was, in the gloaming, with no sound audible but her quiet tones hushed to the solemnity of the subject, the narrative made a deep impression upon me. Yet in the very desire for assurance of the fact, it was difficult to avoid the question—

" Do you not think it was a dream ? "

" I am convinced the spirit of Sir Walter actually appeared to him, and they met on that fateful night," she replied. " My father was as calm and clear-headed as he had ever been in his life. With some the mind weakens at the approach of death, with others it strengthens; they see things with a clearer vision, and the veil is half undrawn. It was so with my father. Scott had been his dearest friend; their affection was strong and undying. When separated by death, Sir Walter's influence never lost its hold upon my father's mind. He talked of him frequently and he was no doubt very constantly in his thoughts. They were still bound to each other by a chain powerful enough to bring them together in these last hours. Yes, he certainly appeared to him. Nothing less than the actual presence of his old friend would have brought that look into my father's eyes."

" Then do you believe in ghosts so-called ? "

" I believe in supernatural apparitions," she replied. "How can we doubt them ? With Dr Johnson I would say that if all reason is against it, the weight of evidence cannot be set aside. I hold that the world of spirits is closer to us than we are aware of, and if the veil were withdrawn from our eyes, we should see ourselves surrounded by a crowd of ' ministering angels.' To my mind there cannot be any doubt about the matter." And she herself dwelt so near the spiritual world that her unshaken belief was almost a matter of experience.

Yet there was a time when Felicia Skene might have developed into a mystic. She hovered on the very borders of the " world between." With her vivid imagination and passionate nature, we cannot wonder at this. It was her real strength of mind which saved her from becoming a visionary. Her power would have been unbounded. I can conceive her working by signs and wonders, with a following devoted as that of Irving of old, when he saw visions, spoke in unknown tongues, and set his congregation thrilling and weeping by turns. But her mind was too vigorous to lose its balance; life on earth was too earnest and practical to be wasted in mere dreams and visions, however nearly they might approach the realms of

positive existence. This was not her idea of
fulfilling the command that we should bear one
another's burdens. She saw too much of the
sin and misery, want and care, everywhere
abounding. If ever inclined to mysticism, these
sad but wholesome experiences into which she
deliberately threw herself effectually and for ever
averted the danger. Nevertheless she was one
in whom one might have expected "manifestations"; the power of seeing beyond the veil.
"These things go not out but by prayer and
fasting," said our Lord to His disciples. And the
life of Felicia Skene was one long prayer; and, it
may be added—so utterly frugal were her meals
—it was also practically one continued fasting.
Not from any penitential motive; far from it; but
because she simply seemed to have the power of
living almost without food. This was another of
the marvels of her very extraordinary existence.
Therefore I confidently expected to hear that she
too had had visions, seen apparitions, heard voices.
"No," she said, "I have never experienced anything of the sort. Nothing of the supernatural
has ever approached me, neither in dreams nor in
waking hours. With all my imagination, I
believe I am too practical. I don't think I have
ever desired to see what we call a 'ghost.' If I
could do the poor troubled spirit any good, then
let it come; otherwise I would rather wait my
own hour. It will come soon enough. Until
then let me give all my thoughts and energies to
work, and let dreams and visions visit those who
have nothing to do."

"Yet you see how the apparition of Sir Walter
brought consolation to your father?"

"His work was ended," she returned. "His last hour was approaching. He had done with the world. When my last hour approaches and I lie upon my death-bed, though crowds of beloved friends appeared to me from the unseen world, I would welcome them all."

This was strong language for one who might once have become a mystic, and proved the wholesome influence of a life of constant occupation. Inward and spiritual experiences she had had, almost amounting to revelations, but no "outward vision or token" had ever come to her. Nevertheless, she firmly believed in the possibility of supernatural appearances.

Years after this apparition of Sir Walter to James Skene, I visited Frewen Hall with his daughter. Though a little altered, it retained much of its old character: a quaint, old-fashioned building such as one could scarcely expect to find in the Oxford of to-day. We wandered from room to room, from floor to floor, and as she passed on it was very visible how utterly her mind and spirit had been thrown back into the days gone by. Even to me the place seemed crowded with ghosts as she vividly described people and scenes that had themselves become mere shadows and memories. Here her father had sat, there her mother; this had been her own favourite room; on that bench in the garden they had watched the afternoon shadows lengthening as they talked of things past, present and future. Especially she lingered in the room in which her father had died. "There he lay," she pointed; "and there Sir Walter sat and looked at him. I never enter this room without feeling it in some way still haunted; that is imagination, of course; but it is not imagination that it seems more sacred to me than other rooms; and here if anywhere I lose myself in the days that are no more."

That visit to Frewen Hall was an experience strangely pleasant, singularly exceptional, of which the impression remains to this hour. It seemed to bring me more intimately into her past life, when as yet we were unknown to each other, and even she herself had not attained to that "fulness of perfection" which comes as a rule only after much trial and testing of the refiner's fire, and the hair has grown grey, and the eyes have put on that ever-questioning look, as though asking a reason for all this mystery of sin and suffering, these tangled threads of life. "It is all for some wise purpose," she would say, whenever we touched upon the point. "We are assured of that. We see through a glass darkly. It is not given to us to see the end from the beginning. Our finite minds can judge nothing properly. And after all, if the world is full of wrong it is man's doing. We are suffering for man's disobedience, which in a sense has to be worked out. All one can do is to try to lessen that suffering, and bring erring mortals to a knowledge of the truth."

It was her constant endeavour. She was not one who preached and did not practise. On the contrary. She was to all intents and purposes a worker. Even to the criminal women in prison, whilst trying to awaken them to a sense of sin, of moral and personal responsibility, the punishment that must follow now, the certainty of retribution after death, she

was never the condemning judge, but addressed
them, each separately, in quiet tones of sympathy
and sorrow; sorrow for the sin, sympathy with
the sufferer. Many a hardened woman would
be moved to tears under her ministrations,
the influence of the sorrowful pain she saw
beaming upon her—perhaps for the first time
in her chequered life—from those kindly eyes;
and if the momentary contrition passed away,
and the promise of amendment was often
broken, yet we shall never know how much of
the seed sown in faith bore fruit after many
days. All effort is not lost; on the contrary,
there is the promise that it shall be found
again.

Apart from her ministrations, it was amazing
how Felicia Skene found time for all she
accomplished. These daily tasks would have
been sufficient occupation for many, and were
indeed far more than many ever attempt. Above
and beyond this her life was full of thought,
work and effort. She wrote much and power-
fully; whether prose or poetry, whether fiction
or papers on social subjects, all came to her
naturally and easily. Gifted with strong imagination, she weaved her tales and stories, made
them real and lifelike, delighting the readers of
the magazines to which she contributed for
many a long year. This again would have been
sufficient with many for the life's work, but
with her, all literary labour was looked upon as
intervals of rest and refreshment in what she
considered her real and more serious occupation:
visiting those who were sick and in prison, trying
to discover the sorrows of others for the sake

of carrying them herself as far as she was able to
do so.

And her literary gift was made use of by her
friends for their own purposes. For years she
helped Sir Henry Acland—much her senior—
in his work, and once when spending the day with
her, she told me that she expected him. On the
occasions of our meeting, visitors as a rule were
denied. It was very usual for a constant stream to
appear, and we should never have had a moment's
freedom for conversation, all the interchanges
of thought and experience which place those
meetings amongst my happiest recollections.
But Sir Henry Acland was too old a friend to
be denied. " I have, however, warned him," she
laughed, " that there will be no three hours for
him to-day, but a stern limitation of five minutes."
Then she so explained the nature and object of
his present work, that when he called and alluded
to his purposes, I was acquainted with them.
He was so far true to the restriction that, when
thrice five minutes had elapsed, he rose and took
his leave, but on the landing stopped to say to
Miss Skene : " I had not spoken for two minutes
with your friend before he understood and saw
the importance of my scheme." " I firmly
believe," she added, relating this on her return to
the room, " that he thinks you unequalled in
perception."

" That is gaining credit on false pretences, and
you will have to undeceive him."

" Oh no," she replied. " Your appreciation
has only confirmed him in the justice of his
views, though I fear he will never live to mature
them. You see how frail and feeble he is."

No one thought then that she would be the first to cross the border.

We were standing in the quaint little drawing-room, listening to the echoes of Sir Henry's carriage as it went swiftly down the narrow street. "Its name seems a stumbling-block to strangers," Miss Skene laughingly observed. "I often have letters addressed to me New Inn, with a fresh line for Hall Street, as though I lived at an hotel in a certain Hall Street, Oxford. One meets with curious experiences in life."

Her keen sense of humour was, indeed, unsuspected by those who were not intimate with her. It formed a delightful and necessary relief to the more serious views of life she was too often obliged to take; and her earnest and noble face would sometimes, as a humorous thought struck her, or a humorous anecdote was repeated, suddenly irradiate, and she would break into very real and cheering laughter. It was well that she possessed this buoyancy of spirit, this gift for seeing the bright side of things as well as the more sad. Without doubt it carried her through trials and strains and scenes of misery—those criminal waifs and strays to whom she devoted herself—which otherwise might have broken her down.

When the sound of Sir Henry Acland's carriage had died away, she turned to two cages in the room, each containing a parrot. Both had belonged to him, and he had insisted upon giving them to her. To refuse anything she could possibly grant was impossible, and so the birds were transferred to a new home. The only other live creature about her was her little long-haired terrier Tattie, but the old saying in this case could not be carried out. With all my affection for her I could not endure Tattie. And yet he had once done her a great service, for which he ought to have been canonized in the dog calendar. It is more than probable that he saved her life, and to Tattie we were all deeply grateful. Nevertheless he dwelt not in our affection. To do him justice, it was a matter that seemed to give him very little concern. He possessed the affection of his mistress, and apparently cared for nothing beyond.

I have alluded to her constant stream of visitors; not on one special day of the week, but on all days and through all the daylight hours; for as a rule she made a point of never being denied to any one if at home. But there was one day in the year that she invariably spent alone, yet never felt less alone: though she would add that she was thankful when it was ended. This was Christmas Day. The morning services over: Holy Communion and the usual prayers and sermon: she would return to her house and remain secluded for the rest of the day. Here she was face to face with her own thoughts; a crowd of past recollections; momentous thoughts of the world to which she was hastening; the numberless friends and relatives to whom she would so soon be reunited; by whom on this day of days she felt specially surrounded, and with whom she seemed to be brought into spiritual, almost visible, communion. Many a letter she wrote to me describing how her day had passed, with its bitter-sweet recollections of the years gone by for ever, yet filled with all the hope of the future. For like St Paul she knew—she could but know—that she had nearly run her race and finished her course: had almost passed from the cross to the crown.

The little drawing-room was full of charming mementos of the past. Tattie lay upon the hearth-rug in front of the blazing fire, happy and indulged. The parrots were climbing inside or outside their cages as fancy led them, feeling that their lines had fallen in pleasant places. In one corner was a bookcase filled with volumes given to her by a friend. Here a piano had once stood, but generous in this as in all things, she had given it to one who, in her opinion, needed it more than she herself, and could not quite afford to buy one. The walls were hung with exquisite water-colour drawings which her father had sketched in Greece in the years gone by; drawings of extreme refinement, care and skill, and delicate colouring. These she held amongst her greatest treasures. To every small portrait and minia-ture, new and old, a special interest and a romantic story was attached. Charming photo-graphs of relations, beautiful women from all parts of the world, and especially Greece and Russia, abounded. On a side table, carefully enclosed in a case, was a translation of the Greek liturgy by herself and Lord Bute, one of her great friends. When the work was finished, he caused a special copy to be mag-nificently bound for her and adorned with illuminated pictures taken from the old masters,

This she left as a memento of herself to the
writer. The room was usually filled with
flowers. A few old chairs stood about of remarkable work, dating back to the days of
Rubislaw and Frewen Hall. So the small
room was transformed into something beautiful
and refined. But nothing graced it like the
presence of its owner. Dressed, as I always
saw her, in rich black silk, she was very much
of a queen : essentially the *grande dame*. Tall
and commanding, upright in carriage until the
last years, she looked extremely imposing. Her
head was well set upon her shoulders, and her
large eyes looked out from a pale, high-bred face.
Perhaps the most remarkable feature about her
was her expansive brow, white as pure marble,
over which fell her abundant grey hair. No
photograph has reproduced this or in any way
done justice to her. When dressed for walking
the hair was rather severely drawn beneath the
bonnet, in great part concealing the fine breadth of
brow. Her beautiful expression of face could not
be hidden ; and I do not remember ever to have
seen her wearing a veil. But the head, under
any circumstances, could only be called magnificent, bearing witness to her comprehensive
intellect. In mind she was as far above ordinary
women as in her ceaseless labours. In her
manner there was a sweet graciousness exceedingly winning, as her kindly gaze fastened itself
upon you. In moments of repose she became
abstracted. The eyes seemed to see things afar
off; she might have been holding communion
with spiritual beings invisible to others. Nothing
was more striking than her remarkable ap-

pearance. She never failed to meet me on the platform on the days I came down to Oxford. Invariably at one end, apart from the crowd, her tall, venerable figure would stand out majestically, and the face, with its saintly calmness and repose, would strike me, each time with more and more wonder, as that of one who almost belonged to a holier order of beings. On our way through the streets people would pause and marvel who was the remarkable woman that passed along as though in the world, yet not of it. She herself was unconscious of the attention she attracted; and I have already said that her self-obliteration was at all times one of her greatest charms.

I have mentioned the sketches that adorned the walls of her little drawing-room. We often examined them together. They recalled her Greek life to her. She was never tired of dwelling upon these early days—that lovely country where some of her happiest years were spent. Looking back, these years must have seemed a paradise on earth; Elysian fields given up to romance, the healthiest and most delightful of pleasures, where she was surrounded by all she loved best; the father and mother to whom she was devoted heart and soul; brothers and sisters who came next in her affections. I have every reason to think the subject that troubles most young women at that age—love and matrimony and settling in life—never crossed her thoughts for an instant. She was too intensely happy at home to bear the contemplation of any change. Suitors she could not fail to have, but all were rejected. Her life was a

dream of high-souled happiness. Those about
her gradually married, she herself would not.
Probably few men were worthy of her, and she
did wisely and well to remain single. It was
here that her magnificent voice was cultivated,
into which she threw all her intelligence and
feeling, charming her hearers as long as she
possessed it. I, alas, had never the privilege of
listening to that wonderful voice. When we first
met she had ceased to sing. She was gifted, however, with what singers very frequently are not
blessed with—a musical voice in speaking. But
there are those still living who remember her in
the days of her glory, though not in those earlier
days of Greece, when her life passed as a dream,
and she grew to love with all the strength of
her impassioned nature the Greek islands and
the blue waters of the Mediterranean that
washed their base. All her romantic ideality
expanded and strengthened amidst these classic
scenes. She loved Athens especially, where all
doors were open to her, from the Palace downwards. Her spirit of adventure she kept to the
very end of life, and her written and published
stories were often the mere transcription of
dreams that came to her during sleep, in which
she was the heroine of wonderful adventures.
Almost the very last story she ever wrote was
one of these vivid dreams.

Here, too, her love for poetry was fostered,
for she was deeply poetical. It seemed that no
gift had been denied her, and if actual genius
was not hers, her versatility approached very
near to it. Again her gift of languages was conspicuous. Greek she spoke as a native, French

also, and there we met on common ground; to
French we would often turn in our conversations. It was her native language, as it was
mine. She was born almost within sight of the
Rhône, in the warm, sunny, imaginative land of
Provence; and in certain papers that were appearing in 1896 on the Valley of the Rhône she
took a most lively interest; was never tired of
talking of the scenes visited within sound of the
river on whose banks she had first seen the
light of day. It was one of our oft-spoken
dreams that we should travel together to these
places, and together revive past recollections;
but, alas, it never was more than a dream, never
could be more. Her days of travelling had long
been over. She could scarcely enter a railway
carriage, and when, every now and then, for the
sake of others, she took a short journey up to
town, it was at the risk of her life. All the last
years were lived on sufferance. She knew that
any day, without warning, the end might come.
Yet she never spared herself. The idea of
death, nevertheless, was always present with her.
She said to me more than once: " I do not fear
death, but I am haunted by its shadow. It
seems so cold and lonely, and never leaves me.
I continually ask myself when that change will
come; what it is; what I shall awaken to."
She had no real fear. Perfect love casteth out
fear, and such her love must have been.
But the greater the depth of feeling, the more
the Majesty of the Unseen is realised, so
much more will the mind dwell with constant
awe upon the subject. Her faith was absolute,
therefore again she had no fear, but she could

never contemplate the change that must surely come without the very utmost seriousness and almost alarm : alarm at its irrevocable nature : the flight from mortal to eternal regions. And so she was mercifully taken through the Dark Valley in her sleep. There was neither coldness nor loneliness for her. The great change came to her gently, as a wonderful awakening.

Our friendship was firm and lasting. It was established at our very first meeting, and strengthened with every interview. Some of our happiest hours, most delightful conversations, passed in the gardens of one or other of the colleges. Now it would be Christ Church Meadows, now perhaps the lovely gardens of St John's or Worcester. She loved them all, and in all was a familiar figure. Seated in a quiet nook, in view perhaps of some exquisite Gothic building of the days gone by, she would lose herself in recollections of the past. We discoursed on a thousand subjects, thoughts and ideas connected with this world and the next, until perhaps the sudden chiming of the hour from some neighbouring tower would remind us both that time has a troublesome way of flying when we most wish it to stand still. Then reluctantly we would make our way under the spreading trees or across the velvet lawns, and pass out of this dream-world into the prosy streets of Oxford ; and by-and-by would come the inevitable farewell. And next morning would bring a letter reviewing the past day, anticipating our next meeting. After our very first interview she had sent me as a memento a pencil-case on which was engraved F.M.F.S. to C.W.W., to which, some years after, she added the words *Semper Fidelis*. A steadfast faithfulness of friendship that remained true to the end, as everything about her was true, and real, and earnest. Not least amongst her gifts was that of letter-writing. Her handwriting was clear and open and unstudied, like her own pure and beautiful self. She possessed the faculty of rapidity, and expressed exactly what she wished to say in the happiest language. Her admirable style extended itself to her letters; if indeed they were not even superior to her imaginative efforts.

Such was Felicia Skene to the writer, and he believes that he knew her best, with perhaps the exception of two or three of her nearest relatives and friends who had borne her company for yet longer years; had watched her pass from comparative youth to middle age, and from middle age to those days when the noble form began to be bowed, and the beautiful face to assume the far-off expression of those who seem to be listening for a Voice which is soon to bid them close their eyes upon the world to reopen them in Paradise. Infinitely pathetic was the figure in its latest days; and as she moved through the streets of Oxford, her step growing slower with advancing age, but always stately, never looking to right or left, many a gaze would follow her and feel that she was something beyond and above the world. Many a grave dignitary would bow down as he passed and went on his way, as though he too felt that she was one who almost censured others by the dignity of excelling.

2 B

She is seen no more, and Oxford is the poorer; for never again will such a face and form pass before them, and never again will so ministering a spirit dwell amongst them. Much as we all loved and appreciated Felicia Skene, much as we saw how far she soared above others, it was yet insufficiently realised that we were in very truth entertaining an angel unawares. These great souls never are valued to their utmost until, passing away, we suddenly find they have left behind them a void that cannot be filled again. All that may have been said in this volume is yet faint and feeble in comparison with her actual presence; her spiritual gift and her mental charm. She was truly an embodiment of St Paul's 13th Chapter to the Corinthians: and having entered into her rest, she now sees face to face all that she so fervently believed in; all that we see in life "as in a glass darkly," yet that she perceived with so great faith and zeal. "Rock of Ages cleft for me," was one of the hymns sung at her funeral, and it has lately been well written to me by one who was her close friend and companion for half the years of his life: "That October 6th was a dreadful day to me too. The one recollection of peace that I have was during the singing of the hymn *Rock of Ages*, and an underlying sense of thankfulness that her rest had come, and death was over for her."

This lengthened eulogy reads almost as an exaggeration. It is not so. We must bear in mind that all whose faces year after year are steadfastly set towards the higher life, must eventually attain in a great measure to that perfection of character which we are told, on the highest Authority, may become ours even in this world. The wonder therefore is, not that Felicia Skene should so nearly have approached this perfect state, but that so comparatively few are able to grasp it. "The spirit indeed is willing, but the flesh is weak." That is the difficulty, the stumbling-block by which so many are sore let and hindered in running the race that is set before them. In earlier days Felicia Skene had had her conflicts; her battles with self; her victories to gain. Like all human beings she possessed her faults and failings; self-will was one of them, a love of power and ruling; her strong nature often bearing down all opposition. But in the school of affliction and self-discipline all this passed away, and a nature rich and mellowed, softened, charitable, sanctified, was the result. Thus it might truly be said of her, as her favourite and much-loved Sir Walter wrote of one of his best and happiest characters, that she was only "a little lower than the angels." Her price was indeed far above rubies. To the writer her friendship was a continual delight and privilege, her loss an abiding sorrow. But the end had to come for her, as it must come for us all in turn; and then, to quote words of her own written at the death of one who, like herself, had passed the refining fire and come out seven times purified:

"Her soul like a white perfumed blossom sprang to heaven."

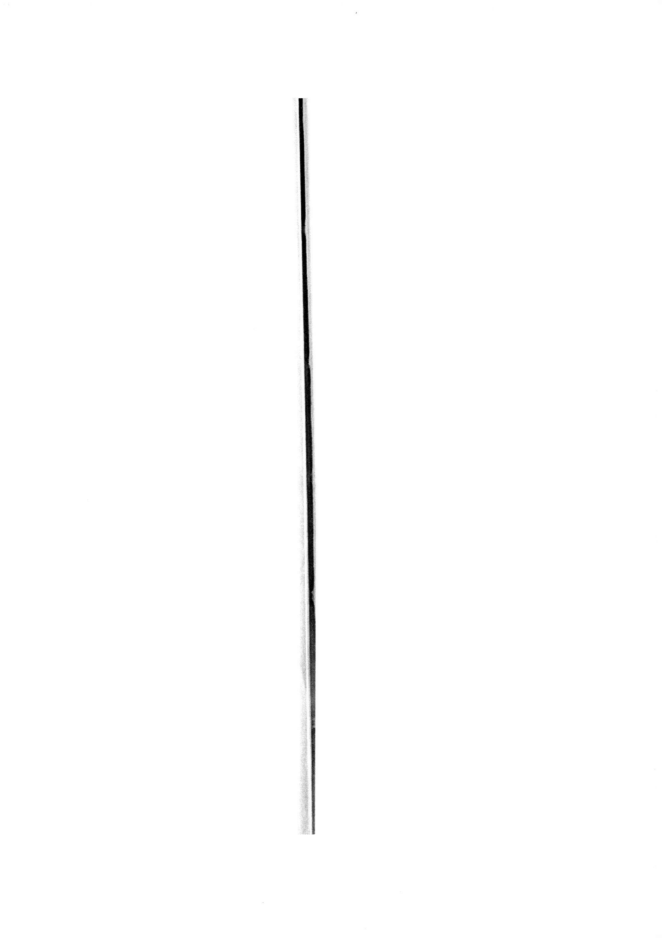

INDEX

Lightning Source UK Ltd.
Milton Keynes UK
05 November 2010

162478UK00006B/122/P